T0374896

BACKCOUNTRY GHOSTS

California Homesteaders and the Making of a Dubious Dream

JOSH SIDES

UNIVERSITY OF NEBRASKA PRESS   LINCOLN

© 2021 by the Board of Regents of the University of Nebraska

A portion of chapter 8 first appeared as "The Sunland Grizzly" in *Natural History* (June 2014): 36–46, http://www.naturalhistorymag.com/features/182751/the-sunland-grizzly. A portion of chapter 15 first appeared as "Hit by a Volcano" in *True West* 22 (January 2019), https://truewestmagazine.com/lance-graham-volcano/.

All rights reserved
Manufactured in the United States of America

Library of Congress Cataloging-in-Publication Data
Names: Sides, Josh, 1972– author.
Title: Backcountry ghosts: California homesteaders and
the making of a dubious dream / Josh Sides.
Other titles: California homesteaders and the making of a dubious dream
Description: Lincoln, NE: University of Nebraska Press,
[2021] | Includes bibliographical references and index.
Identifiers: LCCN 2020024000
ISBN 9781496213211 (hardback)
ISBN 9781496225481 (epub)
ISBN 9781496225498 (mobi)
ISBN 9781496225504 (pdf)
Subjects: LCSH: Land settlement—California—History. | Pioneers—California—Biography. | Ranchers—California—Biography. | Farmers—California—Biography. | Land tenure—California—History. | Homestead law—California—History. | Frontier and pioneer life—California. | California—Rural conditions. | California—History, Local.
Classification: LCC F864 .S586 2021 | DDC 979.4—dc23
LC record available at https://lccn.loc.gov/2020024000

Set in New Baskerville ITC by Mikala R. Kolander.
Designed by N. Putens.

To Sarah and Jesse

The history of California is American history *in extremis*.

—WALLACE STEGNER, 1967

CONTENTS

ILLUSTRATIONS

INTRODUCTION

In 1862 President Abraham Lincoln signed the Homestead Act, the most ambitious and sweeping social policy in the history of the United States until the passage of the Social Security Act in 1935. "In so far as the Government lands can be disposed of," Lincoln said, "I am in favor of cutting up the wild lands into parcels, so that every poor man may have a home." Intended to encourage the settlement of small farmers in the vast American West, the Homestead Act granted 160 acres of public lands to almost anybody who wanted them, for only $18 in filing fees, or about $450 in 2020 dollars. By the time Congress repealed the act in 1976, more than 1.6 million Americans had acquired about 270 million acres of public land through its generous provisions. To put this acreage into some perspective, a single homestead plot was about the same size as Disneyland, or roughly 120 American football fields, and if you could gather all of the homestead plots into one clump, it would be about the size of Ethiopia, Colombia, or South Africa.

Given the massive geographic scale and generous financial terms of the Homestead Act, it is not surprising how large it looms in the national memory. Few American children reach high school without having heard of it, and thousands of tourists flock to celebrate it every year at the Homestead National Monument near the small town of Beatrice, Nebraska. In a recent poll co-sponsored by the National Archives for an initiative called Our Documents, Americans ranked the Homestead Act of 1862 the sixteenth most important document in American history, just after the Articles of Confederation and just before the monumental Fifteenth Amendment, which prohibits racial discrimination in voting. Documents farther down the list include the Marshall Plan, the Voting Rights Act, the Federalist Papers, and George Washington's First Inaugural Address, just to name a few.[1]

Indeed, among famously harried Americans, the very term "homestead" still induces an involuntary nostalgia for a slower, simpler, more wholesome—and much less expensive—time. Countless baby boomers read Laura Ingalls Wilder's Little House on the Prairie series of autobiographical children's novels in their youth. Published between 1932 and 1943, the novels mined the purported virtues of the homestead existence in the Midwest. "Running through all of the stories, like a golden thread," Wilder wrote, "is the same thought of the values of life. They were courage, self-reliance, independence, integrity, helpfulness. Cheerfulness and humor were handmaids to courage." Even more Gen Xers watched the television adaptation of Wilder's work, *Little House on the Prairie*, which aired from 1974 to 1982 and featured *Bonanza* star Michael Landon. *Little House* was saccharine fare but also exactly what Landon sought in the violent seventies. "It was the first one of some 80 pilots I'd read," he told the *Los Angeles Times* in 1974, "that wasn't totally involved with killing people."[2]

Of course national mythology is rarely a good guide to truth, and all of this celebration of the Homestead Act has surely distorted its modest achievements. The terms of the act were deceptively simple: in order to receive a "patent" ("a clear title" in modern terms) for a 160-acre plot of public land, homesteaders had only to "prove it up" (improve it). The exact degree of improvement the act required changed throughout the years, but it was always mandatory that a homesteader reside continuously on the land for five years, cultivate a small portion of it in crops, and build a crude house on it, no smaller than twelve feet by fourteen feet in size. As one would expect, homesteaders rarely got the best lands, those having been indiscriminately sold off or gifted by the federal and state governments to cronies, wealthy individuals, and massive corporations. And most homesteaders lived so close to the bone that even one bad crop, one unusually cold winter or hot summer, one insect infestation, could sabotage the entire endeavor. It is no surprise then that well over a third of homesteaders failed somewhere along the way, never receiving a patent, their land ingloriously returned into the public domain. For these reasons and numerous others, American historians have been justifiably skeptical about the impact of the Homestead Act.[3]

But a close look into California history reveals just how important homesteading really was, particularly in the most cutthroat real estate market in the American West. The gold rush generated extraordinary fortunes for a select few, and drew eastern capital to California, where investors quickly understood the speculative value of land in a state destined for western, even national, dominance. Naturally they set prices for land that the legions of workingmen crowding the new state could rarely afford. And so more than one hundred thousand Californians tried their hand at homesteading between 1863 and the late 1930s, by which time almost all the public land was exhausted. Remarkably, more than sixty thousand homesteaders succeeded, most of whom might never have been able to afford land otherwise, and some of whom, frankly, used the act to augment their existing holdings. Either way, they claimed about ten million acres—roughly 10 percent—of California land, and they contributed significantly to agriculture, accounting for about 65 percent of new farms.[4]

Looking backward from today—when about one-third of American home owners are house-poor, rents are unsustainably high, and home-lessness is an epidemic—the homestead moment seems inconceivable. But homesteaders cut some of the first roads and dug some of the first ditches and wells. They planted some of the first crops in the region and contributed to the food supply of nearby towns. Their toil and enormous patience, agricultural experimentation and innovation, doggedness in the face of natural elements and disasters, and resolve to defend hard-earned land for themselves and their children left us a powerful legacy.

But Americans also inherited from the homesteaders something more ambiguous: the notion that virtually every American could and must own land, regardless of their background or station, no matter the sacrifice. There is little doubt today that home ownership is financially prudent for most American families, but the California stories that follow also suggest that it remains an open question whether the lifelong pursuit of private property, its constant and costly maintenance, its perpetual defense, and all the anxiety and energy devoted to those endeavors have really served the best interests of Americans. It was the Homestead Act that first gave Americans the idea that almost anyone could own land and put the nation on the trail toward the modern American Dream. But it was a trail of never-ending switchbacks, perilous drops, and it was always boggy in winter. How many of its travelers, boot-deep in nighttime mud, looked up to the infinite stars and asked, *goddammit, is it all worth it?*

BACKCOUNTRY GHOSTS

1

Not Much Else Beside

Rose Trujillo Wiley's cabin sits at the end of a pockmarked private road in Topanga Canyon, California, nestled amid the sage scrub, oak, and black walnut trees of the Santa Monica Mountains. Her ten-acre ranch is surrounded by the city of Los Angeles, the second most populous city in the United States, but you would never know it. A brush rabbit darts across the entrance to the hillside property and a few horses mill about a rare patch of flatland. It is quiet: you can hear lark sparrows singing in the near distance, red-tailed hawks crying closer.

"I feel blessed," she tells me, and it is easy to see why. Her spot above the tree line is a sanctuary from the city. A gentle breeze blows through the center of the property, where she planted apple trees, bougainvillea, jacaranda, and brilliant blue morning glories. It is late afternoon, and soon the sun will set like a slowly bursting plum. Wiley points to my iPhone and proudly tells me: "You'll get no reception here." Except for the telephone wire running into her cabin and the jerry-rigged irrigation pipe that delivers graywater from her washing machine to her garden, you could be forgiven for thinking you were in an earlier century, and in another place.[1]

Born in 1931 in the depths of the Great Depression, Wiley watched Topanga transition from a land of humble subsistence, to a counter-cultural retreat in the 1960s, and then to what it is now, a bastion of understated affluence, quiet wealth sprinkled with patchouli oil. The aesthetic of life in the canyon is still Old West, but the money is chiefly new Hollywood: the median income of Topanga Canyon is now more than twice the Los Angeles citywide average, as is the median home price. One of Wiley's newest neighbors up the road is film and television star Benjamin Bratt. Wiley has no intention of selling her land, but if she did, she could easily fetch a small fortune.[2]

Wiley owes her peaceful existence in Topanga Canyon to the most unlikely benefactor: her paternal grandfather, Francisco Trujillo, a Mexican immigrant who first arrived in Los Angeles as a boy with his parents in 1867. There were only about five thousand people in the city—an eccentric mixture of American whites, Europeans, Mexicans, a smattering of Chinese, and a morbidly dwindling population of Chumash and Tongva Indians—mostly surrounding the town center, known as *la plaza*. Afflicted by a small-pox outbreak late in 1862 that killed at least two hundred residents, Los Angeles was also roiled by perpetual violence. "Men hack one another to pieces with pistols and other cutlery," the founding editor of the *Los Angeles Star* newspaper complained back in 1852, "as if God's image were of no more worth than the life of one of the two or three thousand ownerless dogs that prowl about our streets and make night hideous." Not enough had changed in the intervening years: in October 1871, while Francisco was still a boy, whites and Mexicans shot, and then hanged, somewhere between seventeen and twenty Chinese men in one of the worst mass lynchings in American history.[3]

Across *la plaza* from Chinatown was the rough tenement district known as "Sonoratown" after its Mexican inhabitants. It is there that the Trujillos most likely settled when they first arrived in Los Angeles. They appear to have escaped the violence of the era, but Francisco was the victim of at least one scam in which a man named Santos Silva sold a horse to another man named Estephan Piña, then stole the horse back and sold it again to unsuspecting Trujillo, whom Piña naturally dragged to court on charges of larceny. It was a saw, but no less true, that frontier Los Angeles might have been more properly named "Los Diablos."[4]

By the time Francisco reached early adulthood, he had abandoned the mean streets of frontier Los Angeles and taken a job as a ranch hand

1. View of a man with a group of ostriches at the Kenliworth Ostrich Farm, Rancho Los Feliz, showing hills in the background, ca. 1885–89. USC Libraries—California Historical Society Collection.

at Rancho Los Feliz, about six miles upriver in the rugged eastern edge of the Santa Monica Mountains. One of more than about seven hundred ranchos established by Spain and Mexico throughout California between the 1780s and the 1840s, Rancho Los Feliz covered more than six thousand acres. Originally granted to José Vicente Feliz for his service as a Spanish soldier and administrator, the rancho passed through many hands until a wealthy eccentric named Griffith Jenkins Griffith bought the remaining four thousand acres in 1882. The Welsh-born immigrant had made a fortune in mining investments throughout the state and was well positioned to take advantage of the Southern California land boom that was just beginning in the early 1880s, reaching its frenetic zenith in 1886 to 1887. Spurred chiefly by a price war between the Southern Pacific and Santa Fe railroads and the exuberant promotional efforts of both railroad and real estate interests, the boom more than quadrupled the population of Los Angeles. As the population surged, land prices rose even faster, reaching roughly $200 per acre for unimproved land on the fringes of the city and much higher prices in the center of the city and south of *la plaza*.[5]

Griffith made out well: he netted more than $1 million by selling off plots of his ranch, and he still had enough land remaining to gift more than three thousand acres to the City of Los Angeles in 1896 for the "rest and recreation of the masses," the chief attraction of which was one of America's first ostrich farms. But laborers like Trujillo watched the Southern California land boom from the sideline. California actually had some of the highest farm labor wages in the country, but that was not saying much. Trujillo probably earned a little more than $40 per month—about $1200 in today's wages—and it would have taken him too long to earn enough to pay the customary 30 percent down payment on one acre of undeveloped land, the price of which would surely have increased by the time he had the money. And anyway, western land was rarely sold in single acres, the size being prohibitive for profitable farming, particularly for wheat or corn. But Trujillo—now married with two young boys—would not be so easily discouraged.[6]

Exactly what inspired Trujillo to visit the Los Angeles Land Office is lost forever to history, but it is certain that he pored over the *Official Map of the County of Los Angeles, California (1888).* Roughly five feet wide by five feet long, the map spanned four large sheets of paper, each one smudged with the grime of thousands of searching fingers. It was richly illustrated and colorful, but very discouraging: so much of the land beyond Sonoratown and *la plaza* was still engrossed by dozens of massive land grants—Rancho San Antonio, Rancho Tajuata, Rancho Santa Gertrudes, Rancho Las Cienegas, and so many others. And filling the spaces between the ranchos were smaller but extraordinarily valuable tracts owned by men whose names dotted the map like so many trees: Brickman, Hough, Furlong, McKinlay, Tomkinson, and Slauson, men who had been in the right place at the right time with the right amount of money and the right skin color. But just when it must have seemed hopeless to him, Trujillo eyed the sprawling range of unsurveyed public land between the Pacific Ocean and the San Fernando Valley that the Tongva had called "Topanga," the "place above." Better yet, the land office clerk must have told him, the land was open to settlement under the Homestead Act of 1862.

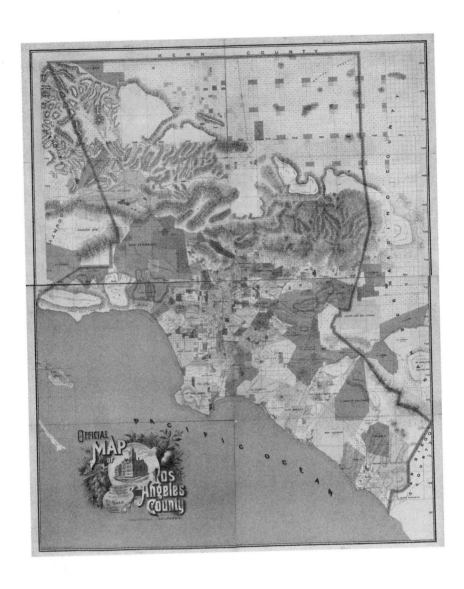

2. Official map of Los Angeles County, California: compiled under instructions and by the order of the Board of Supervisors of Los Angeles County (1888). Library of Congress, Geography and Map Division.

Francisco rushed to survey the Topanga land and soon returned to the land office at Spring Street. He signed documents, and then he, his wife Manuela, and sons Delores and Polito packed up their possessions and made the twenty-six-mile journey back across Los Angeles and up the winding and dusty trail leading to their Topanga plot. Like virtually all homesteaders throughout the West, Trujillo and Manuela worked themselves to the bone and lived humbly for the next few years. Granted, they did so under the perpetual California sunshine, never knowing the brutal winters that Midwestern homesteaders suffered. Nonetheless, life as a subsistence farmer in the Santa Monica Mountains presented unique challenges, the most formidable being drought and the annual threat of wildfires in summer and fall. But there were also the thieving deer, gophers, voles, and rabbits, as well as the livestock-hunting coyotes and mountain lions. Despite the challenges, the Trujillos maintained six dairy cows, grew beans and corn, made wine, and even harvested the dense greasewood and chaparral choking their property. Francisco hacked away at it, bundled it up with twine, and traveled back to Los Angeles on muleback, selling it off as firewood to Chinatown cooks. The toil paid off, and in spring of 1899 Francisco received the patent for his 160-acre plot in Topanga Canyon, signed by President William McKinley's secretary. It was an achievement that would have profound and felicitous ramifications for Trujillo's progeny.

Francisco died in 1916, kicked to death by his horse, and Polito and Delores inherited the ranch. The brothers sold off parcels over the years, but Delores lived out his days on the remaining ten acres. It is also where he raised his daughter, Rose. "My father," Rose Wiley said of Delores, "never entered the twentieth century," though he lived until 1959. Francisco had taught Delores and his brother how to grow corn and beans, how to tend cattle, and how to find work when it was needed. Delores also rented out his mule team to aide in construction of the main road through Topanga Canyon, which became Route 156 after 1933. And even as Los Angeles hurtled into the space age, Delores remained defiantly antimodern. He refused to electrify the house, claiming that electric light was unnatural and injurious to the eyes. He bought a car,

3. Homestead Land Grant Certificate for Francisco Trujillo, 1899. Topanga Historical Society, County of Los Angeles Public Library.

reluctantly, but only because he was thrown from his horse outside a New Year's Eve party in 1928 and vowed not to follow his father's fate.[7]

Francisco Trujillo probably never imagined being described as a legatee of a self-sustaining agrarian vision dating back to the founding of the United States, but that's what he was. Indeed, Thomas Jefferson believed that property should be widely distributed because, as historian Edmund Morgan put it, "he believed the citizens of a republic must be free from the control of other men and that they could be free only if they were economically free by virtue of owning land on which to support themselves." "Whenever there are in any country uncultivated land unemployed poor," Jefferson wrote to James Madison in 1785, "it is clear that the laws of property have been so far extended as to violate natural right. The earth is given as common stock for men to labor and live on. . . . The small landholders are the most precious part of the state." For Jefferson, this was no mere abstraction. "Every person of full age neither owning nor having owned [50] acres of land," he wrote in *Notes on the State of Virginia*, "shall be entitled to an appropriation of

4. Francisco Trujillo (*left*) with a hired hand on Trujillo Ranch, Topanga, California, ca. 1912. Topanga Historical Society, County of Los Angeles Public Library.

5. Delores Trujillo sitting on the footsteps of the old house in Topanga, California, 1952. Trujillo wore a homemade leg brace because of arthritis. Topanga Historical Society, County of Los Angeles Public Library.

[50] acres in full and absolute dominion, and no other person shall be capable of taking an appropriation."[8]

But a soaring national debt in the early republic doomed Jefferson's initial vision of free and equitable land distribution. This was most evident in the Land Ordinance of 1785, adopted by the United States Congress of the Confederation principally to raise much-needed revenue through the sale of land, and secondly to establish a uniform system of land distribution as settlers leaned westward. The primacy of the first goal, as Jefferson himself appreciated, militated against the free distribution of land to small farmers. Instead the land ordinance provided that unlimited 640-acre (one square mile) sections be auctioned off at a minimum auction price of $1 per acre—the total section price being roughly $17,000 in contemporary dollars. Even though economic inequality in the United States was less pronounced than it is today, median household income in the former colonies was less than $300.[9] The high cost of land relative to income, and the absence of purchase limits, virtually guaranteed that wealthy speculators and large land companies would be the principal consumers of the public lands. Even after Congress passed the Harrison Land Act of 1800—reducing the minimum plot size to half sections (320 acres) and easing the terms of payment—the price was still prohibitively high for most Americans.

And so, many Americans too poor to buy land simply took it, government and Indians be damned. Among the hundreds of thousands of migrants to the Trans-Appalachian West in the early nineteenth century were countless squatters, men who believed "that title passed directly from God to the first who put the land to beneficial use," as historian Donald J. Pisani aptly put it. After the Louisiana Purchase in 1803, settlers pushed west of the Mississippi, even as Congress tried to restrict their expansion. Fearing that sparse settlement in the remote wilderness would lead to "chaotic settlements" and the "dissolution of Government," Congress initially resisted the call of territorial governments to grant settlers land through "preemption"—a preferential right to buy the claim they had already settled upon and improved at a modest price. Additionally, in 1804 Congress passed the first of several statutes designed to curb squatting on government land, authorizing the army to eject squatters and further subjecting them to steep fines and even imprisonment. But federal anti-squatting laws were nearly impossible to enforce in the vast lands of the West, and so the squatting continued virtually unabated. "Despite prohibitions against intrusions," historian Paul W. Gates wrote of squatters, "they continued to precede the surveyor and, before the public sale, to take possession of land wherever they found an attractive spot for a good farm or a site for a gristmill or sawmill." American squatters demanded something for virtually nothing, and on a grand scale.[10]

As squatting flourished, the federal government—if merely to keep pace with the reality on the ground—reluctantly endorsed the practice of preemption. Beginning in 1830 Congress passed a series of acts sanctioning preemption on surveyed land, and in 1841 it passed the Preemption Act, allowing squatters to purchase up to 160 acres of the land upon which they resided for $1.25 per acre before the land was available for sale to the general public. "Tenantry is unfavorable to freedom," preemption advocate and Missouri senator Thomas Hart Benton had written: "It lays the foundation for separate orders in society, annihilates the love of country, and weakens the spirit of independence. The tenant has, in fact, no country, no hearth, no domestic altar, no household god. The freeholder, on the contrary, is the national supporter of a free government and it should be the policy of republics to multiply their freeholders as it was the policy of monarchs to multiply tenants."[11]

The Preemption Act of 1841 certainly fulfilled the dream of private landownership for more middling Americans than any land law ever had. But for western farmers and others organized under the banner of the National Land Reform Association, it was not enough. They pressed for more, and they lobbied Congress for a feasible homesteading policy in which settlers could acquire western lands for no more than a nominal administrative fee. By 1854 the newly organized Republican Party placed free western lands into its platform, a move that would surely aid Lincoln's presidential victory in November of 1860. Meanwhile southerners resisted vociferously, fearing that competition from western farmers would be ruinous to their own, slave-driven, operations. The secession crisis in 1860 and 1861 resulted in the depletion of southern Democrats in Congress, allowing for easy passage in both the House and Senate of the Homestead Act in 1862. Two months later Lincoln also signed the Railway Act and the Morrill Act, providing federal subsidies for transcontinental railway construction and federal land for agricultural colleges, respectively, further reshaping the American West.[12]

Long after Lincoln's assassination in 1865, both the spirit and the policies of homesteading intensified. That year New York Tribune editor, statesman, and longtime supporter of the homestead concept, Horace Greeley, famously popularized the phrase "Go West, young man," and he reiterated it in 1871: "Of course, I say to all who are in want of work, Go West!" Lesser known but probably more influential were the campaigns among eastern workers and their representatives for free land in the West, particularly after the depression of 1873 and the massive labor strikes of 1877. In this context many believed that the Homestead Act could serve as a kind of "safety valve" for unemployed workers teeming in the East. Meanwhile Congress continued to expand the scope of the Homestead Act. Because dryland farming in the Far West generally required more than 160 acres to be profitable, Congress passed the Enlarged Homestead Act of 1909, which granted settlers 320 acres. And because cattle raising took so much land, the federal government authorized the Stock-Raising Homestead Act of 1916, granting 640 acres for settlers to raise livestock. Far from losing relevance in the twentieth century, the Homestead Act and its ancillary acts only became more important.[13]

However, as countless homesteaders would find, very little is truly free. "The gift of soil," the noted American political scientist Arthur Fisher Bentley wrote in 1893, "is by no means all that is needed as the foundation for a farm." He estimated the cost—which included purchasing horses and implements, small stock, stables, seed, and the labor costs of breaking forty acres—to be no less than $1,000 (more than about $25,000, in today's dollars). In 1909 Arthur H. Dutton of the *San Francisco Chronicle* sounded a similarly cautious note for aspiring California homesteaders:

> The public lands are not available for the poor man, that is, for the penniless man, with or without family, who yearns for a home of his own in the country, where he may work for himself, emancipated from the thrall of employer, landlord, butcher, baker, and candle-stick maker. At the lowest possible standard of living for an American, $750 in cash is the least amount that the prospective homesteader, a single man, should have on hand before he makes his first settlement on the land. After that he may be able to earn a living from the land itself, but that amount is essential at the start. It will give him but the barest necessities. A thousand dollars will be needed for a man with a family. Fifteen hundred dollars will give some sense of security to a single man and $2500 to a man of family.

Indeed it might be said that homesteading was the American dream most Americans could not actually afford.[14]

Furthermore the geographic and environmental diversity of California guaranteed that homesteading would be an imbalanced affair across the state. There are dozens of ways to divide the pie of California, each of which reveals unique environmental, climatological, and land-use distinctions. The most familiar, and the broadest, of these is the distinction between Northern and Southern California. Although there are fifty-eight counties in California, just four Southern California counties claimed 22 percent of all homesteads: Kern, San Bernardino, Los Angeles, and San Diego, respectively. The patents for those emanated from the Los Angeles Land Office on Spring Street, the same one Francisco Trujillo visited to find his Topanga tract. Another, perhaps more useful, way to divide California is by its four major regions, and homesteaders spread throughout all of them: the coast (31 percent), the mountains (30 percent), the central valley (29 percent), and the desert (10 percent). If you add in the countless microclimates affecting each region, the variance in homestead experiences was wide.

Whatever their precise geographical and environmental circumstances,

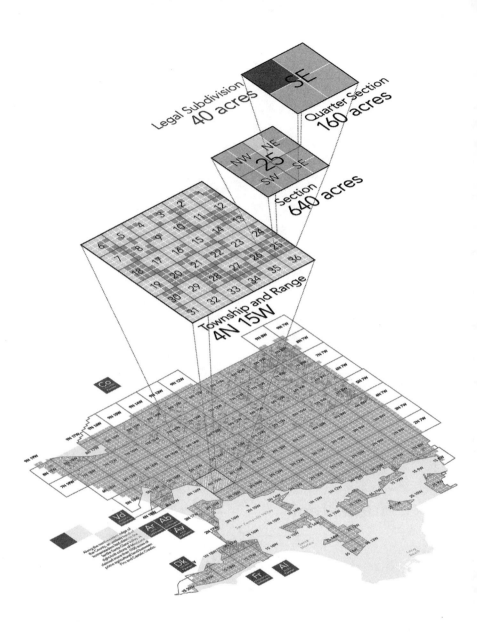

6. A homestead parcel. The Land Ordinance of 1785 established the Public Land Survey System (also known as the Rectangular Survey System) in which the land of the West was divided into townships that contained six square miles, and was further subdivided into thirty-six sections, each containing one square mile (640 acres). David Deis, Department of Geography, California State University, Northridge.

Crescent City •

Eureka •

Mendocino •

Sacramento •

San Francisco •

• Fresno

• Bakersfield

Number of
Homesteads
PER SECTION

- 1
- 2
- 3 or more

each section
is approximately
1 square mile,
or 640 acres

Los Angeles

San Diego

7. The homesteads of California. David Deis, Department of Geography, California
State University, Northridge.

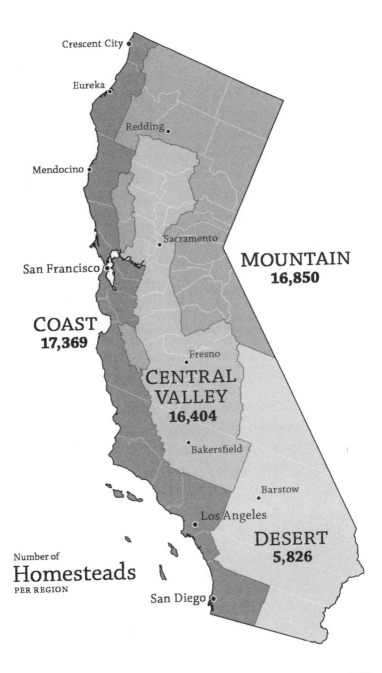

Crescent City

Eureka

Redding

Mendocino

Sacramento

MOUNTAIN
16,850

San Francisco

COAST
17,369

Fresno

CENTRAL
VALLEY
16,404

Bakersfield

Barstow

Los Angeles

DESERT
5,826

Number of
Homesteads
PER REGION

San Diego

8. California homesteads by region. David Deis, Department of Geography, California State University, Northridge.

California homesteaders knew the odds were against them. "Uncle Sam bets you 160 acres of sand that you can't live on it for three years without starving," one morbid homesteader saying went. And in the American popular imagination, the "homesteader" became a member of a social class of people instead of what he or she really was: an individual claimant of public lands under the Homestead Act. At its most benign this class perception generated condescension toward homesteaders. They were folks to be pitied. Newspapers frequently described them as "lonely," and in December of 1921 a group of women working at a Northern California land office decided to write letters to isolated Humboldt County homesteaders in order to spread Christmas cheer. At its worst the perception generated contempt—they were "white trash" or "sandlappers," a term for a bird that scratched the sand for seeds. Both shades of the perception—condescension and contempt—were evident in the "cowboy poetry" of Elliot C. Lincoln, a Harvard graduate, Pomona College English professor, and onetime Claremont city councilman. In 1920 Houghton Mifflin published his first book, *Rhymes of a Homesteader*, in which he included this poem with the same title:

Buried up to his ears in debt,
Fighting the heat and cold and wet,
His chances worse than an even bet—
You'll find the homesteader.

Eyes burned out in the summer sun,
Skin like a beefsteak underdone;
You'd think him fifty—he's thirty-one—
But then, he's a homesteader

Winter comes, and his note is due
(Summer was dry, so nothing grew),
So he sells his gun, and a cow or two,
And hopes, does the homesteader.

Rough and broken his acres lie,
Half of them white with alkali;

But they mean that thing he couldn't buy—
A home—to the homesteader.

One part hero, and three parts fool,
All of him bulldog grit, as a rule.
He's slow to learn, but he stays in school.
"Here's How," Mister Homesteader.

Another poem written by a Southern California desert homesteader
was more charitable, though no less sardonic:

Jim Travers had a homestead,
A square half mile of land,
The desert stretched on every side
With greasewood, sage and sand.

Jim Travers had a homestead,
And not much else beside,
But a shack a man has made himself
Can fill his heart with pride.

He had no need of many things,
He didn't wear a shirt,
He hauled his water in a can;
Clean sand is not like dirt.

Boiled beans will fill a belly up
With salt pork for a treat.
He had a rabbit now and then,
Or turtle for fresh meat.

He worked for wages when he could,
But neighbors lend a hand
And sort of pass themselves around
Out in this desert land.

The air was sparkling clear and clean,
The sun was hot as noon.

Red sunset blazed across the sky,
Came dusk, and then the moon.

Bare mountains fifty miles away
Shone white beneath its light.
Jim slept beneath the vast round sky.
He loved the desert night.

The desert's wealth is for the poor,
Alone-ness without bars;
Aloneness in a friendly land;
Wide spaces and the stars.

Jim Travers had the sort of wealth
That comes where lands are wide,
Jim Travers had a homestead—
And not much else beside.

Among the 1.6 million men and women throughout the American
West who acquired homesteads, many were like Travers and Francisco
Trujillo, folks who sought to better their lot in life by acquiring and suc-
cessfully "proving up" 160 acres of land granted to them by the United
States federal government because they had "not much else beside."[15]

2

A Country of Plantations and Estates

When Lincoln signed the Homestead Act late in May of 1862, many Americans were anxiously reading the news of Confederate general Thomas "Stonewall" Jackson's audacious campaign through Virginia's Shenandoah Valley. Even way out in remote Los Angeles, sectionalist tension ran high, and the most influential newspaper editor of the moment, Henry Hamilton of the *Los Angeles Star*, openly denounced Republicans as "n—— worshippers." But for the overwhelmingly Mexican population around *la plaza*, there was more interesting news: their countrymen's defeat of the French at the Battle of Puebla earlier in the month on May 5, Cinco de Mayo. The liberal San Francisco–based newspaper *La Voz de Méjico* described a wave of patriotism among Mexicans living in California, claiming that "there are more than a thousand Mexicans ready and willing to march to Mexico to offer their services in defending their country against the foreign aggression." In truth, Mexicans were deeply divided about the event, but for the elders among them, those who could still remember the bruising 1848 conquest of California in the Mexican-American War—*la invasión*, as they called it—the vanquishing of the French had surely given them some satisfaction.[1]

If Mexican and American patriotic sentiments quickened the pulse, daily life in frontier Los Angeles was slow going. Folks were still talking about the ferocious forty-three-day storm the previous winter that brought more than sixty inches of rain and massive flooding to arid Los Angeles. "Rivers were formed in every gulch and arroyo," the *Los Angeles*

Star reported. "The Los Angeles river, already brimful, overflowed its banks, and became a fierce and destructive flood," washing away livestock, roads, orchards, vineyards, waterworks, and probably a handful of long-forgotten laborers. But now it was spring, and the elder Mexicans basked in its fragrant warmth, under the Peruvian pepper trees of *la plaza*. Sonoran farriers and carpenters, and bakers from Sinaloa plied their trade while Americans and European immigrants milled about, many still hungover from their gold rush dreams of the previous decade. Upstate, San Francisco thrummed with humanity, but daytime Los Angeles was somnolent. Historian Leonard Pitt described Los Angeles as a "country village," where only the "creaking caretas and barking dogs," "galloping horses," and "a commotion in a country saloon" broke the rural silence. An earlier historian named James Miller Guinn wrote of Los Angeles: "It was like the earth on the morning of creation, 'without form.'"[2]

Over on Spring Street, a jaunt from *la plaza*, the Los Angeles Land Office was similarly dull. Though it would ultimately distribute more acreage and more homesteads than any of the other seventeen federal land offices spread throughout the state from San Diego to Shasta, you would never know it in 1862. The Land Office had opened in 1853, the same year in which John Bigler, California's first full-term governor, proffered a Jeffersonian vision for the new state. "The interests of both State and nation," he proclaimed, "will unquestionably be best served by thus donating the public domain in small tracts." He continued:

It will induce emigration to the State; greatly increase the amount of taxable property; and, above all, secure to us an abundance of the necessaries of life produced at home. . . . An additional argument . . . is found in the fact, that in consequence of the inadequate cultivation of the vast and productive lands of the State, it is now and will hereafter be in the power of the unscrupulous capitalists and speculators to monopolize the very necessaries of life, and thus to reduce the laboring classes . . . to the verge of starvation.

Indeed, the rapid, efficient, and equitable disposal of the public lands would have been a great boon to California's "laboring classes," whose membership was large and needy: miners, general laborers, and farm laborers alone constituted well over half the new state's workforce. For most of them, the hope of ever buying land was a long shot, even with California's relatively high wages.[3]

And until late 1862—nine years after opening, twelve years since statehood, fourteen years since American conquest—the Los Angeles Land Office had not granted even one acre, not to the laboring classes or to anyone else. In fact its meager staff of well-connected locals did little more than file survey field notes and respond to letters from squatters outside the city straining to secure titles to their sometimes-dubious claims. Finally in December of 1862 the Los Angeles Land Office realized its first sale, a cash purchase of six lots totaling about 360 acres in the Antelope Valley, unremarkable land near a sag pond known as the West Elizabeth Lake (today Hughes Lake). The buyer was Edward Fitzgerald Beale, a privileged Naval Academy graduate–turned–swashbuckling officer, Mexican-American War veteran, California explorer, surveyor, and future founder of Tejon Ranch, the largest private landholding in the state at the time. Other than that, though, the staff of the Los Angeles Land Office had virtually nothing to show for its near decade of negligible work, nor was it alone: not even the land offices in Stockton or Marysville—both in the heart of populous gold rush country—issued any land patents until 1859, nine years after California became the nation's thirty-first state.[4]

To be sure, California real estate was a land-office business, just not at the land office. By contrast the sale of *private* land from the courthouse steps of towns across California had been red hot since statehood. In fact city leaders in Los Angeles could not even wait that long, conducting their first auction of lots in November of 1849, almost a full year before statehood and well before the city had a legitimate courthouse. Operating instead out of the scrofulous Bella Union hotel—a glorified flophouse for rough customers and, later, Confederate sympathizers—the *ayuntamiento* (town council) auctioned off 19,000-square-foot plots for between $50 and $200, a good deal for men who had already made their fortunes in cattle ranching and land acquisition long before American conquest, including Benjamin David "Don Benito" Wilson, Francisco Figueroa, and one of the richest men in Los Angeles County, Jonathan "Don Juan" Temple, the first American mayor of the city during the Mexican-American War and one of its first developers. The *ayuntamiento* also granted large parcels to individuals and companies that provided services to the city, including the Pioneer Oil Company, the Canal and Reservoir Company, Phineas Banning, and Ozro W. Childs, who built the city a new canal. By the early 1860s the city of Los Angeles had sold off almost all of its patrimony, the first of many steps toward its legendary privatization.[5]

North of Los Angeles, in the San Joaquin Valley, the landgrab was more spectacular. During California's first two decades, a coterie of wheat, land, and cattle barons—"land pirates," as critics called them—acquired vast acreages of prime agricultural land, sometimes through fraudulent means: the cattle company Miller & Lux claimed 328,000 acres; land speculator William S. Chapman, 277,600; "Wheat King" Isaac Friedlander, 107,000. And because controlling land required controlling water, Miller & Lux infamously acquired both banks of the San Joaquin River in an unbroken strip of more than one hundred miles. "Cattle of every kind and age ran wild," one observer in Fresno wrote. "They multiplied and in great herds grazed on the hills and roamed the valley and plains as freely as deer." At its height the range stretched roughly from Chowchilla to Kings River and from the foothills of the Sierra to the Coast Range. "Our land system," Governor Henry Huntly Haight railed in an 1869 speech to the California Legislature in Sacramento, "seems to be mainly framed to facilitate the acquisition of large blocks of land by capitalists or corporations either as donations or at nominal prices." Opposition to "land monopoly" would soon become a potent political rallying cry in Gilded Age California.[6]

Literally, of course, there was not a monopoly on land in nineteenth-century California. Instead a clique of very wealthy and aggressive men manipulated federal public laws and corrupted public officials in order to hoard land and water. But "land monopoly" clearly made a better slogan, and it was soon decried in the editorial pages and repeatedly investigated in the state capital. Henry George further popularized the term "land monopoly" in his best-selling book *Progress and Poverty* published in 1879. George and other critics of "land monopoly" were surely righteous, but it is also worth understanding how far gone the land problem really was by the time they discovered it. At its birth California inherited a vexing legacy of Spanish and Mexican land claims that immediately dashed any hope of an even vaguely equitable disposal of land. The "land pirates" would certainly exacerbate the problem later, but it was already in the blood.

Even before the signing of the Treaty of Guadalupe Hidalgo—the peace treaty ending the Mexican-American War in February of 1848—it was clear to Americans in California that reckoning with property in the territory and state was going to be devilishly complex. "It will produce distress on the land," a young William T. Sherman observed in 1847 while stationed in Monterey, but "will offer plenty of employment for lawyers." Although the treaty promised that Mexican property would be "inviolably respected," executing such a policy would be a tall order because of the peculiar legacy of Spanish and Mexican land claims: in the 1780s the Spanish had issued a handful of land grants to prominent citizens to encourage settlement in what they called "Alta California," and after Mexico gained independence from Spain in 1821, the Mexican government intensified the practice, particularly in the 1840s. By the end of the war there were about seven hundred fifty grants covering a staggering fourteen million acres of prime California land. Many of the grants were "truly baronial in their extent and surroundings," as one contemporary described them.[7]

The "Californios," as the Mexican land grantees referred to themselves, lived in a sumptuous fashion much more feudal than modern. Take the case of Don Mariano Guadalupe Vallejo, born to influential Spanish parents in Monterey in about 1807. Groomed for leadership as a teenager, Vallejo quickly rose through the ranks of the Spanish and Mexican governments, ultimately founding the bucolic town of Sonoma and becoming the director of colonization in Northern California. As a reward for his dutiful service Vallejo acquired several ranchos, which, when combined, constituted about 175,000 acres, or about 275 square miles. The lifestyle of the Californios—the state's first leisure class—comported with their vast landholdings. "Labor of any kind they regard as dishonorable," one mission padre said of the Californios, and so they relied exclusively on the toil of the American Indians cast out of the missions after Mexican independence. These laborers were sometimes called *emancipados* for their dubious freedom. Their numbers decimated by mission-era contagions, their landscape destroyed by roaming Mexican cattle, and their culture nearly erased by captivity, the American Indians of California were easily, shamefully, exploitable. It was almost exclusively by the sweat of the *emancipados'* brows that the ranchos became the hubs of a vast statewide cattle empire, shipping out millions of hides and millions of barrels of tallow, the rendered fat of cows used chiefly for making candles in the pre-electrical era. During the gold rush Californios turned to selling live cattle to the meat-starved markets in gold country, realizing a handsome profit for a spell. And they rewarded themselves fittingly, hosting large fiestas with musical accompaniment, serving roasted pig, red and white wines, and pickled olives, with regularity. "He lived in a luxurious style and had a large household of trained servants, chiefly Indians," a dinner guest at the San Fernando Valley home of Andrés Pico recalled. "His silver and china table-service made a brilliant display." Mariano Vallejo had silver spoons, too, his having been smithed and monogrammed for him in Russia.[8]

But the days of silver and fine china were short-lived; *la invasión* and the gold rush changed all that. The war severely disrupted Californios' cattle operations and scattered their American Indian laborers, forcing about a quarter of them to sell off their ranchos to well-heeled American newcomers in the months immediately following the Treaty of Guadalupe Hidalgo. For the rest of the Californios the most immediate threat came from American squatters who exploited—by the thousands—the vague boundaries of the unfenced ranchos and loudly rejected the legitimacy of grants handed down by a vanquished enemy anyway. In fairness to the squatters it was often impossible to know who owned what in California immediately after the war, and a man who had risked life

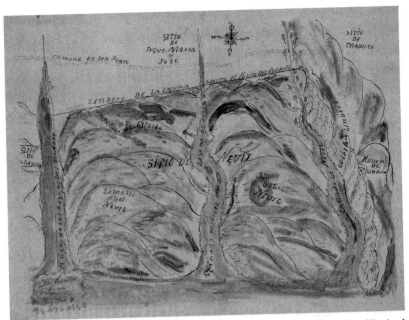

9. *Diseño* map of Rancho Niguel, 1872. The casual *diseños* bespoke an era of limited litigiousness among Mexican landowners. American conquest, by contrast, brought with it careful land surveys and the Public Land Survey System. Though the vast majority of Californios secured title to their land under the California Land Act of 1851, they paid a very high price to do so, often mortgaging land or selling parcels outright to cover legal costs. They also strained under the weight of new land taxes and, occasionally, gambling debts. *Diseño* map of Rancho Niguel, with certification by J. R. Hardenburgh, Jan. 17, 1872, SR_Map_0087A, Solano-Reeves Collection, Huntington Library, San Marino, California.

and limb to cross the plains, then had failed as a gold miner, and then had subsequently improved a plot of land that was neither cultivated nor occupied had good reason to feel possessive of his investment of time, energy, and capital. Indeed, millions of acres of rancho lands throughout California had no sign of inhabitation, cultivation, or even grazing, a function of the peculiar Spanish and Mexican system. In sharp contrast to the precision of the American system—specifically the Public Land Survey System laid out in 1785—the Spanish and Mexican system was extremely casual, as the property maps, known as *diseños*, from the period reveal. Hand drawn and colored, without reference to longitude or latitude, and loosely bound by natural landmarks that might move or disappear without warning—a creek bed, a fallen tree, a cow skull—the quaint maps appear to the modern viewer as an invitation for future chaos. At the very least they suggest that Sherman had been right, that there would be "distress on the land."[9]

Indeed distress soon became a full-blown crisis in which thousands of squatters fanned out across the state, engaging in sporadic violence to defend their presumed rights. "The good ones were few," Mariano Vallejo said of the incoming hordes, "and the wicked many." Nor were the Californios the sole target of land-related violence: in 1850 at least seven men were killed in Sacramento in the so-called squatters' riot against speculators and local law enforcement. Finally, a long three years after the end of the war, Congress stepped in and passed the California Land Act of 1851, which created the Land Commission appointed by the president to adjudicate Mexican claims. The Land Commission worked as efficiently as it could, but because documentation for the 813 cases was often lost or destroyed, and the *diseños* were vague and unofficial, the process was a slow one, averaging about five years per case. Appeals ended up in the district courts and occasionally the United States Supreme Court, further dragging out the affair. Ultimately the Land Commission process was surprisingly solicitous toward the claimants, and in the end about 80 percent of the rancho claims were upheld. But the victories were often pyrrhic: defending those claims was very expensive, potentially costing thousands of dollars in lawyer fees, surveys, and boundary litigation. For example, Manuel Dominguez, heir to the roughly 43,000-acre Rancho San Pedro in southern Los Angeles County, incurred more than $20,000 in fees to secure his claim, which he finally did in 1858. Because Californios were often land-poor, lacking the money to pay legal fees, they offered up land instead, and about a quarter of rancho property quickly passed into the hands of American attorneys in the process. Finally it must be said that the Californios were infamously spendthrift, borrowing heavily to pay their new state land taxes, racking up horse-gambling debts, and simply refusing to tighten their belts. When the Californios lost their land, en masse, their lifestyle quickly followed, and soon they died off or melted into the masses of landless and struggling mestizos. "Most of the old families sank into obscurity," one observer wrote of the Californios in 1891, "and it is now difficult to trace their connections." It was not long before advertisers seized upon the romanticized image of the Californio for this or that insipid ad campaign, but there were almost no Californios around to enjoy their revived popularity, such as it was.[10]

If the Californios disappeared, the legacy of their land system emphatically did not. "California is not a country of farms," Henry George lamented in 1871, but rather "a country of plantations and estates. Agriculture is a speculation." Indeed, although the new rancho owners could have profited handsomely and immediately by subdividing the lands and selling parcels off to the legions of land-seekers, they generally sat on the land instead, speculating on even bigger future returns. "Across many of these vast estates," George wrote, "a strong horse cannot gallop in a day, and one may travel for miles over fertile ground where no plough has ever struck, but which is all owned." A study of landholdings in Southern California in 1919—seventy-one years after the Treaty of Guadalupe Hidalgo, forty-eight years after George's observation—revealed that surprisingly little had changed. "The dominant form of the large holding," the California Commission on Immigration and Housing concluded, "is the tract which has been held the greater part of its boundaries undisturbed from Mexican times," and in some cases several former ranchos had even been "joined into one immense holding." Nineteen complete and undivided ranchos still existed as late as 1944, and many more thousands of acres of former rancho lands were still owned by a handful of individual owners or corporations. As late as the 1970s only 257 individuals or corporations owned 25 percent of California land.[11]

But for members of the laboring class—the overwhelming majority of whom could not afford to buy former rancho land even if it had been quickly subdivided and sold off—it was the failure of *public* land disposal that was the most immediate cause of their frustration and landlessness. The California State Legislature bears significant responsibility for this failure. Initially operating out of a mud-splattered hotel in San Jose, the "Legislature of a Thousand Drinks," as it was known, absolutely lacked decorum. "It is of the style of rump parliament," an English visitor observed, "with very little dignity, very little sense, and still less honesty." In fairness, the legislature did establish the basic features of state government, including a tax collection system, a board of education, and a prison system, no mean feat in an immense and mostly lawless new territory. But the legislature's failure to centralize the process of public land sales in the first eight years of statehood was an unmitigated disaster that would stain California indelibly. By leaving the chief mechanisms of the land business—surveying, assessing, selling, and recording—entirely in the hands of county-level officials, the legislature invited cronyism and other forms of corruption, and that is precisely what it got, on a grand scale. One after another surveyor took bribes from so-called land jobbers and granted free lands to employees, friends, and, of course, themselves. Even lowly clerks wreaked havoc on the system by entering falsified information into the property rolls for the right price. In one brazen instance an anonymous rogue intercepted a bill en route to the governor's office and scratched out a provision limiting the total allowable acreage per sale. Unaware of the change, the governor signed the bill, and it would take another three years until the legislature restored the original intent of the law.[12]

The legislature finally got around to creating a centralized state land office in 1858, but it was chronically underfunded and understaffed, and too late: untold acreage of public lands had been lost forever to swindlers and their confreres. The Swamp Land Act of 1850 only intensified the calamity. A well-intentioned federal law designed to bring annually inundated lands under cultivation in Florida, the act had great potential in California, particularly in the marshy tule basins of the Sacramento Valley. Shortly after the passage of the act, Governor Bigler—that stalwart of generous public land distribution to the laboring classes—urged the legislature to institute "stringent restrictions" on swamplands to prevent speculation, which it quickly did by establishing a purchase limit of 320 acres. These restrictions, coupled with state and federal disagreements over what, precisely, constituted swamplands, created uncertainty about title, slowed land sales, and drove the cash-strapped legislature to create a centralized swamplands board in 1861. But money talked, and influential land speculators soon exerted so much pressure on legislators that they ultimately voted to restore local control, thereby killing any hope for a systematic and unified system of swampland disposal. As a result a staggering 2.2 million acres—more than 3,400 square miles—passed into the hands of fewer than three hundred men under highly dubious circumstances. "The simple presence" of water, a legislative committee concluded ruefully, "is all that is necessary to show to the speculator that the land is 'swamp' and it therefore presents an inviting opportunity for his grasping cupidity." There are no historians of California unfamiliar with the tale of cattle baron Henry Miller's alleged voyage across the San Joaquin Valley on a rowboat strapped to the top of a horse-drawn wagon, an absurd but successful effort to secure occasionally damp lands under the Swamp Land Act.[13]

Meanwhile Congress gave away the farm to get the transcontinental railroad. About two months after signing the Homestead Act, Lincoln signed the Pacific Railway Act granting the Union Pacific Railroad and Central Pacific Railroad companies enormous tracts of public land in the West, more than six thousand acres for each mile of track completed— ultimately more than 175 million acres. By 1870 the railroads owned twenty million acres of California land, approximately 20 percent of the entire state. Little wonder critics described the railroad as an "octopus" whose tentacles stretched across the state lands and whose influence stretched into the courts and the California State Legislature. Statewide outcry about "land monopoly" only intensified.

South in Los Angeles, where civic leaders openly fretted about the small size of the population, the railroads brought the promise of a brighter future. At the time of the 1870 census Los Angeles had only about six thousand residents, far fewer than San Francisco's 150,000, but also fewer than Sacramento, Stockton, Oakland, and even Fresno. The completion of the Southern Pacific Railroad line from San Francisco to Los Angeles in 1876, followed by the completion of the southern Santa Fe Railway in 1886, changed all that by bringing thousands of white

Americans and Western Europeans to the small city. Their arrival also accelerated the demise of the Californios, hastened the subdivision of the old ranchos, and dramatically intensified farming. "Only within the past few years," an 1886 railroad promotional pamphlet read, "has emigration come to California, an emigration seeking homes where industry would be rewarded by a comfortable living for the agriculturalist and his family, and where thrift, diligence and economy would eventuate in a competency for age, education of his children, and that period of release from toil which should be the reward of very well-ordered and industrious life." These "agriculturalists"—in stark contrast to the wheat and cattle barons of the San Joaquin Valley—generally operated smaller-scale intensive farms, building markets for honey, wine, citrus, and dozens of other fruits and nuts. Ultimately, according to historian Leonard Pitt, "more than a hundred towns and thousands of orchards and farms were platted out in Southern California during the 1880s"[14]

Urban development moved in all directions, but because surveying was not completed until 1871 and most of the available land had been picked over by speculators during the booms, aspiring homesteaders found very little in Los Angeles on which to settle. Fewer than twenty homesteads existed in the city proper. The small collection of Los Angeles homesteaders concentrated around contemporary Hollywood, straddling Normandie Avenue and bounded on the north and south by Melrose Avenue and Wilshire Boulevard, respectively. At the time of homestead settlement, this "far western" region was surveyed but not part of the City of Los Angeles until 1910, shortly before film production began in the area. In the late nineteenth century it was known alternately as Cahuenga Valley or Cahuenga, both in reference to the Cahuenga Pass—named by the Tongva Indians—which allowed passage between the San Fernando Valley and Los Angeles. Among the first and certainly the most successful of the Cahuenga homesteaders was a Danish immigrant named Ivar A. Weid.

Weid arrived in Los Angeles in 1871, soon finding work as a gauger for the Los Angeles County Surveyor, a post that made him a rare expert on land division and sale in Southern California. Most importantly Weid

10. Location of homesteads in the context of modern Hollywood. David Deis, Department of Geography, California State University, Northridge.

knew where the few remaining parcels of public land were in Los Angeles, and he soon filed on an eighty-acre homestead. Weid built a substantial house, thirty-six by twenty-four feet, worth about $600, fenced forty acres, and planted wheat and later two hundred fruit trees.[15] Clearly savvy, Weid invested his income from fruit sales in shares of a mining company that evidently paid dividends, because he soon purchased a beachfront block in Santa Monica, which he held on to for a few years before selling it for $5,000. With the money from that sale he easily bought an additional 240 acres around his homestead. The Chevalier wheat he produced in 1876 earned accolades in the *Pacific Rural Press* for its heft and plumpness. Soon his portion of Cahuenga Valley was commonly referred to as Weid Canyon, and by 1880 he listed his ranch for $15,000 as a "well-known farm." "For a gentleman's home or for speculation," he advertised, "no better opportunity is offered." The homestead having catapulted Weid into new echelons, he changed his occupation in the city directory from gauger to "capitalist" and bought a house downtown. Today Ivar Street in Hollywood still bears his name, and he is credited for naming Sunset Boulevard. It is a remnant of an exceptional homesteader, at an intersection today simultaneously associated with grittiness, celebrity, expensive sushi, and the Los Angeles Film School.[16]

Shortly after Weid's death in 1903, the Historical Society of Southern California—founded by a group of visionary memory-keepers in 1883—published a biographical sketch of the pioneer. As was the nature of the form, the biography extolled the virtues of Weid's character. His "snug fortune" was the product of Weid's "untiring energy and liberality," his "temperate habits," and his "careful investments." To have read Weid's biography in 1903 must have warmed the cockles of other prominent men in Southern California because it was proof of their belief that through virtue, prudence, and discipline anyone could amass great wealth and place "himself in an enviable position socially." Yet, without diminishing Weid's impressive wealth-building, it is also an obvious point that he benefitted from the only topic Americans still will not discuss: the importance of random good fortune. Weid arrived at precisely the right time, just before all the public land in Los Angeles was gone; the federal government gave him an eighty-acre gift through the Homestead Act, and it was the foundation for all his future success; and nature rewarded him: Weid's wheat crop did not fail. The man obviously worked very hard and avoided ruinous and expensive habits, and for that he fairly earned the accolades of the Historical Society. But it was wrong to imagine Weid's life as a simple parable about the rewards of virtue; it was also a story about simple good luck, a lesson that would never be lost on homesteaders.[17]

3

Instant Relics

It was late in the summer of 1916 when homesteader Charles Decker awoke, hitched his horse, pushed through the salt brush and horsetail, and then drove his wagon down a dusty trail from the mountains into the town of Santa Monica to buy supplies. He was approaching the pier when a Pacific Electric streetcar slammed into his wagon, shattering it into a twisted wreck of wood and iron. Fortunately Decker escaped injury, and in the annals of American traffic collisions the incident does not even warrant a footnote, but it is an irresistible metaphor for the awkward spot homesteaders occupied in rapidly modernizing California. By the time of Decker's accident, horse-drawn wagons were oddities in Los Angeles. It had been almost thirty years since electric trolleys began replacing them, and more than a decade since automobiles began replacing the trolleys. Futurists in Europe and the United States, inspired by the Wright Brothers' inaugural North Carolina flight in 1903, were already predicting flying cars. Indeed the automobile was so common in Los Angeles that the Board of Public Utilities urgently sought the removal of traffic-clogging trolleys from the streets, hoping to put them into underground tunnels or onto elevated tracks. In other words, witnesses to Decker's accident surely regarded his splintered wagon as a curio, and him a living relic.[1]

The early twentieth century brought extraordinary advances in manufacturing technologies that drove rural Americans toward cities where they joined millions of new European immigrants in the urgent pursuit of steady and gainful employment. As a result the proportion of Americans living in cities rose from 40 percent to 51 percent in the years between 1900 and 1920. But in California the transformation was far more dramatic: the proportion of urbanites in the population rose from 52.4 percent to 68 percent in the same period. As most Californians raced into the modern age, homesteaders generally lived like humble pioneers of the mid-nineteenth century, hunting for food, curing meat, hauling water, chopping firewood, and cultivating small farms without the aid of the new, but prohibitively expensive, internal combustion tractors. Still, as Decker discovered, modernity had a nasty way of crashing into you. Conquering nature in the Santa Monica Mountains was hard enough: choked by highly flammable coastal scrub oaks and greasewood, miles from law enforcement or professional firefighters, and fed by unpredictable creeks, the range rarely even appeared on maps of the region. But the twentieth century also brought vexing man-made challenges to the homesteaders of the Santa Monica Mountains. New restrictions on land use bedeviled them, as did new state hunting laws and the new property interests of elite Angelenos. For the homesteaders of the Santa Monica mountains the future was always a cur, nipping at their livelihood and lifestyle.[2]

Homesteaders like Charles Decker were not the first inhabitants of the Santa Monica Mountains to feel the future bearing down on them. Indigenous people had lived there for thousands of years before Charles Decker's father and mother, Marion and Emma, arrived by wagon in the early 1880s. Natives of the Chumash and Tongva groups ate yucca bulbs, soaproot, tule, acorns, small game, deer, and on the Pacific Coast, shellfish and mussels. Savvy hunters, they carefully preserved the heads of deer and wore them like crude caps, easily luring deer into close range. And to acquire what they lacked, they traded shell beads, stone mortars, seeds, and baskets with one another, as well as with indigenous people from the Tataviam, Serrano, and Yokut tribes in the region. All this is to say that natives thrived amid the bounty of the Santa Monica Mountains, and we might imagine that the homesteaders invaded and destroyed their arcadian paradise, leading to their dispossession. In fact by the time Marion Decker started homesteading the range, there were virtually no American Indians left in the area, and very few anywhere else in California. In Southern California, and throughout the state, the catastrophic damage caused by disease-infested Spanish missions was irreversible, and it was further exacerbated by the arrival of Americans who slaughtered California natives mercilessly. Statewide the native population dropped from about 300,000 before the Spanish arrived, to fewer than 25,000 by the dawn of the twentieth century. The latest date for which there is any archeological evidence of the Chumash and Tongva in the Santa Monica Mountains is 1809, though there remain about twenty sites of Chumash rock art to this day.[3]

Marion Decker was born into poverty in rural Kentucky in 1843 and worked his way to California's San Joaquin Valley by the 1860s. The valley was full of hungry men in those years, failed prospectors, struggling farmers and farmhands, forced to take up work for the big operators— Isaac "The Wheat King" Friedlander, Miller & Lux, and the like. But Decker was probably too proud to stay on as a laborer and a tenant, or perhaps too ornery. Decker and his new bride, Emma, moved to Southern California in the 1870s and, after a failed farming venture in Los Nietos near modern-day Whittier, headed for the hills. With five children, Decker claimed a plot high in the Santa Monica Mountains above Malibu in 1885 at the age of forty-two, and proved it up by 1890.[4]

The semiaridity of the Santa Monica Mountains profoundly shaped the homestead experience there. There was not then—nor is there now—a reliable, year-round, native water source in the Santa Monica Mountains. Malibu Creek, Topanga Creek (formerly Garapito Creek), and their tributaries comprised a significant watershed in wet years, but wet years in Southern California were uncommon. Recently scientists have found evidence of multiyear droughts in Southern California as early as AD 850, with one lasting more than two hundred years, and dozens more lasting ten to twenty years in a row. In Southern California there simply never has been anything like "average" rainfall. So Decker and his few neighbors were able to acquire water from the creeks— whenever it came—in large wooden barrels that they drew upon for human and draft animal consumption, and for fire control.[5]

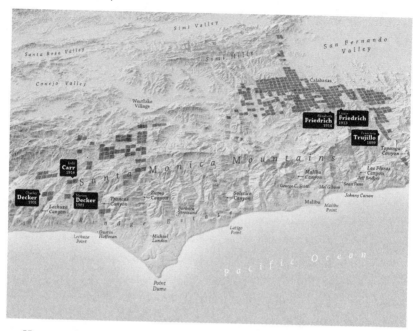

11. Homesteaders of the Santa Monica Mountains, with modern sites and celebrity addresses. David Deis, Department of Geography, California State University, Northridge.

But agriculture was another story, and in dry years homesteaders' options were few and far between. "Marion Decker, who lives up the coast," the *Los Angeles Times* reported in April of 1894, a drought year, "was in town Thursday. He brings no very glad tidings from the ranches of his neighborhood. The lack of rain has now reached a point where there remains no hope for the grain crop. Barley will make a little hay and the corn a little fodder, but that's about all." The livestock of the region was scrawny, and the farming output episodic and always underwhelming. Adding to the agriculture problem in the Santa Monica Mountains were the misty mornings, which caused "rust" on wheat crops, effectively ruining them. Finally, armyworms began infesting Southern California farms in 1899, destroying beets, corn, and beans.[6]

Because so little of the homestead land in the Santa Monica Mountains was arable or irrigable, homesteaders consumed lots of meat. The

Deckers joined poor people in other parts of the country for whom chicken was becoming an increasingly popular source of protein. Nationally the cost of beef, mutton, and pork rose dramatically at the turn of the century, largely because of the diminishment of western grazing lands. As such, Americans began to see chickens as "food for the laborer" and not simply producers of eggs. Agricultural newspapers emphasized the importance of cultivating "broilers," and most homesteaders kept a coop. One newspaper account insisted that every homesteader have "his wife and daughters and young sons raise chickens, while he and his older sons cultivate the fields, clear the forest and do the other heavy work." With proper techniques, maintaining chickens even became a fairly easy business, augmenting homesteaders' meager incomes. Small farmers throughout the United States began to focus on "finishing" (fattening for more flavor) their poultry. That process involved cramming a dozen young chickens into a tiny crate to deprive them of exercise and then feeding them large amounts of meal, oat, bran, and dried chicken blood.[7]

The Deckers also enjoyed a bountiful quarry of deer, rabbits, and ground squirrels, just as the Tongva and Chumash had before them. A full-size buck could produce up to 150 pounds of meat, some of which would be eaten fresh, some of which would be dried and cured. The bones, gristle, and blood could be ground into a nutritious animal feed. Naturally in this environment hunting became a prized skill, and gunplay a favorite pastime. Few were better at it than Marion's son, Charles Decker, but he developed his extraordinary skill at precisely the wrong time in the history of California. Born in 1870, Charles Decker filed for his own homestead next to his father's in 1901, the same year that the California State Legislature proposed what the *Los Angeles Times* referred to as "radical changes" to the existing game laws of the state. Although California had enacted game laws as early as 1851, it was not until January of 1901, when Theodore Roosevelt entered office with a commitment to conserve natural resources, that the California State Legislature began proposing truly transformative rules to the Department of Fish and Game. Specifically, Assembly Bill 625 initiated so-called bag limits for bucks, ducks and doves, and quail. "The pot hunter," the *Los Angeles Times* opined, "and his equally unprincipled confrere, the man who shoots in season and out, will be things of the past." But for Decker and others in the mountains, the three-buck-per-season rule would be stifling, and unlimited hunting of protein-rich deer was such a fundamental right that it needed articulation or defense.[8]

To the chagrin of the Deckers, the region's hunting regulation regime was surprisingly influential. Although law enforcement was very scarce in the range, citizens' groups down in Los Angeles and Santa Monica kept a wary eye on the spoils of hunters returning from the Santa Monica Mountains. Most significant was the Los Angeles County Fish and Game Protective Association, which had nearly one thousand members by 1902, only a year after its founding. Unlike other game associations whose purpose was simply to regulate hunting seasons for the sportsmen, the Fish and Game Protective Association also welcomed "every man or woman who is interested in the protection of the state's game, fish, and song birds" for more than the incentive of sport, and those concerned that birds and other animals "are being rapidly exterminated." The organization, according to *Forest and Stream* magazine, "so influenced public opinion that any violator of the game laws is almost certain of arrest and conviction." As the secretary of the organization explained it, part of its goal was to educate hunters, and particularly landowners, "that all game and other wild life belongs to the State of California, and not to those property owners upon whose land it may roam, and neither does the possession of such land invest any special privileges in regard to shooting out of season."[9]

Charles Decker resisted the new game enforcement regime emphatically. Not only did he reportedly brag that he could kill meat "whenever he desired to get away with it," but he "soonered"—the practice of hunting before the official season began. More egregiously, he and his father welcomed influential men from Los Angeles who craved a "frontier experience" in the modern age. Charles hosted weekend hunting parties, some of which respected Fish and Game seasons, others of which did not. Charles and five of his guests from Los Angeles were dragged before the court in 1916 to face charges of soonering. He admitted to the crime but argued that he had a large family that "demanded meat and that deer was the only meat available." The judge levied fines against the five others hunting at the Decker ranch but spared Decker, evidently sympathetic with his need to feed his family. But he warned Decker that he suspected that his homestead was "in reality, merely a rendezvous of illicit deer slayers."[10]

Illicit or not, hunting at the Deckers' homesteads became a regional pastime for affluent Angelenos. Newspapers relished accounts of prominent men returning from the Deckers', having bagged bucks and quail. Beginning in the late 1890s scarcely a weekend passed without a society page account of one or another scion visiting the Deckers for a hunting adventure. "Seven fat bucks is the record made by a party of Los Angeles and Santa Monica sportsmen who returned yesterday morning from a five days' sojourn on the Malibu above Santa Monica," the *Los Angeles Times* gushed in 1904. "Finer deer never came into the beach city, and the hunters were naturally very well satisfied with their journey." Accounts in the *Times* were so common that the newspaper encouraged others to settle in the Santa Monica Mountains: "If there is a man in the city who hasn't made use of his homestead privileges," the newspaper quoted one "man of affairs" as saying, "he is losing a great opportunity if he does not make a homestead entry on some of the Santa Monica Mountain land. I am as certain of its future value as I am of the development of this city. The time will come, and not a long way off, when these mountain lands will be in demand, with their beautiful elevations, overlooking the sea."[11]

If the Deckers and their homesteading neighbors resisted new hunting rules coming up from the city, they were largely helpless in the face of new land policies in the region. Specifically, beginning in the 1890s they found their access to the coastal road blocked by the new owners of the vast Rancho Malibu Sequit. The ensuing conflict over Malibu's coastal road—later the Pacific Coast Highway—would last more than twenty years and become the subject of Los Angeles lore. Today it is difficult to imagine Malibu as anything other than what it has become and what it has represented for the last half century. A collection of premium-priced beachfront, hillside, and canyon homes, Malibu is more than a locale—it is the American Dream on steroids. For Californians and many Americans there is no locale more synonymous with wealth, beauty, and luxury than Malibu. Not even the fires that periodically rage through Malibu—indeed that have raged since long before the arrival of the Spanish in the eighteenth century—can shake the collective faith that no place is better than Malibu.

Stretching along more than twenty miles of pristine coastline, and spanning more than 13,000 acres, Rancho Malibu Sequit was magnificent. Granted to José Bartolomé Tapia in 1804, the rancho initially passed from its Spanish owner into the hands of a Frenchman named Leon Victor Prudhomme, and then to Don Mateo Keller, a vintner-cum-banker. The coastal road on the far western edge of the property had remained passable for public use since construction in 1804. It was the essential route to the market of Santa Monica, and without it homesteaders and other settlers in the Santa Monica Mountains would have to make the arduous and time-consuming trip over the mountain, into the San Fernando Valley, and then east to the Sepulveda Pass. Even with the best horse and the fairest conditions, the route took at least six hours. For Decker, who would testify to the same effect many times, the coastal route had been a public thoroughfare as long as he could remember. But this all changed in 1891, when Frederick Hastings Rindge bought the rancho.

Rindge, the sole heir to the vast estate of British textile magnate and billionaire Samuel Baker Rindge, traveled from Massachusetts to Los Angeles in 1887, settled in Santa Monica, and purchased Rancho Topanga Malibu Sequit as a "weekend home" for his wife, May Knight Rindge. Immediately, the Rindges insisted that the roadway was their private property, and they soon erected a gate. Marion Decker—who had built his own winding road, Decker Canyon, to connect to the coastal road—was incensed and told Rindge as much. Frederick Rindge conceded and gave Decker and select homesteaders keys to the gate. But when Frederick died suddenly in 1905 and May Knight Rindge took over, concessions to the homesteaders quickly evaporated. "Today, if a stranger attempts to travel up the old road of the Malibu Rancho," the *Los Angeles Times* reported in 1907, "he is likely to be turned back by padlocked gates or by agents who make him declare his business and destination." In a failed effort to block further settlement of the Santa Monica Mountains, May Rindge even petitioned the United States Department of Forestry to declare the Santa Monica Mountains a forest reserve.[12]

Rindge ignored multiple county requests to remove her gates, thus triggering a nearly twenty-year legal battle between the county and Rindge's small army of lawyers. Summoned many times to testify to the long-standing public nature of the roadway, Marion Decker and his fellow homesteaders appeared to the *Los Angeles Times* as relics. "Bronzed and bearded pioneers and their families, their health and cheerfulness calling to mind memories of mountain and stream, appeared in . . . superior court yesterday." Even with the support of the U.S. secretary of the interior, the county lost several key trials to the Rindge lawyers. As the trials dragged on, homesteaders complained increasingly about going hungry for lack of access to the markets of Santa Monica. In 1917, by which time Charles Decker and other "belligerent mountaineers" had finally upgraded to automobiles, they participated in a blockade, in which they turned the tables on Rindge by chaining their cars together outside her home, preventing her access to the road. She responded in kind and had the road dynamited so that it was impassible.[13]

At one point in the long trial, Superior Court judge Paul John McCormick, several attorneys, and the bailiff took a three-day trip to the road in question. Even by 1918 the range was still regarded as serious backcountry. "This trip will not make the history that the Lewis-Clark exploration did," the *Los Angeles Times* reported, "but horses will pack their outfit, and if necessary the court will sleep on the ground beside a camp fire. Flapjacks, beans, bacons and coffee will be the bill of fare." Ultimately the 1923 Supreme Court decision settled the affair, and construction on the roadway commenced. It slowed briefly, however, when a construction crew dug into a Native American burial site. Human bones, shell beads, and arrowheads spread across the ground, "valuable relics of a departed race," according to the *Los Angeles Times*.[14]

Beginning in the 1920s something happened that the Deckers could never have imagined: the Santa Monica Mountains became gentrified, although the term was not yet in currency. First the home place of natives for thousands of years, then a frontier of desperation for homesteaders like the Deckers, the Santa Monica Mountains finally became a wilderness playground of the rich. The gentrification of the Santa Monica Mountains was a function of elite culture and tastes but also of an 1891 amendment to the Homestead Act itself, the so-called commutation clause, which allowed for cash purchase after fourteen months' residency. Seldom used in California until the early twentieth century, the clause allowed elites to buy up parcels of public land as extended vacation properties. "Los Angeles Business men become squatters," the *Los Angeles Times* teased, but the effects were real. By 1923 all public land in the Santa Monica Mountains had been claimed. "The whole face of the Santa Monica mountains," the *Los Angeles Times* reported that year, "has been changed." That development, coupled with the gradual dissolution of the Rindge estate in the 1930s, set the region on its modern course toward subdivision as an elite bastion.[15]

Among the gentlemen who increasingly inhabited the Santa Monica Mountains was a man named Charles Crutcher, an aspiring writer who self-published a collection of stories called *Tales from Topanga* in 1927. In the story "The Man on the Mountain," Crutcher tells the tale of an old Topanga homesteader. The man lives in a small shack "in quiet and solemn grandeur," imparting wisdom and smoking "a yellow cob pipe, with a peaceful expression covering his round face." Crutcher was unabashed in his romanticism: "'Do you live here all alone?' he asked the homesteader. He replied, 'Just my thoughts, my rabbits and my birds, they are my companions, my friends.'" In Crutcher's soft hands, men like Decker became artifacts of a pioneer past, as distant and noble as the Chumash and Tongva, whose bones were strewn across paradise.[16]

4

Hard-Bitten Country

George W. Ozmun followed all the rules in a county where nobody else seemed to give a damn. During a warm October day in 1910 he marched into the land office at Visalia and filed on a forty-acre homestead near the Kern County town of Taft. The small size of his plot was uncommon, but land was moving fast in Kern—oil was booming—and Ozmun wanted his own farm before it was too late. To support the upkeep of his small farm and the cabin he had built, he worked as a prospector in the foothills east of Taft where more than a few prospectors had made thousands of dollars from gold, borax, and gypsum strikes in the county. And so Ozmun toiled, both on the farm and beyond, as most homesteaders did. But when he returned home from work with his family one afternoon in 1911, he found that his labor had been in vain. More specifically, he found that his cabin had disappeared.[1]

The implausible theft of Ozmun's house likely inspired a few giggles in town, but among homesteading farmers it was no laughing matter, and they knew exactly who was to blame: oilmen. Indeed, as the sheriff soon discovered, the theft was a conspiracy by a cabal of oilmen who sought to dig wells on Ozmun's land, and they realized that removing his house would undermine his effort to attain a land patent. For the homesteader the cabin was not just shelter from the elements but was also proof of improvement, and losing it could be devastating to a homesteader's claim. Ozmun was worried, and he was not alone: "The authorities have been having considerable trouble," the *Los Angeles*

Times reported of Kern County in 1911, "looking after the interests of agricultural homesteaders whose rights are being violated by those in quest of oil." Ozmun took them to court, but he would lose.[2]

A year earlier, Kern County homesteader Bernard L. Snepp—a veteran of the Spanish-American War—awoke to the sound of splitting wood. Outside, twenty workers for the Los Angeles–based Midland Oil Company—convinced there was oil beneath Snepp's property—tore down his handmade fence and drove a team of mules across his property to begin laying pipes. "He rushed over, gun in hand," the *Petroleum Gazette* reported, "and he ordered them off, but they laughed at his lone firearm against their score, and consigned him to perdition." Like Ozmun, Snepp's next step was to take Midland to court. He rushed to Bakersfield, the seat of Kern County, and filed a suit against Midland. As the trial began, Judge Charles Wellborn ordered the sheriff to eject the oilmen from Snepp's property until the matter was resolved, a ruling that the Midland workers entirely ignored, returning to work on Snepp's homestead the very next day. Judge Wellborn then ordered the Midland workers back to court to face charges of contempt of court. While they were there, Snepp loaded Midland's new $18,000 well with dynamite and grinned as it exploded in a shower of oil, dirt, and twisted metal. The well was a total loss.[3]

Judge Charles Wellborn might have ruled in Snepp's favor before the dynamiting, but it was not likely: today, in the archives of the University of Southern California, Wellborn appears in a chummy photograph with Edward L. Doheny, the famous Los Angeles oil tycoon who had drilled the first successful well in the Los Angeles City Oilfield in 1892. By 1911 Wellborn was a partner in the firm of Doheny-Canfield, owner of Midland Oil Company in Kern. But it scarcely mattered because Snepp dropped his case after a rumor spread through the county that his badly decomposed body was discovered a few miles from his homestead, a dagger still firmly lodged in his heart. He could not be sure who started the rumor, but he understood the message loud and clear. Like Ozmun, Snepp lost his homestead, but in 1923 he was able to buy a plot in Lost Hills, a small farming community and later a rest stop for weary travelers on Interstate 5.[4]

The injustice of the Ozmun and Snepp incidents was not unusual in Kern, the most hard-bitten county in California. The arrival of impoverished Okies during the Great Depression and, later, the emergence of the raw "Bakersfield sound" in local honky-tonk bars indelibly linked the county to working-class struggle, but Kern was a land of inequities long before. Because of its deep, well-drained, and loamy soils, because of early and successful efforts to divert water from the Kern River, and because the process of land distribution was so poorly regulated in the years after American takeover, much of the land was sold off by the state, with no purchase limits, long before the passage of the Homestead Act.

Land speculators William S. Chapman and Haggin & Tevis, the "Wheat King" Isaac Friedlander, and cattlemen Miller & Lux were the first to the trough, and they gorged themselves on cheap and fertile land. Chapman, Friedlander, and Miller & Lux claimed more than two hundred thousand acres in Kern alone. Readers inclined to celebrate the foresight and business acumen of these land barons might be humbled to know that some of them shamelessly manipulated the Desert Land Act of 1877, which, because it lacked the residency requirement of the Homestead Act, was ripe for massive fraud through the use of "dummy entrymen." The scheme was simple and highly effective: the land baron offered poor men cash to claim parcels of arid lands, lie in affidavits that they intended to irrigate the land, secure title under the Desert Land Act, and then transfer the title to the land baron. From the very beginning fair play was just an aberration in Kern.[5]

Today Kern County occupies a peculiar place in the California imagination. Most Californians chiefly associate it with the Grapevine, a steep roadway that grudgingly connects Central and Southern California. But it has also long been California's most agriculturally productive county, and today it grows more almonds than any other place on earth. Less appreciated is the fact that in the early twentieth century, Kern became California's leading oil producer, and today pumps out more than eight million barrels from more than 155,000 wells. It was also the most-homesteaded county in all of California, with more than thirty-seven hundred patents issued. But, as the Ozmun and Snepp incidents revealed, the high-stakes nature of agricultural and petroleum production in Kern often wreaked havoc on the simple homestead dream.[6]

The story of James Munroe Elwood was a reminder that even a poor man could get lucky, sometimes. Elwood and his wife homesteaded near Delano beginning in 1886, cultivating twenty acres of hay, mostly for the subsistence of their cattle. Elwood built a humble sixteen-by-twenty-four-foot house, a thirty-six-by-twenty-four-foot barn, a "chicken house," and a pump windmill. He also generated income by running a small lumberyard from the property. In almost every respect Elwood and his wife lived the unexceptional lives of toiling homesteaders. But their fortunes were about to change. One night in May of 1899 Elwood overheard two drunkards talking about an oil prospect on the property of a man named Thomas Means. The next morning Elwood approached Means about securing a lease to drill for oil on his land. Elwood secured the lease and wrote immediately to his father to come down from Fresno to help him. "He knew I liked to prospect," the elder Elwood later recalled. They dug a well with nothing more than a hand auger comprised of lengths of one-half-inch iron rod. They hit oil sands at thirteen feet and immediately recruited others to help in the endeavor. The senior Elwood later recounted the next steps:

We then went up onto the bluff and commenced a shaft, and at the depth of forty-three feet we again struck the oil sand. . . . We were obliged to put in an air blast to furnish fresh air to the men below, on account of the strong odor of gas. At the depth of seventy-five feet there was so much oil and gas that we concluded we had better get a steam rig. We got this and went down 343 feet. . . . The first oil taken away was when I took four whiskey barrels of it to Kern City and shipped it to Millwood for skid grease, getting a dollar a barrel net.

Thousands of men soon crowded the area around what they now called the Kern River Oilfield, but to the Elwoods went the biggest prize. Among the faces in the crowd was Edward Doheny, who quickly cut a check in the amount of $2,500 (about $70,000 in contemporary dollars) to the Elwoods. "This, of course," the senior Elwood recalled, "was an agreeable surprise to us." But Doheny definitely got the better end of the deal: he purchased several other oil leases in the area and sold them as a package to the Santa Fe Railway company for $12.5 million. More significantly, the Kern River Oilfield—principally operated by the Chevron Corporation today—is now the fifth largest oil field in the United States, having produced in excess of two billion barrels of oil.[7]

The success of the Kern River Oilfield strike triggered a flood of prospecting migrants to Kern County. Between 1900 and 1910 the population of the county more than doubled from 16,480 to 37,715, the fastest growth in the county's history. And subsequent strikes in 1910 and 1912 further intensified the population surge. But, as the *Los Angeles Times* observed in a 1912 article entitled "Why Kern County Is the Land of Opportunities," Kern suffered from uneven development in which agriculture was not properly valued. "Right now is an excellent time to buy land in the San Joaquin Valley, anywhere near Bakersfield. . . . It is not that Kern county is lacking in 'opportunities' but there is a lack of persons who will avail themselves of these opportunities."[8] Estimating that there were more than a million acres of uncultivated farmland, the *Times* urged readers to get to Kern, quickly. Inspired by this kind of boosterism and word of mouth about quick riches, Californians and others rushed to Kern to prospect, buy government land, or homestead. The Agricultural Entry Act of 1914 that allowed homesteaders to claim public lands that had previously been reserved for mineral purposes also drew them. Indeed in 1914 and 1915 more Americans filed for homesteads in Kern than in any other year.

A few homesteaders like James Elwood benefitted from the oil boom. But most were threatened by it, just as George W. Ozmun and Bernard L. Snepp were. This was the function of an unfortunate omission in the Homestead Act of 1862: it did not assert the rights of homesteaders to subsurface resources like minerals and petroleum during the five-year improvement period. In fact, it said nothing on the subject. Luckily for homesteaders, both the courts and the Department of the Interior consistently ruled that homesteaders who had patented their land *after* the five-year period owned both the land and what lay beneath it. However, *during* the five-year improvement period, the outcome was unclear. Frequently, as in the case of Ozmun and Snepp, oil companies built derricks on the land of homesteaders, removed signs of homestead improvement, and then took their chances in court, where they usually prevailed, mineral rights being regarded as paramount by the Department of the Interior. "If an entryman lives on the land and is able to keep the oil prospectors away from his holdings, well and good," the *Los Angeles Times* reported grimly, "but there is nothing in the law that will prohibit them from going to the land and boring for oil by force of arms."[9]

Exacerbating the high-stakes nature of landownership in Kern was the fact that many men with capital exploited the Homestead Act to augment their already large landholdings, rather than to start a family farm. The career of William N. Cuddeback is a case in point. Born in San Bernardino County a year before the passage of the Homestead Act, Cuddeback took some schooling in Los Angeles before his parents moved to the Tehachapi region of Kern. By the time he reached his midtwenties, he and his brother had developed a thriving cattle business. He claimed his first homestead at the age of twenty-nine in 1890, after his initial financial success. "Aside from what his father left to him," the *History of Kern County* (1914) reads, "he has become wealthy in his own right." With that wealth Cuddeback then purchased the 3,200-acre Norboe Salt Lake ranch, five miles east of Tehachapi, where he kept a herd of cattle, raised grain, and shipped thousands of tons of salt from the lake. A portion of the Norboe Salt Lake ranch was comprised of pure clay, which soon attracted the City of Los Angeles, which soon bought part of the ranch site for a cement plant. Not easily satisfied, Cuddeback next invested in Imperial County: he bought a 280-acre alfalfa and dairy farm that he quickly sold "at a high figure" and finally bought a 580-acre alfalfa ranch in Riverside County. After all these sales, Cuddeback consolidated his Kern cattle operations in the 1920s with another 320 acres courtesy of the Stock-Raising Homestead Act. He would later send his son to Stanford University.[10]

And families naturally perpetuated their small dynasties to their children. Clarence C. Cummings claimed his homestead in Tehachapi in 1922 at the age of forty. His homestead application reads like a testament to the hardscrabble life. He claimed only a nine-by-twelve-foot two-room house made with logs and a "second-hand iron." He claimed no furniture but an "old cot" and reminded the General Land Office (GLO) that the land "is located up in extremely rough and precipitous mountains and is difficult to reach even on horseback there being no way of placing building material on the land without carrying the same over rough trails on the back of animals."[11]

But Cummings—whose father had shipped him to Los Angeles as a child for proper education—had already inherited his father's five-thousand-acre ranch. Additionally he and his brothers had purchased another five hundred acres of grazing land. In short, a traditional homestead claim represented to them merely a way to augment their success, whether earned or inherited. Furthermore it appears that Cummings rarely resided on the land, naturally preferring the ranch house on his father's acreage. Indeed, an agent for the General Land Office wrote to the commissioner of the GLO in 1921: "The indications about this claim were that it had not been resided upon to any great extent and it is likely that the claimant spent more of the time at this ranch house than he told me." Ultimately the land agent recommended the homestead patent, but only because the land was of so little apparent use.[12]

Both Cuddeback and Cummings were entirely compliant with the letter of the Homestead Act, and the strategy of using the Homestead Act to augment existing holdings in California was not uncommon. But it clearly violated the spirit of the act by removing land from the public domain that might have been used for the "poor man," and Abraham Lincoln would likely have wagged his head at the arrangement. On the other hand, those with more money and more preexisting landholdings were also more likely to make semiarid western land productive, a key goal of the act.

5

Violent Paradise

Refugio "Babe" Campo watched, helplessly, as his dog writhed on the ground in pain. He looked at the remainder of the dough he held in his hand, a treat he rolled for the dog, and knew that the flour had been poisoned. Campo's dog survived, but the next night all three of his horses died of strychnine poisoning. A week later all of the lumber he had hauled to his remote homestead in the hills above Santa Paula was doused in kerosene and torched. Somebody wanted Campo off the land, and he had a good idea who it was: a cattle rancher from nearby Somis named Jose Cananas. Campo had watched from a distance one night as Cananas tried to poison his well. Jose Cananas and his wife, Minnie, had lived there long before Campo claimed his homestead up the hill in 1914, and they had become accustomed to grazing their cattle free, far, and wide. They possessed that curious sense of entitlement to vast grazing lands that was acute among cattlemen. And Campo was surprisingly patient, never reporting their assaults to the authorities, until his wife ate a potato from their provision shed and began to convulse violently. Campo raced her on horseback to a doctor in El Rio and she was narrowly saved. This time Campo reported the crime to the sheriff, who soon arrested Cananas.[1]

To understand this madness, you have to take a drive. If you follow the fertile Santa Clara River west along California State Route 126 from the Santa Clara River Valley into Ventura County, you will enter one of the most agriculturally productive regions of the United States. Among

California's fifty-eight counties, Ventura ranks tenth, with more than two billion dollars in gross annual production, largely due to its strawberry crops. Continue out to the fertile Oxnard plain, marvel at how the coast meets the crops, and then head north on California State Route 1 toward Santa Barbara—long billed by tourism promoters as the "American Riviera" for its spectacular coastline and temperate climate. If you do this, you will have a fairly complete picture of why homesteaders of the late nineteenth and early twentieth centuries frequently found themselves embroiled in violent struggles—both as victims and as perpetrators—over landownership here. Superior agricultural conditions, prime grazing land and a cattlemen culture, ambiguity about several large Mexican-era land claims, and the discovery of oil created a set of circumstances in which discord and violence became virtually inevitable.[2]

One of the earliest and highest-profile conflicts occurred when arriving homesteaders tried to evict a long-standing Mexican landowner named Julio Peralta. Unlike many Californios who sought to defend their land claims after the Mexican-American War, Peralta had enough money to pay his lawyers in cash and avoid the pyrrhic fate of paying debt with landholdings. And unlike most, he actually expanded his landholdings, purchasing property in Santa Paula in 1864, a tract that contained an old but fully functional Spanish irrigation system. But as aspiring homesteaders and other settlers arrived, they complained about Peralta's near monopoly of both land and water in a valley that had been advertised as open to homesteaders. They began squatting on his property and filing overlapping homestead claims and eventually taking him to court, arguing alternately that he promised to sell off his land to them, that he was not a citizen, and that they had prior appropriative rights in what might be called a kitchen-sink legal strategy.[3]

In the first case, *Santa Paula Water Works et al. vs. Julio Peralta* (1893), the water company and neighboring homesteaders argued that Peralta had no right to either the land he inhabited or the water he had been using for twenty-five years. In that Superior Court case the judge upheld Peralta's right to the land but decided that he was obligated to share the water of Santa Paula Creek. Dissatisfied with this outcome, the petitioners—who now also included investors in a lemon ranch dependent on the creek's water—sought to remove Peralta's rights entirely and appealed to the State Supreme Court. The Supreme Court upheld the lower court's ruling.[4]

During the legal proceedings, homesteaders and other small farmers had diverted water from Peralta's ranch, and they forcibly prevented him from watering his cattle. Peralta hoped that his victory would inspire these interlopers to clear away from his property, but it did not. The local sheriff simply refused to follow the court order. Even more devastating for Peralta was the fact that the Supreme Court case broke him. "From an opulent stockman and rancher," the *Los Angeles Times* reported in 1897, "he has been reduced to a penniless man." Unable to pay even the interest on his two mortgages, he was foreclosed upon, losing everything. Peralta held out longer than almost any other Californio, but even he could not stop the onslaught of Anglo settlement, investment, and litigiousness.[5]

Homesteaders in Ventura also lashed out against Thomas Wallace More in one of the most sensational acts of violence in the region's early history. More and two of his brothers had made handsome fortunes for themselves in the wake of the gold rush, mostly through the purchase and sale of cattle-grazing lands. For a time, one of More's brothers, Alexander, owned the entire island of Santa Rosa, one of the eight Channel Islands off the coast of Santa Barbara and Ventura. Together the brothers saw a great financial opportunity when the Santa Barbara County probate court (Ventura County did not incorporate until 1873) ordered the sale of a vast cattle ranch known as Sespe in 1854, near Santa Paula. For a song, the brothers bought the six-league (more than twenty square miles) estate of Carlo Carillo, and Thomas soon bought them out and became the reigning cattle rancher of Santa Paula.

More lived in peace until the 1870s, when homesteaders began to claim land adjacent to his ranch. Skeptical about the extent of More's claim, they road horseback to the land office in Los Angeles and did some digging. What they found was a Mexican document indicating that the original estate only contained two leagues and not six. Now, even a cursory glance at the map associated with the land grant clearly indicated six leagues, but because Spaniards often only listed the most productive land in the grant, there was a second document indicating only two, and that was the only document homesteaders needed to support their assertion of fraud. They began taking up claims on More's historic—but in their eyes, fraudulent—holdings, and More responded by shooting at livestock and occasionally rousting squatters. Homesteaders responded by organizing under the banner of the Sespe Settlers League and openly threatening More in local newspapers, as they did in this July 1871 announcement in the *Daily Alta California*: "While in session a complaint was brought against you for trespassing upon settlers' rights who are living quietly and peaceably on Government land. Resolved, therefore, that a Committee of three be appointed to wait upon T. W. More and notify him that he is not to injure, molest or insult any settler that is settled upon land in Santa Clara River Valley, between Santa Paula Creek and the Piru Creek. And if said T. W. More does, he is doing so at his peril." The threats became more pointed, but in the meantime the United States Supreme Court ruled that the estate would be limited to only two leagues. This was a great victory for the homesteaders and should have resolved the issue peacefully. However, there were long delays in surveying the land after the court decisions, and homesteaders lacked the patience to wait until a proper survey was completed before staking their claims. More, for his part, refused to budge until all surveying was completed.[6]

Leading the Sespe Settlers League and the campaign against More was a settler named Frank Sprague, whose son owned a homestead near the More property and who would later claim government land himself under the Stock-Raising Homestead Act of 1916. But at the time, Frank Sprague was simply a squatter, and a notorious one at that, having started numerous brawls in Santa Paula. He was a fiery speaker and a member of the Grange, and he reached his boiling point in the drought year of 1876 when he discovered that More intended to build a dam and create his own water district. Finally, in March of 1877 Sprague and several homesteaders decided to take matters into their own hands.

In the middle of the night More awoke to find his house and barn on fire. He raced outside in his drawers to untie the horses. There, a group of three or four masked men—the witnesses could not be sure—shot him in the hip with a shotgun. He writhed on the ground and the men approached. The masked man with the shotgun pointed it at More's head, yelled "Now die, damn you, die!" and shot him in the face, his skull shattering into a dozen pieces.[7]

Though Sprague and several others were convicted of murder, public sympathy in the region firmly supported the settlers. The local newspaper, *Free Press*, openly sympathized with the defendants and called upon the region's large landholders to "cut it up and sell it at reasonable rates." The *San Francisco Post* argued that More was "so obnoxious" that nobody would warn him of the danger to his life, and characterized the settlers as victims of "armed retainers of a man, who, under the color of an admittedly forged Mexican grant, endeavored to turn them out of house and home, and seize upon their realty." Nor did the threat of violence against elites subside. Sarah Eliot Blanchard, the daughter of land mogul and Santa Paula founder Nathan Weston Blanchard, recalled that her father spoke out against the "cowards" who killed More and was warned by settlers that he would meet the same fate. "Father still went to Ventura twice weekly," Blanchard remembered, "and if he were delayed, I can still see Mother's terror."[8] Oil magnate and later United States senator Thomas R. Bard was shot at when he returned to the valley one evening.

The intensification of oil extraction in the region amplified antielite sentiment among homesteaders. First discovered in the 1860s, oil became big business in Ventura County in the 1880s, with strikes in Ojai, Santa Paula, and the former Rancho Sespe. As in Kern, Ventura homesteaders had to worry about losing their claims to oil companies during the first five years of improvement. For example, aspiring homesteaders Andrue L. Jump and Elisha O. Coats lost their Fillmore claims to the Santa Paula Oil Company in 1917. The oil company had presented the land office with photographs showing that the land was made primarily of rock buttes, was entirely without agricultural potential, and had in fact "barely enough soil between them to allow for the erection of an oil derrick." But the company found room for its derricks. Here the land office adjudicated based on the potential value of the land rather than on its potential value to settlers. Neither Jump nor Coats had ambitions for large-scale agriculture; they simply wanted a place to live, and followed the homestead laws to the letter in good faith. Subsequent oil strikes in Orange County would further test the limits of homesteading in an age of massive oil extraction.

In fact field agents from land offices sometimes worked in concert with oil interests and explicitly against those of the homesteader. Frank R. Rodriguez of Piru learned this lesson the hard way. In 1918 the chief of the Field Division of the San Francisco Land Office sought to bar Rodriguez—a decorated World War I veteran—from filing his final proof because he was absent for two years in the service. At first glance the chief's opposition seemed merely officious, a clear instance of favoring the letter over the spirit of the law. The chief's position aroused the ire of the National Service Division, which weighed in on Rodriguez's behalf. "It seems very strange," a staff person wrote, "that a man who did his duty, entered the service because he felt it was his duty to do something for the Government which was allowing him to own land and has been deprived of everything that which should be rightfully his."[9]

Rodriguez's claim sat atop an old oil-prospecting site, a fact that became widely known in the area during Rodriguez's absence. That the oil prospects had never been realized seemed to bother none of the wildcatters, who began to apply for leases on oil claims, though not one of them ever sank a well, a testament to the triumph of ambition over achievement. Nonetheless, the chief of the land office remained firm that the potential should be played out and that Rodriguez should be denied his claim. Rodriguez's attorney, Frank C. Prescott, appealed to the Department of the Interior arguing that Rodriguez typified the precise sort of homesteader that the Homestead Act was supposed to reward. "This district as a whole, and the entrymen therein, are unusual," he wrote, "in that the entrymen being mostly native born California citizens, of Spanish or Mexican descent, have actually cultivated their homesteads and raised their families thereon." Rodriguez had already proved up one claim successfully, planting forty acres of barley, building a twenty-by-thirty-foot house, and a digging a thirty-foot well. The Department of the Interior was sympathetic and reversed the land office decision.[10]

Recognizing the inevitability of conflicts like these, the Department of the Interior had separated surface and subsurface rights in the 1916 Stock-Raising Homestead Act, creating "split estates" in which homesteaders owned the land but the United States government retained ownership of subsurface rights. Nonetheless, traditional homesteaders in Ventura County, as in Kern, often lived in a state of perpetual anxiety about being challenged by oil companies' deep pockets and legions of attorneys. These threats, and the perceived arrogance of men like More and Bard and the wildcatters on Rodriguez's homestead, fueled vigilante sentiment. As one editorialist wrote in 1891: "The right to a quarter section of land—to a homestead—is one of the few privileges remaining to a poor man in this country: Let land-grabbers and speculators take warning . . . and keep their grasping fingers off of the homes of honest settlers. . . . Let it be generally understood that those who go to deprive a settler of his home by force take their lives in their hands."[11] This public sentiment burned hot in the early years of the twentieth century but cooled into the 1920s as traditional homesteaders proved up their claims and new settlers under the Stock-Raising Homestead Act understood that they had no subsurface rights.

Having dug, tilled, planted, toiled—and sometimes litigated—to secure their landholdings, homesteaders and other Santa Clara River Valley settlers never imagined dying in one of the worst man-made disasters in American history. But that is what happened to Jefferson Hunick, dozens of other homesteaders, and ultimately more than six hundred people in all. Born in 1846 in Pennsylvania, the son of German immigrants, Hunick migrated to California to farm and claimed a homestead in the Santa Clara River Valley in 1910 at the age of sixty-four. He had worked hard, following the letter of the Homestead Act, proving up his land, building a suitable home, and digging a well. He provided shelter for his siblings and a nephew. Then one night he awoke to a rumbling sound, walked outside, and was carried to his death by an eighty-foot-high wall of water.[12]

In the early morning hours of March 13, 1928, the St. Francis Dam, upstream at San Francisquito Canyon, failed, sending millions of gallons of water and debris through the Santa Clara River, filling the serene valley with thousand-pound chunks of concrete, livestock, and human bodies. "Never in the history of America," a committee would later report in 1929, "has there been a disaster more tragic, nor one which came so quickly and brutally, than the roaring flood of water which . . . swept down the narrow San Francisquito Canyon, through the fertile, peaceful Santa Clara Valley, down through the historic Newhall Ranch, over a portion of the city of Santa Paula and onward to the sea."[13]

The dam's chief engineer was William Mulholland, a man deeply revered at the time for his miraculous delivery of water to Los Angeles from the Owens Valley via a 233-mile aqueduct he completed in 1913. The Los Angeles Aqueduct, as it was called, paved the way for the growth of modern industrial Los Angeles and made Mulholland a household name. But the St. Francis Dam disaster changed all that. Though cleared of criminal liability, Mulholland had surveyed the dam mere hours before the disaster and determined it to be safe. His credibility destroyed, Mulholland retired from the Bureau of Water Works in 1929 and died in 1935 in relative obscurity.

6

Swindles and Salvation in the Antelope Valley

Today the Antelope Valley represents the last frontier of Los Angeles County. On the far western edge of the Mojave Desert and a good forty miles from downtown Los Angeles, the Antelope Valley is home of two of America's fastest growing cities, Palmdale and Lancaster, which grew by a phenomenal 122 percent and 61 percent, respectively, between 1990 and 2010. The sprawling valley is now home to more than half a million people. But at the turn of the twentieth century, the Yucca-studded valley seemed unredeemably remote, grotesquely barren. "As seen from the railroad," the *Los Angeles Times* reported in 1891, when fewer than four hundred souls, mostly homesteaders, inhabited the entire valley, "it presents an uninviting appearance, with its great stretches of arid soil." In 1910 scientists from the United States Geological Service arrived and identified a massive artesian water belt under the valley, a discovery that hastened settlement and expansion. But until that time homesteaders had faced daunting challenges. "Many people in the county arrived at the definite conclusion," George Wharton James wrote of the days before the discovery of the artesian belt, "that this was part of the irreclaimable desert, was totally unfit for agriculture, and therefore had no future."[1]

But for homesteaders of the late nineteenth century, the Antelope Valley beckoned, and not because it was naturally appealing, as the Santa Clara River Valley was. Instead, the chief appeal of the Antelope Valley was simply the overwhelming availability of land, and it soon became

12. Yucca mohavensis forest near Palmdale. Men and women gathered under yucca trees, ca. early 1900s. C. C. Pierce Collection of Photographs, Huntington Library, San Marino, California.

one of the densest outposts of homesteading in Southern California. And unlike the lone pioneers of the Santa Monica Mountains, many Antelope Valley homesteaders followed the advice of irrigation expert Harry Bowling. "To reclaim the desert on a large scale," he wrote in 1916, "is too big an undertaking for any single man, it must be done by large combinations." Indeed the failure rate for individuals in the Antelope Valley was very high. First, it was expensive to drill a deep well, and of the 353 wells in the Antelope Valley in 1911, only thirty belonged to homesteaders. The rest were owned by well-capitalized farmers and large entities, including schools, cattle companies, and the Southern Pacific. Second, it was also very expensive to ship produce to market. The Southern Pacific Railroad charged the same amount to haul grain or produce on a short run from Lancaster to Los Angeles as it did to haul it four hundred miles to San Francisco because of the greater economy of scale on the longer route. So most individual homesteaders often took the ninety-mile wagon ride through the passes, a hard route, and sometimes a perilous one.[2]

The geography of the Antelope Valley was felicitous to a cooperative spirit: with hundreds of homesteads spread across a flat valley, there were no natural barriers to cooperation as there were in the mountains. But the greatest facilitator of cooperation and communal ownership in the Antelope Valley, however, was the Wright Act. Passed by the California State Legislature in 1887, the act allowed for California residents to pool their resources, incorporate, and bond irrigation districts. The proceeds of the bond sales would be used to build canals, dams, and reservoirs. In the era before large-scale municipal state and federal irrigation programs like the Owens Valley aqueduct or the California Aqueduct, the Wright Act was a godsend. It was particularly important in light of the 1886 California Supreme Court decision in *Lux vs. Haggin*, which subordinated appropriative rights to riparian rights except when the appropriator had begun using water before a riparian owner acquired his property. The resulting policy, known as the "California Doctrine," guaranteed that lawyers would be kept very busy and that riparian owners would usually prevail, but the Wright Act tipped the scales in favor of newcomers who were not able to acquire waterfront property or dig their own wells but still desperately needed irrigation. The California Department of Engineering generally regarded the Wright irrigation districts, which soon numbered in the dozens, as successes. However, it noted, several of them were purely speculative in intent, were "dishonest and fraudulent," and lacked neither "physical nor agricultural, nor even moral justification." A chief offender in this category was the Big Rock Creek Irrigation District in the Antelope Valley, the brainchild of a schemer named Harlan Page Sweet.[3]

Born in New Hampshire in 1850 and raised in rural poverty on the outskirts of Chicago, Harlan Page Sweet turned his back on the plow and became a newsman, assuming the role of general manager of a new Chicago-based agricultural weekly, *Farm, Field and Fireside,* in 1884. A gifted talker and tall in stature, with quick, dark eyes, Sweet evidently concluded that he would find faster fortune in Los Angeles, so he moved there a year later, reinventing himself as a banker. The move was propitious, and soon Sweet owned a house in Boyle Heights that an architectural writer described as one of the "largest and best-finished houses in the city." Had Sweet continued banking, he might have enjoyed a life of modest wealth and anonymity, but his financial ambition was ravenous. In August of 1887, just five months after the passage of the Wright Act, Sweet entered claims on two eighty-acre parcels under the Desert Land Act, at the foot of the San Gabriel Mountains. But Sweet had no intention of farming: instead he concocted a plan to incorporate a Wright Act irrigation district around his property and then sell the property at a higher value once it was irrigated. It was an abuse of the Desert Lands Act, but it was not illegal. The illegal action would come later.[4]

The water source for Sweet's irrigation district was Big Rock Creek, the main fork of which begins at Mount Baldy, the highest peak in the San Gabriel Mountains. When it flows, it flows northwesterly until breaking northward into several tributaries that spill into the Antelope Valley near the site of Llano, which was uninhabited at the time. When the California Engineering Department later investigated Sweet's scheme, they found the "direct flow of this stream to be altogether undependable." And although Sweet's proposed district promised to irrigate 30,000 acres, it never had the capacity to water more than about 150 acres. But 1888–89 was one of the wettest years in Southern California's recorded history, with more than thirty-four inches of rainfall, and then, as now, nobody planned for drought when it was wet.[5]

And so in July of 1890 the Los Angeles County Board of Supervisors approved the creation of the Big Rock Creek Irrigation District and the district's issuance of $300,000 in bonds to support the construction of ditches, tunnels, pipes, and flumes to divert water from the creek. Simultaneously Sweet incorporated the Columbia Colonization Company with the purpose of selling lands in the new district. Using the pages of the *Farm, Field and Fireside*, Sweet promoted the activities of the Colonization Company, but the irrigation district was a ground game; he needed buy-in from the homesteaders of the region, who would be taxed for the maintenance of the district, once constructed. One of the most successful homesteaders at the outflow of the creek was man named Lewis C. Tilghman, a migrant from Illinois.

Tilghman was a straight arrow who lived with his wife and a family of German boarders and aspired to become a postmaster for the Antelope Valley. Tilghman's land was not optimal, sitting as it did on "ordinary farming land of a desert nature." The previous occupant had cultivated the land but had eventually abandoned it. But Tilghman improved it quickly, earning enough money from his seven acres of alfalfa and a vineyard to plant about one thousand fruit trees. Soon he replaced his twelve-by-eighteen-foot homesteader shack with a five-room house and also built a cattle shed. Much of Tilghman's success was attributed to the ditches he and his boarders dug from the creek to his property. Because Tilghman was successful and trustworthy, and probably a little naive, Sweet invited him to become secretary for the Big Rock Creek Irrigation District.[6]

The problems started almost immediately after the district was formed. Upon the order of the board of supervisors, the property holders within the boundaries of the new district were to vote on the organization and maintenance of the district, but the principals in the matter—including Sweet—ignored the election results and appointed themselves as the leadership, quickly negotiating an expensive contract with a defunct water company that owned water rights, pipes, and flumes in the district. When Tilghman, acting in his capacity as secretary, asked to see the records, the treasurer refused, forcing Tilghman to sue to get the records. Once he got them, he discovered what he already suspected, that the district had entered into contracts illegally but also that they had failed to pay the interest on the bonds sold for construction. A judge ordered a temporary halt to the sale of bonds until the debt was paid, further slowing progress, while the principals sorted out these and other financial irregularities.[7]

The second major problem was that Sweet and the principals of Big Rock Creek Irrigation District refused to recognize the riparian rights of homesteaders and other settlers upstream. Consequently the chief activity of the district in its initial years was suing upstream users, always in the amount of $10,000. "Judging by the multiplicity of suits in the courts," the *Los Angeles Herald* reported, "the folks up there would rather fight than eat." In each case, the judge ruled in favor of the upstream users, consistent with the riparian doctrine of *Lux vs. Haggin*. In an important case that went to the California Supreme Court, a settler named Fritz Boehmer preemptively sued Big Rock Creek Irrigation District in 1894. Judge Lucien Shaw, the chief justice of California, ruled that Boehmer's rights to a portion of the water flowing into Big Rock Creek were superior and paramount to those of the irrigation district by virtue of riparian rights but that the contiguous government land he purchased did not carry with it riparian rights. "Quarter sections, derived by separate titles, through which the stream does not flow, cannot be classed as riparian," Shaw concluded. It was an advance in California water law and added further clarification to the murky California Doctrine, but from Boehmer's perspective it was a disappointment.[8]

But the real problem was that Sweet attempted to sell land in Llano to which he did not have title and which did not, as he had promised, have adequate irrigation. In this Sweet was shameless, as his letter to an investor who asked about the unpaid bond debt found out: "There is no question about your title," Sweet wrote. "The colonists are expecting us to continue the tunnel, and this can only be done by all those who owe us obligations meeting them promptly, as we are putting all out ready cash, and some more, into the colony enterprise, and are borrowing large sums besides. We will send you a warranted deed if you want it. We write this because we really need the money and need it badly to continue the enterprise." H. P. Sweet's sweet, unfulfilled promises eventually caught the eye of the United States District Court in Los Angeles and a grand jury indicted him on charges of mail fraud in August of 1897. And it was high time for Sweet's comeuppance, as many observers noted. "Next to bottling the air and sunshine," William Smythe (about whom more later) wrote in the *Atlantic Monthly*, "no monopoly of natural resources could be fraught with more possibilities of abuse than the attempt to make merchandise of water in an arid land."[9]

Yet, those delighting in Sweet's downfall would have to wait another day for satisfaction. His lawyers effectively argued that Sweet had not, in fact, been in violation of Section 5480 of the United States Code—the postal fraud provision. First, they argued, the intent of the code was to prevent the sale of counterfeit currency and not "frauds committed by selling of land." And second, as to Sweet's claim that there would be sufficient water, this was "the merest estimate" of the quantity of water and in no way intended to be a representation of fact. Finally, it was true, attorneys conceded, that he did not possess perfect title to the lands he was selling, only the "color of title." But this was immaterial, they argued, because "the court may know that lands in the Antelope Valley or Mojave Desert, where the big Rock Creek is situated, are for the greater part utterly barren and worthless . . . and all kinds of crops are withered up and destroyed by the hot winds of the desert." Remarkably Sweet's attorneys prevailed and the case was dismissed in 1901. But it scarcely mattered: the last tract at Llano had been sold in 1898, the fifth driest year on record between 1877 and 2012.[10]

Neither Sweet nor Tilghman, nor any others associated with the failed Big Rock Creek venture, were ever convicted, probably because even a stern judge could not find malicious intent in an era when so many land claims were in a confused state of imperfection. But the lesson for Tilghman and other homesteaders was clear: there were no quick or easy ways to deal with water shortage in the Antelope Valley, and no water laws could change nature.

Llano would eventually become famous, but not through the efforts of H. P. Sweet or the Big Rock Creek Irrigation District. Instead politician Job Harriman established a socialist colony there in 1914, a model of the ostensible advantages of a communal society. Llano Del Rio, as it was called, promoted its natural advantages. "The property lies for the most part between Rock Creek and Mescal Creek," a company brochure read, "on the plain below, and running to the base of the mountains that form a magnificent watershed and which are snowcapped for several months of the year." Eventually more than one thousand people joined the largely self-sustaining colony. Ultimately political discord soured the venture, but it was water that ended the colony. Harriman, like H. P. Sweet and others before him, argued that the waters of Big Rock Creek would be sufficient for the colony, but they were not.[11]

Other homesteaders were more successful. Olin L. Livesey was a rare, silver-spooned homesteader, who chose the agrarian life and saw great potential in the Antelope Valley. Born in Massachusetts in 1850, the son of English immigrants, Livesey graduated from Wesleyan—where he co-founded the exclusive Wesleyan chapter of the Skull and Bones Society—in 1873. He later moved to Pasadena where he became a clerk in the Superior Court and wrote extensively about his first interest, horticulture, in his spare time. Evidently tired of urban life, Livesey claimed a homestead in 1890 in the Antelope Valley, adjacent to what is today the Antelope Valley California Poppy Reserve.[12]

A devout Christian, Livesey soon saw in the Antelope Valley a chance to pair agricultural innovation and Christian values in a new agricultural colony. In 1892 he joined local politicos, churchmen, and Bohemians including Charles P. Edson—father-in-law of suffragette Katherine Phillips Edson—to incorporate the Manzana Colony, a Christian agricultural commune. From the outset Manzana was radically different from Harlan Page Sweet's Llano. Most significantly Livesey and the others forbade the sale of land to anyone not planting, in order to discourage speculation. "They are in no sense speculators," a favorable account in the *Los Angeles Herald* reported. The Manzana Colony furnished land and water, bought trees, and kept the land free from weeds. Success, the Manzana principals insisted, depended on natural factors "and the intelligent application of Christian energy, enterprise and capital."

> Another feature to note in the purposes of the colonies is the provision made in advance of religious education. A stipulated portion of money, or land to set our trees, is made over to the Colonizing Superintendent, an income from which is for the common benefit of the community. A church, school and library and their attendant expenses are to be provided.

13. Pioneers of the West End. *The Almond Colonies of Southern California* (Los Angeles: Almendro, 1893). Huntington Library, San Marino, California.

A photograph of settlers in the promotional tract featured the following caption: "It will be perceived that they are not bushwackers, in an intellectual sense, though they are in muscle and determination to convert the savageness of nature into the delights of Christian civilization." Manzana advertised regularly in *The Churchman*, targeting readers as far away as New York.[13]

Manzana was the first of several agricultural Christian colonies to emerge in the Antelope Valley, and it was not long until the region developed a reputation for rectitude that contrasted markedly from the real and imagined vices of Los Angeles. A keen observer of this trend was the colorful California traveler and writer George Wharton James. An Englishman and an ordained minister, he had a checkered past, including allegations of adultery and fraud, and was subsequently defrocked. He turned to writing, churning out several important books that stand today as classics in the study of the American Southwest. He also hired out his talents to various promotional interests, one of which was the Southern Pacific Railroad, eager to sell its share of land in the Antelope Valley. James produced for them a tract that highlighted the characteristics of the residents, and if he is to be believed, he was impressed.

"The Antelope Valley regards itself as superior to many regions in social conditions," James wrote. "In the first place there are no saloons, with their almost certain accompanying evils of gambling dens and haunts of vice. And such is the vigilance of the county officers that there have been few complaints, even, of blind pigs."[14] This was at least partially the work of homesteader Reverend John E. Robbins, beekeeper and frontier preacher from Ohio, who settled in 1888, claimed a 160-acre homestead plot, and led the Union Moral and Religious Association of Acton for more than twenty years.

Materially, Manzana thrived for a spell. Fed by the waters of Lake Katrina and Kings Canyon, the colony produced mightily. In 1901 alone, it produced 80,000 pounds of almonds. But, as always, water was destiny, and the drought year of 1903–4 killed crops and ambitions. Although deep well drilling would ameliorate circumstances after the 1910 artesian belt discovery, it was too late for Manzana. Furthermore, water shortage would be endemic to the region until the arrival of the California Aqueduct in the 1950s. Today the northern tip of the Antelope Valley in Kern County produces most of the nation's almonds and pistachios, and the Los Angeles County portion produces billions of dollars' worth of milk, grapes, cattle, strawberries, alfalfa, lettuce, walnuts, and tomatoes, all through the magic of irrigation.[15]

7

Mexican Lands in Mexican Hands

Nobody was sure exactly how the fight began, but it ended with Juan de dios Verdugo badly bloodied, firing his revolver wildly about the barroom. He had been on so many drunken sprees, brawling his way across Los Angeles County, that nobody was particularly surprised. But this fight in September of 1887 nearly killed him. At some point he was hit in the head with a rock, and the blow, according to the *Los Angeles Times*, "not only knocked him silly but cut through his hat and drew much blood from a scalp wound in his head." Verdugo composed himself enough to pull out his gun and fire off a few rounds, but onlookers subdued him and likely prevented the melee from becoming homicidal.[1]

Verdugo was a descendent of California royalty, but you would not know it that night. He was the great-grandson of José María Verdugo, a revered Spanish soldier who had been handsomely rewarded by the Spanish Crown for his service in California. In 1784 Governor Pedro Fages had granted him Rancho San Rafael, a 36,000-acre ranch that hugged the foothills from modern-day Glendale, through Eagle Rock, and into La Cañada. When he retired from military service, José María operated a vast cattle-ranching operation that might have produced wealth for generations to come had his son managed it with even a modicum of fiduciary sense upon José María's death. But Julio—Juan's grandfather—was an unmitigated disaster. He mortgaged the vast property in 1861, according to noted historian Leonard Pitt, "for sprucing up his casa, buying provisions, and paying taxes." That spree, coupled with

68

ballooning debt, ended in "foreclosure, sheriff's sale, and ruination." Naturally Julio Verdugo's avaricious lawyers were the first to the auction house and bought the entire ranch. For Juan, who came of age in the 1870s as white men swarmed over the landscape, nostalgia for a world he had never known must have weighed heavily on him, maybe even put a chip on his shoulder.[2]

Even after his near-fatal scuffle, Juan Verdugo refused to stay out of trouble. He briefly courted Teresa Figueroa, likely another descendant of Californio royalty. But, as with the Verdugos, the onslaught of American men and new laws had been cruel to the Figueroas. Teresa was either desperate to claim his name for her own or madly in love, or perhaps very impatient, because when Verdugo failed to act speedily enough in proposing to her, she sued him for $10,000 and demanded that he marry her immediately. A judge dismissed the case, and Verdugo decided, wisely we might say, against the marriage.

When he was not fighting or drinking or breaking promises to marry someone, Verdugo was toiling away like most Mexicans of that era, doing odd jobs for white property holders, digging mines, and farming. But by the age of thirty-five his brawling days were behind him, and he thought carefully about the future of his now large family, which consisted of him, his wife, and seven children. Verdugo vowed to get his own land and claimed a homestead in the Santa Clara River Valley in 1896—then described as Soledad Township. Juan sought more than a new place to live; he likely also sought redemption, for himself, for his family name, and for his people. And though Verdugo's neighbors described his plot as "hilly and rolling" and only "part level," he vowed to cultivate enough of it to complement the cattle pasturage. He cultivated twenty acres of land and cleared another twenty of brush, and built a three-room, eighteen-by-twenty-four-foot lumber house and a corral.[3]

In the late nineteenth and early twentieth centuries the descendants of the displaced Californios struggled to find prosperity in the rapidly Americanizing landscape. By the 1880s most were absorbed into what whites generally saw as an undifferentiated mass of Mexicans. They were tillers of fields, layers of tracks, and makers of bricks. And yet, despite all that effort, they were somehow also—as one white observer judged—"lethargic," "a somnolent collection of human beings." The vast majority of Latinos in California at that time were renters in the city of Los Angeles because poverty kept most of them from becoming home owners. And it also kept them from becoming homesteaders—the cost of implements, seed, and stock was usually prohibitive. But those who did upended the social order, effectively bringing former Mexican lands back into Mexican hands.[4]

Mexican homesteaders were no more or less enlightened than their white counterparts, but homesteading often meant something different to them—perhaps something more—than it did for others. The opportunity to reclaim Alta California lands was poignant. Take homesteader Francisco de la Guerra, grandson of Californio patriarch José de la Guerra y Noriega. José de la Guerra y Noriega had immigrated to California from Spain as a boy in 1792 and soon became an officer in the Spanish military governing colonial California, and ultimately a captain and military commander of the Santa Barbara presidio. More importantly he became an expert trader and quickly amassed great wealth, owning thousands of acres of prime ranch land in Santa Barbara and Ventura Counties. But the de la Guerras succumbed, as other Californios did, to the drought, and it pushed them into the full cycle of debt and foreclosure. Despite his lineage, grandson Francisco had to start from scratch, eking out an existence as a homesteader in the foothills above Santa Barbara.[5]

Francisco de la Guerra settled on a piece of unclaimed "mountainous, rocky and rough" land in 1868 and lived there alone, cultivating barley and hay for his sixty head of cattle and building a twelve-by-twelve-foot adobe house, shingled with wood shakes, and a wooden corral. Describing himself as a "ranchero and general laborer," de la Guerra generally spent his days tending to the cattle. Though he does not appear to have faced any challenges to his tenure on the land, he probably saw the hordes of Yankees filling up the valley in the early 1880s and decided to secure his land with a homestead patent, proving it up in 1886. He paid his nominal registration fee and the land was his for perpetuity.[6]

Among his neighbors in the Santa Barbara foothills was Jesus Maria Figueroa, descendant of the former governor of Mexican California who is credited with secularizing the missions and dispensing land grants in the early 1830s. The descendants of Californios were heavily represented among Hispanic homesteaders, suggesting that most of them did not inherit land but rather worked up from the bottom, like their white homesteading counterparts. That they did so, quietly but with determination, was a testament to their resilience in an era of rapid social and racial transformation. But not all Californio descendants accepted their diminished social status quietly.

Among Mexican homesteaders in Southern California, the majority lived in the Santa Clara River Valley. Though few had Verdugo's pedigree, most had close connections, through intermarriage, to the old world of Mexican dominance, which made them strive even harder, perhaps, than their white counterparts. Adolfo Alvitre, who claimed a homestead in 1899 at the age of twenty-seven, less than a mile from Verdugo's homestead, was an example of how far one family could travel the opposite direction on the social ladder from the Verdugos. Alvitre was a cousin of Verdugo on his mother's side, but those on his father's side were in constant trouble with the law. If Verdugo tried to reclaim some old glory, Alvitre tried to lift himself out of the criminality of his family.

Adolfo was one of ten children fathered by Tomas de Los Innocentes Alvitre. Tomas's parents were California born and owned a small plot of land in the town of El Monte in the San Gabriel Valley. A common laborer, Tomas was never far from trouble. In 1871 he was stabbed repeatedly but survived to see his assailant convicted. And in another instance a man named José Manriquez hit him in the head with a club. An apparent victim of violence in these cases, Tomas was perfectly capable of turning the tables, and he frequently acted as a vigilante for his family's interests. This was most obvious in the case of his threats to shoot to death an infirm septuagenarian named Antonio Rodriguez.[7]

Rodriguez had seen a lot during his time as a subsistence farmer on a small corner of Rancho Potrero Grande. The four-thousand-acre ranch, which covers modern-day Rosemead and South El Monte, had been the exclusive property of Juan M. Sanchez, from whom Rodriguez rented out a twenty-acre parcel. There, for twenty years, Rodriguez grew corn, beans, and peppers, drawing water through a ditch connected to Sanchez's *zanja*, a larger ditch built by Native Americans during the Mexican era, connecting the property to the San Gabriel River. It had been like this, Rodriguez testified, "from time immemorial."[8]

But in 1879 Sanchez fell victim to one of the worst land losses in the history of the nineteenth century. Sanchez was close friends with William Workman and Pliny Fisk Temple, owners of Temple and Workman Bank. During the financial panic of 1875 the bank faced ruination and Temple and Workman searched for an investor to prop up the failing concern until the tides had turned. They found a willing investor in Elias "Lucky" Baldwin, so named for his Midas touch with investments. Baldwin loaned them $200,000 but demanded that the loan be secured by a mortgage on their friend Sanchez's land. Sanchez was reluctant at first but eventually agreed, against the advice of friends and investors. Sure enough the bank failed again. Temple had a debilitating stroke, Workman killed himself, and Sanchez lost his vast estate and lived out his days in ruinous poverty. Luckily for Rodriguez, Baldwin agreed to sell him the twenty-acre plot he had rented for so long.

Waiting in the wings was Tomas Alvitre, who saw the change in ownership of the rancho as a chance to acquire more water. No sooner had Sanchez left the rancho than Tomas and his cousins paid a visit to old Rodriguez. They brought rifles and pistols and made it clear that they would kill Rodriguez if he took one more drop from the *zanja*, ever. Rodriguez was terrified and watched his crops die, but he eventually built up the courage to take Tomas and his cousins to court. He won an injunction against Tomas Alvitre and reclaimed his water access.

But Alvitre was not done terrorizing the homesteaders. He soon found that he could make better use of his neighbor's only mutton sheep than could his neighbor, and so he lassoed it and dragged it toward his house. Fortunately for the sheep, a shepherd returned it to its owner before Alvitre could do it harm. Finally, to almost nobody's horror, a northbound Southern Pacific train struck Tomas in his wagon, throwing him violently to the ground. He survived the impact but later died from the injuries.[9]

And so, like Juan de dios Verdugo, Adolfo Alvitre had something to prove when he began building his homestead in the Santa Clara River Valley. He started when he was twenty-eight years old in about 1897. His homestead witness, Juan de dios Verdugo, described Alvitre's land as "mainly hilly, part level, agriculture and grazing land." Alvitre built a lumber house of twelve-by-twenty-four feet, with fencing, and cultivated almost thirty acres and sank a well. More significantly, he took in his mother and two sisters.[10]

Ironically, while Alvitre, Verdugo, and other Mexicans labored in relative obscurity, Anglos in Los Angeles became increasingly enamored of a Spanish fantasy past. The Mexican homesteads in Santa Clarita were fewer than seven hundred feet from the original property line of Rancho San Francisco, the estate of Ygnacio Del Valle. It was Del Valle's Rancho Camulos that set the stage for Helen Hunt Jackson's 1884 book *Ramona*, widely credited for sparking regional interest in the Spanish fantasy past and stimulating tourism. Jackson stayed at Rancho Camulos during the brief research phase for her novel, and drew inspiration from Camulos in her creation of the Morena Ranch of the novel. Charles Lummis and other boosters quickly seized on the connection and advertised Rancho Camulos as "home of Ramona." In 1910 D. W. Griffith directed the film adaption of *Ramona* with Mary Pickford, and today visitors can stand inside the chapel where she was wed in the film. Neither Jackson nor Lummis would have known what to make of Verdugo or Alvitre, displaced, flawed as anyone, and yet determined to redeem themselves on the farm. Mexicans like these did not fit easily into the sorts of stories whites told about them.

Farther east near Placerita Canyon there was a contingent of European homesteaders, chiefly Italians, Frenchmen, Poles, Germans, and Jews. Whether or not European immigrants were generally subjected to harassment from native whites is hard to know, but Dutchman George Henry Rehberg certainly believed he was a target. Rehberg homesteaded east of Placerita and sought to build a new house. To raise money he allowed a young man named Elton, powerfully built and ornery but highly recommended by one of Rehberg's friends, to occupy a ten-acre portion of the homestead with payment to follow soon. But once Elton settled on the land, he told Rehberg that he would only see payment "after a lawsuit." Old, feeble, and unwilling to fight it out in court, Rehberg resigned himself to Elton's squatting. But after attending jury duty in Newhall one day in 1896, Rehberg returned home to find that his irrigation pipe had been ripped out and rerouted to the new house Elton was building for himself. "I'm a poor man and will protect my property with a gun," he yelled at Elton, who responded that he intended "to spread Dutch blood about the canyon." The sheriff dragged the men to court where Rehberg broke down in tears over Elton's depredations. The court issued a judgment against Elton for the damage to the pipes but did not evict him.[11]

If remoteness bred danger for homesteaders, as it so often did throughout the state, it also complicated child rearing. This was the case for John L. Vignes, the grandson of Jean-Louis Vignes, the first commercial winemaker in California. Like Verdugo, John Vignes inherited none of his grandfather's wealth and was forced to homestead rather than buy land. He and his wife had five daughters and soon realized that the lack of a schoolhouse would severely limit their opportunities, and so they rented a home in Los Cerritos in southern Los Angeles County where they stayed for a portion of the year while the girls were in school. When John tried to finalize his claim in 1909, he was at first denied because the land officer concluded that he had not met the residency requirements of the Homestead Act. Vignes took the case to court where a judge overruled the land commission. "Both parents were determined that their five daughters should have schooling. They are people of refinement," the judge said, "and would not neglect their children. This gentleman and his wife deserve the home. The office knows of no better distribution of the public lands of this district than to a man with five daughters, who is making such a fight to educate them, and finally to get from rented to fee simple lands."[12]

As was the case across rural America in the nineteenth century, families were big, and intermarriage among homesteaders was common. In Placerita Canyon, homesteader Frank Evans Walker and his wife, Hortense Victoria Walker, had twelve children. Hortense descended from the French Reynier clan of homesteaders. Frank Walker claimed a homestead neighboring the Reynier lands at the age of nineteen and soon began riding horses with young Hortense, and they fell in love. Eventually Walker had to build a second cabin to house all his children. The pastoral beauty of the Walker homestead—nestled in a grove of sycamores—drew the attention of location scouts from Hollywood, and the property soon appeared in dozens of films, most notably *The Range Feud* (1931) and *Two-Fisted Law* (1932), both of which featured a young John Wayne. Both films depict a tough West, where hard-bitten men shoot it out to restore their vision of justice. But the location was ironic because if the Walker homestead said anything about the West, it said that there was space for redemption, a space for peace, and even a place for love.

8

Floods and Utopias

A sprawling range almost seventy miles long and twenty miles wide with rugged peaks and canyons; dense forests of pine, oak, and alder; and abundant game, the San Gabriel Mountains beckoned a different breed of homesteader. These brave types sought near-complete self-sufficiency and had little access to the agricultural market in the San Gabriel Valley because of the condition of the local "roads," if that word even applied to the miserable thoroughfares that prevailed in the San Gabriel Mountains before the late 1920s. Muddy and impassible in much of winter, the roads had been hastily cut by operators of gold, silver, and gemstone mining firms, and by timber companies that clear-cut entire swaths of the forest in the mid-nineteenth century. When the homesteaders arrived at the turn of the century, they adopted this rugged landscape, dotted by abandoned mining and timber villages, as their own. They prepared themselves and their families for a life of rustic isolation, and they usually found it, tenuous though it always was.

In the foothills and lower canyons of the San Gabriel Mountains, isolated eccentrics roamed the landscape, men like homesteader Silas Hoyt, who proved up his claim in 1913. Hoyt was easy to spot on his gray horse, Beelzebub, who ripped tree trunks clear out of the ground and dragged them back to Hoyt's stone-and-log cabin. Because Hoyt was too old and too tired to chop kindling, he guided Beelzebub to drag the entire tree into the house, and he slowly burned it from one end to the other until it was time to get another tree. On occasion a doctor

14. Homesteader Silas Hoyt in the doorway of his cabin in the San Gabriel Mountains. "His story," the original caption read, "of bears or Indians, or was it of Vasquez the Bandit, has captured the rapt attention of his youthful audience." This photograph appeared in *Trails Magazine* (Winter 1938). Will H. Thrall Photographs, Huntington Library, San Marino, California.

visited him to wash out his eyes from the smoke and to trim the bushy eyebrows that were so long they obstructed his already poor vision. "Barefoot Tom" Lucas, a ranger who wandered, shoeless, through the crowded forests of pine and alder in search of grizzly bears, also helped the aging Hoyt around his ranch. At a distance Lucas was often mistaken for an animal because he wore deerskin robes and pantaloons, a risky proposition in a landscape of big-game hunting.

But deeper into the range, homesteaders settled as families—the landscape required it. Cutting timber and clearing land, tending livestock, growing vegetables, cooking, carrying water up from the creek or spring—this was the work of a family and not a solitary man. One of the best-known families of its day was that of Delos Colby, who claimed a homestead in 1902 some twenty miles into the mountains at thirty-eight hundred feet. Colby was born in Michigan in 1851, spent time as a saloon keeper in Wyoming, farmed in Santa Monica, married in 1872, and then tried his hand at real estate during the Los Angeles land boom of the 1880s. He was initially very successful, even owning a hotel for a time, but when the land boom ended in 1888, he was left with virtually nothing. He defaulted on two large debts, and his last tract of city land fell into foreclosure. Colby's was a familiar tale, even a cautionary one, about the turbulent world of Southern California real estate. Those who succeeded usually brought significant capital to the game and then had great luck. Delos Colby had neither.

As a buffer against his financial misfortunes, Colby sought government land, and he found it in the San Gabriel Mountains near a granite promontory called Strawberry Peak. He squatted there through a winter and then brought his wife, Lillian, and only child, Nellie. He built a two-story log cabin and a sawmill, utilizing only lumber from the woodlot above the ranch, and they planted an orchard. To augment their meager finances, they advertised their place as a rest stop for hikers. And for a brief moment, after so many struggles, Delos Colby had it all. "No finer house stood in the mountains, no ranch more complete was carved from the wilderness," one observer wrote. "The house, a two-story dwelling built of stone and shingles, was as finished as many a city home."[1]

15. Delos W. and Lillian R. Colby, ca. 1910s. Will H. Thrall Photographs, Huntington Library, San Marino, California.

16. Colby Ranch, two-story cabin, ca. 1910s. Will H. Thrall Photographs, Huntington Library, San Marino, California.

And then a backwoods doctor diagnosed Nellie with throat cancer, and she died two years later in 1914. Lillian was so grief stricken that Delos insisted they travel twenty miles through the mountains to get her to a hospital in Pasadena. "For the first time in five years," the *Los Angeles Times* reported, "Mrs. D. W. Colby this week will leave her mountain home for a so-journ in civilization. She and Mr. Colby will come to Pasadena for a rest. After two years of constant nursing in the hope of saving the life of their only daughter, Nellie Colby, who was buried last Monday evening as the majestic mountains cast their shadows over the vale where the family has lived for years, the mother is left almost a physical wreck and grief for the death of her only child has made it absolutely necessary that she leave her home for a time."[2]

They returned, still mourning, to their ranch several weeks later. Delos and Lillian had several more years running their rustic resort, but the arrival of World War I killed their business: many of the young men who hiked in the region were drafted for service. Delos became severely anxious about their finances and died from a stroke in 1918. Lillian carried on with the help of her son-in-law, Joe Argay. But she had lost too much. She died in bed when her magnificent home caught fire and burned to the ground in 1928.[3]

The Loomises arrived in the mountains shortly after Colby had. When Lester Loomis staked his claim to a piece of the wilderness in 1913, he was fifty years old with white hair, but at six feet two and more than two hundred pounds, Lester was, as one observer wrote, "Thor-like." And his "mental stature," his longtime friend Odo B. Stade wrote, "rose high above his physical one. How else can one explain his sudden decision to start anew, to engage in the hardest kind of work at an age when others prefer an age of ease in the cities?" Whether Lester was endowed with great "mental stature" or a broad set of interests is impossible to know, but he had lived his life to this point with purpose and determination.[4]

Loomis was born in Peoria, Illinois, in 1863, and when he was eleven his parents brought him to California, first to Los Angeles and then to San Francisco. He took on various jobs in his youth, including cowpoke, carpenter, plasterer, and prison guard, but he was "far from being a jack-of-all-trades," Stade wrote. "Whatever he touched he did well by using his keen mind."[5] Soon after marrying in 1886, Lester and Grace moved back to Los Angeles and he found work in the Los Angeles Police Department at a time when physical size and strength were prized over strict adherence to the law, closing cases, and the efficient processing of paperwork. He soon made sergeant, then captain, and finally acting chief of police, all in the span of two years. But he reportedly tired of the bureaucracy and politics of the force and left the police department to work at the Evergreen cemetery in Boyle Heights, where he helped build one of the nation's first crematoriums. He and Grace both worked at the cemetery for fourteen years, and then he worked as a contractor while she stayed on at the cemetery for several more years before they decided to abandon Los Angeles and take their three children, Hazel, Ruth, and Anna, as well as their two sons-in-law, into the mountains. Lester found a spot with an old miners' shack, verified that it was open to settlement, and filed his initial homestead paperwork.

To prove up the claim, Loomis could not rely on converting the old miners' shack because it was too dilapidated and lacked solid foundations. So he and his sons-in-law immediately set about building his ranch house. Stade described the work involved: the flats on both sides of Alder Creek had to be cleared with "mattocks, axes, and brush-hooks—and backbreaking toil"; logs had to be cut, and rafters, sheathing, and shakes had to be "cut, sawed, and split" at the small town of Chilao, four miles away, "and all packed down to the site over a steep and narrow trail." Meanwhile, Grace and her daughters managed the family farm, alternately growing beans, onions, corn, potatoes, beets, and alfalfa. When the house was finally completed, Loomis threw a housewarming party among the few homesteaders in the region and gave a speech. "His eyes glowed," Stade wrote, "and there was a suspicion of moisture around their corners." The pride of building a homestead from nothing deep in the forest had overwhelmed Loomis.[6]

Whatever "mental stature" Loomis had, he also had good luck; he soon found gold in the abandoned mine on his homestead. It was no fortune, but it was enough for him to buy supplies in Chilao to build his own sawmill. Still, he and Grace periodically traveled down—"with heavy hearts" according to Stade—to the San Gabriel Valley to work odd jobs to keep their ranch humming along. They also supplemented their income by housing hunters and hikers who passed through with increased regularity as the county began paving roads into the forest in the late 1920s. Those travelers often photographed the Loomis Ranch and described its warmth and the hospitality of the hosts. "They lived in a world of their own," Los Angeles Times columnist Lee Shippey wrote, "and have made it altogether lovely."[7]

And then nature struck back: Loomis, who had complained of stomach pains for some time, finally went to a doctor in Los Angeles at Grace's urging. He was diagnosed with stomach cancer and died shortly after their fiftieth wedding anniversary in 1936. Even in mourning Grace insisted on returning to the ranch, to be close to the life they had led together. But neither would that last. In March of 1938 Los Angeles experienced the biggest storm ever recorded, and it caused $40 million in damage and killed forty-nine people. The San Gabriel Mountains took the brunt of the storm, recording thirty-two inches of rain at the height. Even "to old mountaineers," the *Los Angeles Times* reported, "the losses and damage are almost unbelievable. Every road and trail in the mountain area is impassable for any except the most experienced rescue crews." The Department of the Interior noted that the typical drainage areas on the south side of the mountains "are small, short, rough, and steep," meaning that the water ran wild and without course. Half the homesteaders lost their houses. Grace Loomis sought high ground during the storm. When she returned, their house had been entirely washed away.

Not every homesteader in the San Gabriel Mountains tried to create a family homestead. Some, like Sumner Wright, dreamed big. Wright had been mining coal near Redlands in San Bernardino County in April of 1896, and not talking to anybody about it. "Wright is very reticent in regard to the work he is doing, and has tried to keep the matter out of the papers," a *Los Angeles Times* reporter observed, "but coal experts on the ground declare the prospects excellent, the best scene in Southern California." Wright was secretive because be guarded his success jealously and was prone to outbursts. Attorneys with whom he would later work insisted that he could only be dealt with when "his mind is quiet." In his most outsized vision, Wright would attempt to leverage his homestead into a world-class recreational resort. He would fail, though others would take up the mantle and create the modern-day ski resort of Wrightwood, deep in the San Gabriel Mountains.[8]

Wright was born in Ohio in 1858 into a family of farmers. They migrated to California in the 1870s, settling in the sleepy coastal farming community of Santa Cruz to grow fruit. Sumner became an expert at cultivating grapes, even presenting a paper before an agricultural commission about a new form of "grape cancer" he had identified in his Muscat vines. Santa Cruz could not contain his ambitions, and after marrying in 1891 he moved to Colton in San Bernardino County to take up coal mining. Wright bought mining rights to a patch of land near Colton and struck a rich vein of coal only twenty feet down. It was of high enough grade to sell for about $10 per ton, and so he dug furiously.

Eager to grow his business, he incorporated with several other miners and oil drillers so that they could purchase 320 acres adjacent to the original strike. The company bought the land, but Wright did not become rich, though he did buy a racehorse that he named Harry Eaderson.

Wright's fortunes improved ecstatically in 1909, when his wife inherited $10,000 (equivalent to more than $280,000 today) from her deceased brother-in-law, California lumber mogul William W. Van Arsdale. Then as now, there was no substitute for a good inheritance, and Wright saw a way to finally materialize his grand vision. He was no longer the sort of striver imagined by Lincoln, no yeoman farmer, but he claimed a homestead in 1910 nonetheless, in the San Gabriel Mountains in what was known as the Swarthout Valley. He soon bought up surrounding properties and had amassed more than one thousand acres by the time he proved up his homestead in 1915. Whether the notion of a resort town on his property originated with Wright or with the lawyers and investors who would later cajole him, we will never know. But before long Wright was preparing to sell his property to a group of influential men in Los Angeles, all in the name of Wrightwood, the year-round resort town. His lawyer, James Oliver, carried on private communications with investors from Merchants and Farmers National Bank, bypassing Wright, insisting that he was difficult and befuddled, but reminding them that his property "undeniably furnished valuable asset for water development." Indeed the survey commissioned by the men making the deal was very enthusiastic:

> Resting as it does on the edge of the desert, yet in the heart of the high Sierra Madres, this valley would be comparatively useless and unattractive were it not for its wonderfully abundant supply of water, as yet almost wholly undeveloped. Three eminent engineers have all made a study of the water available in the valley . . . and they are unanimous in the conclusion that for all purposes for which this valley can possibly be used, including its highest development as an all-year-round resort or club, there is ample water and to spare for all needs, including the formation of a chain of lakes.

They were acutely aware of the fact that, despite his inheritance, Wright was in debt, and they offered him a price that got him out of that debt, exactly. Additionally they offered him $500 per month to manage the lakeside and ski resort. Wright signed on in 1924, selling his land to the corporation, but they failed to develop the area, for reasons that have been lost to history, and Wright was deprived of his monthly salary. Eventually, another company bought the land, kept Wright's name on the place, and founded the modern-day recreational resort of Wrightwood.[9]

A dreamer of a different kind settled at Tujunga Canyon in the San Gabriel Mountain foothills. He was a social critic, journalist, and irrigation expert named William Ellsworth Smythe, and he co-founded one of the most ambitious agrarian living experiments of the era. A New Englander, Smythe made his way west in the 1880s, settling for a time in Nebraska, where he reported for the *Omaha Bee*. When the region was devastated by a multiyear drought in the beginning of 1890, he watched in horror as both hardworking family farmers and regional speculators lost everything. This experience inspired a near-religious conversion in him, a conversion in which he became all consumed by irrigation. "It was not merely a matter of ditches and acres," he later wrote, "but a philosophy, a religion, and a programme of practical statesmanship rolled into one . . . I knew that I must cut loose from all other interests and endeavor to rouse the Nation to a realizing sense of its duty and opportunity."[10]

Smythe moved quickly, founding the periodical *Irrigation Age* for the National Irrigation Congress, an organization founded in 1891 that advocated for reclamation laws and encouraged national investment in irrigation bonds issued in the Far West. In 1894 he organized the first conference of the sort, a five-day affair at the Grand Opera House in Los Angeles featuring hundreds of delegates from the United States as well as from Russia, France, Austria, Ecuador, and Mexico, all gathered exclusively to discuss irrigation. "We meet not merely to extend our country's frontiers," he said at the opening of the conference, "but to widen the boundaries of civilization. The seed which we shall plant in the arid soil of the desert will bear the flower of industrial independence for millions of the freest men who ever trod the earth."[11]

Smythe's high-profile advocacy caught the attention of Frederick Haynes Newell of the Department of the Interior and influenced the ultimate passage of the Reclamation Act of 1902. But for Smythe, irrigation was not an end in itself, but rather a means to fulfill a broader agrarian vision. Unlike the many socialist-minded reformers of the late nineteenth century, Smythe was enthusiastic about private property. "Ownership and permanence of the home," he wrote, "are essential to the highest dignity of life." But he also believed that Americans would only find true freedom, independence, happiness, and health if they cultivated their own food and lived an agrarian lifestyle. He believed that American farmers took on too much land for speculative purposes instead of farming smaller lands with greater intensity. And he believed that the Homestead Act, while theoretically beneficial, gave homesteaders too much land and that all the good land had been taken anyway. (Much later he lamented that for soldiers returning from the Great War "there was no longer a patrimony of fertile public lands available to homestead entry, and requiring no preparation beyond the means of the individual settler.") And so Smythe found investors to help create an alternative to homesteading, at the base of the San Gabriel Mountains. It was to be, he wrote, "the rarest mountain village on earth."[12]

The Little Landers colony that would emerge in 1913 was the product of Smythe's vision, but it was not his first. In San Ysidro, at the Mexican border and fifteen miles from San Diego, he had established a Little Landers colony in 1908. There he had enticed—through heavy promotion in newspapers—about two hundred families to purchase several acres each at the price of $100–$500 per acre. Although the cost was far higher than the nominal fee traditional homesteaders paid for their land, most bought on credit. Additionally, and central to the Little Landers experiment, residents purchased and sold cooperatively and owned a storefront in San Diego to sell their produce. Finally, unlike traditional homesteaders, they only purchased acreage they could maintain themselves, so there were no onerous labor costs. From an economic standpoint the colony succeeded for a time, but not for long. A massive flood in 1916 wiped out nearly half the colony. Homestead shacks, along with the dreams of the settlers, were washed into the Tijuana River. When the flood waters receded, the once-fertile soil had been buried under feet of sand. Few paid off their homes before abandoning the site, and in 1925 an agricultural economist visiting the site found only one original settler. Three years before the flood that destroyed the San Ysidro colony, Smythe had moved to Los Angeles to find a site for another colony. "Why did God make Southern California?" Smythe asked rhetorically in a promotional tract. "I believe God made Southern California to be the paradise of the common man—the chosen home of those who would work and live in the midst of the most ideal conditions Nature ever devised."[13]

He soon chose Tujunga Canyon because he believed, like many others did, that it provided the most healthful climate possible—numerous sanitariums had opened in the region in the late nineteenth century based on the same belief. There was little science behind the notion, but the placebo effect was as powerful then as it is now. More to the point, Smythe found a developer named Marshall Valentine Hartranft who lived nearby, was sympathetic to Smythe's vision and idealism, and was willing to help with the purchase of a one-thousand-acre site. He secured options for the site, incorporated under the name of Western Empire Suburban Farm Association, and sold bonds to cover the cost of irrigating the land. Smythe, meanwhile, promoted the colony relentlessly in the *Los Angeles Times*, and by the end of 1913 there were more than two hundred colonists, each paying $3 per month ($300 total) to buy an acre in the cooperative colony. Smythe forecasted that "individual independence" would be achieved by residents, that "they and their children shall be proprietors rather than tenants," and that Little Landers colony would "become an important supply point for vegetables and poultry to the homes" of Los Angeles.[14]

Smythe's modest agrarian vision was not realized at Little Landers—the ground proved far too rocky and was littered with boulders interspersed with sand and gravel. "The stones were more numerous in some spots than we had supposed," Smythe later acknowledged. Most families were only able to produce enough yield to feed their own family but certainly never enough to participate in the cooperative marketing that was at the heart of the venture. Instead, beginning in 1916 Little Landers colonists began to subdivide their properties—usually into eight lots—and sell the lots off for $400 to $500 each. In the best-case scenario a colonist could turn a profit of $3,700 on a $300 investment. By 1917 there was barely a Little Lander left, and the name of the town was soon changed to Tujunga.[15]

Adjacent to Little Landers was the homestead of Cornelius Birket Johnson, who bore a fine reputation among all but one of his neighbors in Tujunga Canyon—his younger brother, Alva. Johnson, his father, and Alva had settled in the region in the 1890s and would eventually claim their 160-acre tract in 1905. Alva soon married into a family downstream on Big Tujunga Creek, and shortly thereafter Cornelius and his father built a small dam on a portion of the creek in order to assure access to relatively continuous water supply to their grapes. Alva sued, but the judge agreed that Cornelius and his father were exercising their riparian rights and ruled against Alva. "They tried to beat me out of some water," he later complained. He also incurred a substantial legal debt that he sought to pay by robbing trains. Alva and his accomplice succeeded in their first robbery in 1893, but wrecked the train in their second, killing a passenger and the brakeman. He was convicted in March 1895 and served twelve years before being paroled in 1907.[16]

Unlike Alva, Cornelius was content to live out his days in quiet peace on his homestead, but nature intervened. One morning in October of 1916 Cornelius detected the telltale signs of a big animal traipsing through his farm. The paw prints were bigger and deeper than those of the mountain lion, but he remained skeptical that he was dealing with a bear—the California grizzly (*Ursus arctos californicus*) had been hunted to near extinction in the late nineteenth century, and black bears were scarce in the region. Still unsure of what he was pursuing, Cornelius grabbed his .30 Marlin rifle and followed the animal's tracks for about a mile into the foothills, where he lost them.

The next night Cornelius laid down a heavy bear trap, anchored to a fifty-pound sycamore log, and baited it with spoiled beef. Two mornings later he awoke to find the trap—and the fifty-pound log—gone, and now he knew it was a bear. He easily followed the new tracks for about half a mile, until he found the bear, bloody and exhausted, and he shot it. In his twenty years in Tujunga Canyon, Johnson had never seen a grizzly bear, so few were their numbers at this point, but he quickly recognized the telltale long claws and the grayish or "grizzled" fur and knew what he had. He brought back his horse and wagon to drag the 250-pound bear to the local butcher, had it skinned and butchered, and sold off cuts of the meat to the locals. He saved the hide, the head and neck, and a shoulder of the bear, expecting they might be worth something, but he did not know how rare his find truly was: he had killed the last known grizzly bear in Southern California, and the second-to-last confirmed grizzly bear in the entire state of California. The skull of that grizzly bear today sits safely on a shelf in a back room of the Museum of Vertebrate Zoology at the University of California, Berkeley.[17]

9

Taming the Colorado Desert

In 1931 the beloved *Los Angeles Times* columnist Harry Carr took a tour of Southern California in an airplane, that quintessential symbol of modern Los Angeles. The year before, Howard Hughes's aviation war film *Hell's Angels* had thrilled audiences, making it one of the highest grossing films of the era. And Carr himself was a modern man, a serious journalist who earned a name for himself for his powerful reportage from the 1906 San Francisco earthquake but also a Los Angeles socialite who hobnobbed with Hollywood directors D. W. Griffith and Cecil B. DeMille, among others. He was a man so steeped in the culture, history, and life of Los Angeles that he must have wondered what an aerial view of the region could reveal that he did not already know. But when the pilot flew him past the Los Angeles County line into San Bernardino, and into the vast and foreboding Mojave Desert, Carr was surprised: "Nearly the whole area of the Valley of Twenty-Nine Palms," Carr wrote, "has been pre-empted by homesteaders. Their cabins dot the landscape."[1]

The pilot banked right, headed south, and Carr saw the forest of Joshua trees that would soon become a national monument but were presently crisscrossed by new roads graded by optimistic developers. "Someone had the wild idea of laying out this valley in town lots with boulevards. The coyotes are still playing tag in the boulevards." Had his flight continued farther south, Carr would have entered into the Colorado Desert, much of that in Riverside County, and seen hundreds of additional board-and batten-cabins that were both the proof of improvement and often the sole material possession of the homesteader.

What is remarkable about Carr's aerial tour is not simply how many homesteaders there were in the Southern California desert at that time—the Los Angeles Land Office recorded more than four thousand homesteads in San Bernardino and Riverside Counties between the opening of the twentieth century and the dawn of the Great Depression—but also how surprising that fact was to such a sage. Carr's ignorance bespoke a cultural divide—one that became evermore apparent in the early years of the twentieth century—between the residents of metropolitan California and their far-flung neighbors.

Neither the Mojave nor the Colorado Deserts beckoned many settlers prior to the twentieth century. A small group of affluent health-seekers convinced of the desert's palliative properties settled there in the 1870s, but there were few traces of them by the turn of the century; when Riverside was incorporated as county in 1893, there were probably fewer than six thousand people in an area roughly the size of New Jersey. "The popular conception of a desert," George Wharton James wrote in *The Wonders of the Colorado Desert* (1911), "is that the desert is all sand—barren, desolate, unfruitful, shifting sand, where the heat is frightful and we hear nothing can live save horned toads, lizards, snakes, chuckwallas, and gila monsters." Compounding the effects of this perception was the certifiable fact that until the early twentieth century there was ample land for homesteading much closer to the city of Los Angeles. It was not until most of the free land in Los Angeles County was claimed that homesteaders began looking farther east.[2]

As in the Antelope Valley, homesteaders had to sink wells before any improvements could begin, despite the fact that many natural springs dotted the Colorado and Mojave Deserts and nearby foothills. Particularly in Riverside County, natural springs were an important water source for nineteenth-century settlers and for American Indians, the latter of whom also endowed them with spiritual significance. Today, of course, most of the natural springs in the region have dried up, victims of excessive groundwater consumption and seismic shifts, but even in the nineteenth century they were never sufficient for large-scale irrigation purposes.

According to local history books like *Coachella Valley's Golden Years* (1978), settlement of the Colorado Desert really began in the 1920s when well-capitalized developers—pioneering men of great character—created water districts and wrestled the hostile and arid desert into submission. Today accounts like these fill up entire bookshelves in libraries throughout Riverside and San Bernardino Counties, but the truth of the matter is that these men were latecomers. As in the Antelope Valley on the western edge of the Mojave, it was often the homesteaders who were the first white men to prove that the region could be inhabitable, and they painstakingly laid some of the first rudimentary irrigation projects without the support of banks or investors or local government bonds.

Homesteader Jason L. Rector claimed a plot in the Coachella Valley, a few miles east of the whistle-stop town of Indio in 1898. Even for "Riverside people," the *Los Angeles Times* wrote in a profile of Rector, it was "a big slice of their country which they do not know as much as they do of the Philippine Islands." Until whites mispronounced its original name, it was known as Conchilla Valley because of the "little shells" found there, testimony to its geological history, though it sits more than one hundred forty miles from the coast. Rector, a native of Iowa, was mocked by his peers for the apparent foolhardiness of his venture into the hot and dry Coachella Valley, but he persisted, spending months and every last dollar to sink a two-inch pipe into the desert sand. Recall that in Santa Clara River Valley and the Antelope Valley, homesteaders sank wells of one to two hundred feet before finding water. Rector had to work longer and harder, but he finally penetrated the aquifer at 550 feet—almost the length of two football fields. It was a miraculous achievement and allowed Rector to quickly prove up his land and cultivate sweet potatoes, onions, cabbage, sugar beets, alfalfa, wheat, cantaloupe, and watermelons. In 1901 he netted $2,240 from his cantaloupe and watermelons alone, a bit more than $60,000 in today's dollars.[3]

Rector was not the first to irrigate the Riverside region: a well-funded group of developers had built ditches from the Santa Ana River as early as 1870. But Rector was the first independent homesteader to have such success, and there was nothing like success to close the gap between Los Angeles and its desert backcountry. Rector soon co-founded and became vice president of the Coachella Valley Producers' Association, which held six hundred acres of land devoted to melons. In his new capacity, Rector sought cheap labor to work the fields of association members. By the time of the melon harvest in the summer of 1902, he had hired two hundred local American Indians, mostly among the Cahuilla people. But that amounted to only about one-third of the association's labor demand. The fact that he could not find more American Indians willing to day-labor in the Coachella Valley is a grizzly reminder of how fast the native population of that region had declined. The Cahuilla population stood at only about twelve hundred in the 1890s, cut in half first by exposure to Spaniards and cut in half again by a smallpox epidemic in 1863. And northeast in the Mojave in 1870, the United States military pushed the Mojave people into the Fort Mojave Indian Reservation. Those who survived outside of the reservation lived in abject poverty.[4]

Unable to rely on Indian labor, Rector traveled to Los Angeles to seek Japanese workers, reputed to work efficiently and for low pay. He ultimately hired four hundred of them, which represented approximately a third of their population in the city at that time. Successful farmers in the Colorado and Mojave Deserts would soon draw heavily on the city's untapped, idled, itinerant, and indigent labor pool with profound effects on its Mexican, Japanese, and Chinese populations.[5]

When word of Rector's success reached Los Angeles, and the newspaper publicized his exploits, it triggered a homestead rush to Indio. When he was asked about men eager to emulate his homesteading success, Rector sounded a cautious note: "I am a settler of this land, and I know every foot of it. It won't do our valley any good to have people rushing in there and being disappointed. If it is not on the artesian belt, it is just about as worthless as a mountain of rocks." But few heeded Rector's caution, and hundreds of homesteaders soon relocated to Riverside County. The *Los Angeles Times* observed the lure of the desert with some amazement: "As the good lands have been taken up and developed in various ways, newcomers have been forced farther and farther afield, until at the present time the old question, How much good land is there in Southern California? has been change to a diametrically opposite sense, we now ask, Is there any bad land in Southern California? We have come to realize that there is very little that is absolutely valueless." That migration spoke volumes about the state of the employment in turn-of-the-century Los Angeles, a city that left many behind in its mad dash toward dazzling modernity.[6]

Despite industrialists' boundless optimism about turn-of-the-century Los Angeles's prosperity, it was not—as one Los Angeles machinist put it—"enjoyed by those who toil." There was a vast population of poor and lower-class people in the city, but you would not know it from the headlines. City leaders and developers engineered a raft of monumental infrastructural achievements in quick succession—the incorporation of the Pacific Electric Railway Company in 1901 (and with it, expanded electrification), the completion of a world-class port in 1907, and the completion of the Owens Valley aqueduct in 1913. These developments, coupled with rapid population growth, created a buyer's market for employers, and the *Los Angeles Times*, among other official organs of downtown business interests, trumpeted the "good tidings" of the era, particularly on the heels of the depression of the 1890s. The reality was that most workers were miserably underpaid because of employers' fierce advocacy of "industrial freedom," that antiunion creed that made Los Angeles a stridently open-shop town. Additionally, in immigrant districts like the Macy Street district near downtown, workers were often seasonal and thus unemployed many months of the year. Underemployment and low wages triggered a large strike wave in 1910 and 1911 and the bombing of the *Los Angeles Times* building in 1910, but employers only redoubled their power through the use of private security firms. Finally, the recession of 1913–14 dramatically reduced employment opportunities, with some unions reporting levels of unemployment as high as 45 percent. The workingmen of Los Angeles, in short, had a hard row to hoe.

But it was not merely poverty that drove Californians deep into the desert. Further stimulating the small exodus was climatology—a curious mixture of hucksterism and the Hippocratic. Both the high desert of the Mojave—so called because much of it sits more than two thousand feet above sea level—and the Colorado Desert, much of which sits below sea level, had climates that early health promoters believed to be palliative for those with respiratory disorders, particularly tuberculosis. Both extremely hot in summer, the Colorado also had unusually dry air, believed to be a panacea not only for respiratory but for all manner of disorders, real and imagined. In his 1946 classic, *Southern California: An Island on the Land,* Carey McWilliams listed the rest: "incipient phthisis, chronic pneumonia, tuberculosis, disease of the liver, malarial poisoning, cirrhosis of the liver, jaundice, functional female disturbances, the organic ills of advanced years, simple congestion of constipation, hepatic catarrh, scrofulous affections, insomnia, and enlarged glands." It was little wonder that by the end of the nineteenth century it was common for doctors, promoters, and newspapers to refer to the Colorado Desert as "the desert for invalids."[7]

Although the pseudoscience of climatology lined the pockets of more than a few medical "professionals," the palliative properties of the desert could be real. "There have been indisputable evidences of the benefit derived from the climate of Indio," claimed medical doctors Walter Lindley and J. P. Widney in their 1896 *California of the South,* and countless patients vouched for the efficacy of sleeping outdoors on hot nights. So convinced was Norwegian millionaire and philanthropist Nelson Olsen Nelson of the positive health benefits, that he bought 140 acres near Indio to create a "health camp" in 1904, complete with outdoor sleeping arrangements and a specialized dietary and exercise regime. Nelson appears to have been a victim of his own success, as patients, soon believing themselves healed, rebelled against the regime, became indulged, and demanded—as one writer for the *Los Angeles Times* put it—"a bill of fare of greater lay-out than could have been obtained at a first-class restaurant." Nelson shut the doors in 1907 demanding that the federal government assume the burden of healing his spoiled charges.[8]

The spike in desert homesteading during the 1920s corresponded with the return of World War I veterans, many of whom suffered debilitating injuries. Elizabeth (Betty) W. Crozer Campbell and William (Bill) Campbell, for example, were absolutely desperate. Married in 1920, they lived happily for a brief time in Pasadena. But times soon got tough. Once robust, Bill grew chronically ill—mustard gas had badly burned his lungs in the Great War. His illness kept him from a steady job, forcing Betty to work twice as hard. She lost two babies through premature births, and then, insolvent until Bill's delayed pension kicked in, they lost their house. By December of 1924 they had nothing. "We might have gone begging to relatives," Betty later remembered, "but I was afraid that if Bill felt dependent on those who disapproved of him, it might crush him in his weakened state." Sick, poor, homeless, and too proud to beg, the Campbells drove out to the desert to a barren place called Twentynine Palms in Riverside County, pitched a tent, camped under the stars and cottonwood trees, and resolved to find a homestead.[9]

For the Campbells the palliative healing of the desert was real, and Bill's health improved as he toiled on proving up their claim in the hot, dry air. But for Betty—and so many other homesteaders in the Colorado Desert—desert life induced a kind of spiritual awakening as well. "Nothing that I have experienced," Betty would later write, "is more mystical than night on the desert. The absolute clarity of the atmosphere free from mist, soot or smoke, makes a miracle of common things like starry heavens or moonlight." "To most people the Colorado Desert is not only a place devoid of interest, but absolutely to be shunned, feared, dreaded," John Wharton James wrote in 1906, but "no hall of necromancers can equal the desert in its marvels and revelations. Wonder follows wonder in quick succession."[10]

James's engagement with the desert was emphatically, bitingly, antiurban. "It is true," he wrote in 1906, "that the desert is not for everybody." He continued:

He who loves comfort and ease more than knowledge and power; who is afraid of hardship, solitude, heat, and general discomfort; who values the neatness of his appearance and cleanliness of his apparel more than filling himself with experiences strange and novel . . .

had better remain away. The desert will flout him. Its winds will toss his well-combed locks astray and disarrange his dainty apparel. . . . Its lack of all native foods will offend his epicureanism, for to live on "condemned" foods is not agreeable to a pampered palate. No! No! Pampered and feasted sons and daughters of cities, don't come to the desert.

James, like many homesteaders themselves, came to believe that their mode of life was virtuous and gave them insights to "truth" and "clarity."[11]

But for Betty, daytime loneliness tempered the brilliance of the nights. Raised in Pennsylvania, she often found the isolation and barrenness of the desert depressing: "By far the worst thing was the lack of social and intellectual contacts, a kind of loneliness that staggered me." Furthermore, their homestead was at least sixty miles from the nearest town, which made caring for rations all the more important: "Our nearest town was sixty-one miles away, and forty-five of that wasn't road at all, just ancient wagon track winding in and out among the bushes; two ruts with an appallingly high hump in between. We did not usually go for provisions oftener than every three or four weeks, and I learned to keep vegetables fresh, buried in a paper-lined box in the shade. Every four or five days I took them out and crisped them in fresh water, aired them, and put them back again."

That kind of isolation—both among homesteaders and other desert dwellers—required fortitude. It required that they maintain their provisions, maintain their water supply, and not become injured or ill. Accidentally dropping a tool on a man digging his well, tripping on a crag, or chopping off fingers with an ax could all spell disaster given that help was so far away. "It is of supreme importance," Betty later reflected, "to do the right thing in the wilds."[12]

They lived in a tent until Bill's pension belatedly arrived and then set about proving up the land, first sinking a well and then building a house. They hired a well-digger who found water at seventy-four feet. Next they turned to building their home. Their neighbor drove them sixty miles into town with his truck to buy bags of cement—"they were precious," Betty recalled. Running back and forth to the well to wet the cement, Bill, Betty, and a hired hand poured the foundation, and slowly their fourteen-by-eighteen-foot cabin arose in the desert. "We moved into our 'house' before we had any roofing, doors, windows or lining. We tacked cheesecloth over the door and window openings and trusted to luck it wouldn't rain before we could afford the roofing. For some time I looked at a twinkling star here and there through the cracks and knotholes at night, and wondered about rain. . . . Our first rain came three days after the last shingle was nailed on the roof. We listened to the patter above our dry heads, grinned at each other, and felt like millionaires." The Campbells finished their house in 1926, the same year in which Betty's father died. Unbeknownst to her at the time, Betty's father left her a significant trust that would support the Campbells for the duration of their desert lives.[13]

Frank and Helen Bagley arrived in Twentynine Palms in 1927 to file on a homestead, and they quickly befriended the Campbells. Like Bill Campbell, Frank Bagley was a veteran and a health-seeker, though he suffered from severe asthma rather than combat-induced lung damage. The foliage of Pasadena was a curse to the man, and he had no aspirations for growing more vegetation in the desert, so rather than subsist on crops, the Bagleys decided to open a store in their homestead shack. The Twentynine Palms Grocery and General Store, it was called, and its first offerings were modest in the extreme. "I made a list of groceries for our initial stock," Helen later recalled, "keeping carefully in mind that if no one bought things we would eat them. A few cases and half cases of tinned meats and vegetables, a few bunches of carrots, cabbage and potatoes, two sides of bacon." And then they poured the remainder of their savings into a gas tank. Theirs would be the first gas station and market in a sixty-mile radius.

Twentynine Palms was stark country in 1927 when the Bagleys arrived. "There was not even a mile of straight road," Helen later recalled. "More important, there was no school, post office, or store . . . no group of buildings could be called a village." With their three young children, Helen and Frank slept on a roll-out mattress in the corner of the store.

17. The Bagley's store in Twentynine Palms, ca. 1937. Courtesy HJG/Frashers Fotos Collection.

When Frank traveled for work or supplies, Helen experienced a beautiful and burdensome time at "five in the afternoon," which she described as her "zero hour": "The hour of flaming sunsets, when the Sheep Hole Mountains change to mauve and gold and brooding peace descends upon the desert. The children were tired and wanted supper. The baby wept and refused to be comforted. Wood and water must be brought inside before dark; the gasoline lanterns, which frightened me, must be lit just so."[14] Helen's account is a poignant reminder of the timeless challenges of motherhood, which the homestead life only exacerbated.

Owning a store and a gas pump meant that the Bagley's got to know just about everyone in the region. Individually isolated on 160-acre plots miles from one another, homesteaders in the desert kept surprisingly close tabs on each other. "There came a corps of homesteaders who wanted homes on land they owned and a background of sound community life," Helen recalled. "Most were poor, but they worked together. They shared. They shared water, they nursed and helped each other in trouble. Shared too the joys, had fun in homespun ways." But, as Helen found out, there was a corollary to that generous spirit, that communal sentiment. Collective isolation brought with it hypervigilance in all things but particularly in the defense of personal character. Character—which was a fancy word for trustworthiness and reliability in an emergency—could save your life, and so homesteaders often defended it with their own, particularly when the sheriff was sixty miles away. A man named Robert Furniss learned this the hard way when he questioned the virtue of Tennessean Bernice Tucker.[15]

Helen only knew Tucker as the lady with the Packard and the southern drawl who often visited the Twentynine Palms Grocery and General Store. She had the good sense to give Tucker a wide berth, though she did observe that Tucker had been married five times but insisted on calling herself a widow, "appealing to chivalry," and also that she entertained many male visitors at her home. Some of the men in the area respected the ruse and gave Tucker latitude, probably because she was what the *Los Angeles Times* would soon describe as "comely" and "sunbronzed." But others, like septuagenarian homesteader Robert Furniss, had no truck with how she sashayed about. When he saw Tucker drive off to Los Angeles with her daughter's fiancé, Furniss could not keep his mouth shut: "Any man who comes to her house brings his reputation in his hands." And when she returned from Los Angeles, two other homesteaders informed Tucker of Furniss's remarks and said that she deserved better, deserved a "square deal," as they put it.[16]

The next night Tucker and her two teenage sons visited Bagley's store to buy ammunition, picked up two other homesteaders named Smith and Benioff, and drove out to the homestead of Fred Furniss, Robert's son. Her sons standing guard with shotguns, Tucker jammed her .38 pistol into Furniss's ribs and forced him into the car. They drove to Robert Furniss's place and forced him out into the front yard. Seeing that Robert was frail, she turned her attention to Fred. "Fred," she said, "I went all the way to Los Angeles today to get this black snake whip like we used to whip the n—— with where I came from. I'm going to whip you to the rind and then cover you with tar and feathers." And then, to the amazement and horror of Benioff and Smith—who realized that they were in way over their heads—she opened her trunk to reveal a can of tar, two brushes, and feathers that she had removed earlier in the day from her bedroom pillow.[17]

"I intended to see whether anyone could insult a widow woman who was trying to live right," Tucker later told a judge. But presently, Benioff and Smith had abandoned the party, fearful of how far Tucker would go, and the plot quickly unraveled without their support. So Tucker and her boys fled into the foothills to evade the sheriff, en route from the town of Banning. After a halfhearted escape attempt, Tucker turned herself in. And after a short trial in San Bernardino, a jury acquitted her on charges of assault with a deadly weapon because it believed her claim that she did not force Fred into the car, only that she pointed a gun at him. When asked by the district attorney if her gun was loaded, Tucker answered truthfully: "Why certainly. Everybody in Twenty-nine palms carries a gun. It wouldn't be much use to you if it wasn't loaded." Outside the courthouse an armed crowd of homesteaders stood in solidarity with Tucker, while another group patrolled the widow's property.[18]

Among homesteaders Tucker was probably exceptional in her willingness to commit violence. Homesteaders were more often the victims of violence than they were perpetrators. The residency requirement of the Homestead Act was a strong deterrent to lawlessness: the simple act of appearing at the county seat often meant a day's wagon drive, and if a case dragged on, homesteaders ran a real risk of violating the residency clause. It also exposed them to theft and their properties to vandalism. In short, homesteaders were usually the least likely citizens to rock the boat. Gun ownership among homesteaders was widespread, uncomplicated, and pragmatic—in a land with minimal law enforcement, guns were the only tools upon which homesteaders could rely to protect themselves and their property from criminals and wild animals.

But they took threats to their livelihood very seriously and responded with force when it became necessary, as the case of Joshua Tree homesteader William "Desert Bill" F. Keys revealed. Born in 1879 in Nebraska to Quaker parents, Keys had worked for a time as an American Indian guide before claiming two eighty-acre plots and settling them in about 1913. He raised a small herd of cattle and sold surplus fruit and vegetables from his orchard to a store in the Yucca Valley. When his children reached school age, he built an additional shack on his property and hired a teacher to educate them. Keys was a man of the desert and foothills and was, above all, a man of peace. Until he wasn't.

In the California desert, there was no enmity as intense as that between homesteaders and cattle ranchers. Time and again homesteaders settled—as was their right—on formerly open range, range the cattlemen claimed they owned. The Campbells found this out when they first claimed their Twentynine Palms homestead. The second night in their tent two shots were fired close enough to graze the canvas, and Betty was fired upon again the next day by cattlemen. "Desert" Bill Keys also had his share of run-ins. In the late 1920s, a good fifteen years after Keys had settled his homestead in Joshua Tree, a cattle hand named Homer Urton from Yucca Valley started letting the company cattle graze in the mountains. Several times the cattle had wandered onto Keys's land, and when he fenced it, Urton cut the wires, inadvertently losing Keys's milk cow in the mix. Keys put up warning signs: "Homer Urton. KEEP OUT. You will be shot on sight." This continued for about a year until Urton finally decided to pay Keys a visit, at which point Keys made good on his promise and put a bullet in Urton's arm. Keys was easily acquitted on grounds of self-defense. But it was not the last the world heard from Keys: in 1943 he shot and killed a former Los Angeles County sheriff over the rights to a watering hole. The sheriff drew first, Keys said, and he shot back in self-defense. He served five years in San Quentin State Prison and was later granted a full pardon.[19]

Ranching homesteaders sometimes found themselves up against well-capitalized cattle operations based in Los Angeles and Nevada. This was the case of Bob Hollimon, about whom it seemed everyone had an opinion. Newspapers called Hollimon a "two-gun man," a cowboy who had dueled two brothers over a cattle watering hole and won, even with the horse shot out from under him. His wife, desperate for a divorce, asserted that Hollimon had fired a shot through her open legs, causing her irreparable emotional damage. Some even claimed, fabulously, that Hollimon had once ridden with Butch Cassidy's Wild Bunch. His local detractors maintained that his cattle operation was a front for a bootlegging operation, and his chief competitor, Rock Springs Land and Cattle Company, accused him of cattle rustling. But from Hollimon's perspective, he was just a stock-raising homesteader, trying to survive on the far eastern edge of California on the high desert of the Mojave in a place known as Lanfair Valley.[20]

What was clearly true about Hollimon was that he understood land law and worked hard to acquire his homestead. He was, as one balanced observer wrote, "a sticker at home, and everlasting at work." Born in Kansas, Hollimon found his way to California where he worked in various cattle operations before lighting out on his own. In 1915 he found a plot of land in the Lanfair Valley in the eastern Mojave suitable for stock raising and purchased the squatting rights from two men who'd purchased the squatters' rights from a previous resident who had in turn purchased squatters' rights from the first white occupants of the land, the Clements. Part of the appeal of the land was that it had two natural springs, the more productive of which became known as Clement's spring. When Hollimon applied for a homestead on the land in 1916, he demonstrated that he had significantly improved the land by building a reservoir under Clement's spring to preserve its natural flow. He also fenced in a two-hundred-acre portion with Ajax wire, and close to four hundred posts, and he blasted and dug a twenty-five-foot well. Whatever outlaw reputation Hollimon had, he was a stickler when it came to fulfilling the letter and spirit of the Homestead Act.[21]

But Walter Greening, president of Rock Springs Land and Cattle Company—a company he had inherited from his father, based in the Los Angeles suburb of Norwalk—asserted rights to the waters of Clement's spring on Hollimon's property. Greening maintained that long before Hollimon settled on the land, the first squatter signed a quitclaim deed to the springs for a sum of money. But that deed was misdated, never officially recorded, and not witnessed. Despite the cloud over the deed, the Superior Court of San Bernardino County had ruled in favor of the company, enjoining Hollimon from using the water of Clement's spring. The issue would have remained settled, but

Hollimon claimed a homestead on the land, effectively reclassifying what had been open range. Now, he figured, he had a chance, and in a 1925 letter he implored the Department of the Interior to aid in his fight for the water of Clement's spring: "It is a well known fact that the Rock Springs Land and Cattle Co has in the past deprived the Homesteaders and the public the use of water on the free and open range in this country. During all these years they have harassed and obstructed me in my peaceful efforts of making a living and obtaining title to 640 acres of Uncle Sam's land." Supporting Hollimon's assertion that Rock Springs had "ruthless designs against me and my land and water," John S. Hamman of the General Land Office argued that Rock Springs effectively used the threat of a future expensive lawsuit as "a sort of club over the entryman to force him to leave open a portion of his land so that the cattle of the company may obtain water."[22]

However, as with the Superior Court in San Bernardino years before, the Department of the Interior ruled in favor of Rock Springs Land and Cattle Company. The result was that Hollimon lost thirty acres of the 640 allotted for the Stock-Raising Act, as well as the waters of Clement's spring. Hollimon reacted in a way that gave some credence to the earlier claims of his coarseness: his friends often found fresh cuts of Rock Springs cattle on their porches, the spoils of late-night depredations by "two-gun" Hollimon.

10

Imperial Valley Dreams

Dewitt H. Coe pedaled his bicycle for ten straight days in 1901, from Covina to the Imperial Valley in the far southeastern corner of California. "I did not see a soul," he later wrote, "except from a distance." It was a 150-mile journey, and when he arrived in the desolate valley the thermometer read 117 degrees. "The first man I met and spoke to was a Chinaman," Coe wrote about his disappointing arrival, "but even he looked good to me." Coe had it on good authority that irrigation would soon come to the Imperial Valley, but at the moment it was bone dry. Land was cheap, so Coe bought up 120 acres and filed for a homestead on eighty more. And then something improbable happened. In fewer than ten years Coe became wildly successful. Fellow pioneer and Imperial chronicler Edgar F. Howe watched Coe's progress with delight, observing in 1910 how he soon ditched his bicycle for "a high power automobile." The humble homesteader now had sixty-four dairy cows, thirty more head of young stock, two hundred hogs, and dozens of acres of hay and grain. "Coe is essentially a business-like rancher," Howe wrote. "There is no more enthusiastic booster of the country now than Coe, whom the Valley has helped make wealthy."[1]

Hundreds of homesteaders had claimed land in the Imperial Valley before Coe wheeled into town, and none of them had his easy fortune because they lived in the pre-irrigation era. Much of the valley—which was part of San Diego County until 1907—had been an ancient inland sea, and where there was water, it was brackish, but the soils were silty.

Homesteaders sank wells at great personal expense only to draw up non-potable water. The narrator in Harold Bell Wright's best-selling novel, *The Winning of Barbara Worth* (1911), described the pre-irrigation Imperial Valley as a "dreadful land where the thirsty atmosphere is charged with the awful silence of uncounted ages." But others saw the enormous agricultural potential of this barren land just west of the Colorado River. Advocates of the cause had come and gone by the late nineteenth century, but none was as determined and ultimately successful as engineer-cum-booster, C. R. Rockwood, the founder of the California Development Company in 1900. Coupled with the engineering expertise of George Chaffey—best known for founding the towns of Ontario and Upland—the California Development Company set the Imperial Valley on its modern course as one of the state's most productive farming regions.[2]

Rockwood had been trying to irrigate the valley for more than a decade, but it took the California Development Company—a joint American and Mexican company—to realize his vision. Chaffey completed the first canal—the Alamo or Imperial Canal, as it was alternately named—in 1901. The Alamo was a fourteen-mile canal that ran parallel to the Colorado River in Mexico before cutting northward into the Imperial Valley. The company soon rounded out its system by digging more than six hundred miles' worth of irrigation ditches from the canal, and the results were exponential. In July of 1902 there were six thousand acres of crops; by 1904 there were 150,000. "In every direction," the *Imperial Valley Press* reported in 1902, "houses and tents denote the habitation of some homesteader or desert land entryman." Indeed several hundred homesteaders claimed more than 125,000 acres by early 1902.[3]

San Diego's political and commercial leadership was slow to recognize or appreciate the empire on the edges of its vast county. This was largely because of the Cuyamaca Mountains, whose craggy passes were impenetrable to all but the most daring. It was an eight-mile wagon journey, one that Harold Bell Wright described with only some embellishments: "The only mark of man in all that desolate waste and itself marked every mile by the graves of men and by the bleached bones of their cattle." A more modest assessment by a San Diego businessman was that it was "a difficult and somewhat expensive" journey; regardless, it was a journey that few prospective settlers wanted to make, and as a result few did. Nor did many share Coe's affinity for the bicycle. Instead the majority of the Imperial Valley's early pioneers came from Los Angeles, via the Southern Pacific Railroad. Although Los Angeles is approximately one hundred miles farther from the Imperial Valley than is San Diego—as the crow flies—it was much closer in transportation terms back in Coe's day. The Southern Pacific, which had quietly helped to fund Imperial Valley irrigation efforts, built a spur line to Calexico in 1903. Meanwhile the San Diego and Eastern Arizona Railroad—dubbed the "impossible railroad" because of the engineering and financial challenges it posed—was not completed until 1919.[4]

Among the homesteaders of San Diego County was the eccentric George DeClyver Curtis. Born in Providence, Rhode Island, Curtis moved west after graduating from Harvard in 1893. He worked as a rancher in Arizona during his youth and before heading to California in search of government land. Curtis claimed his homestead at the age of forty, but age would not challenge the hearty man. Settling in the foothills east of the town of Ramona, Curtis set about to prove up the land, planting fruit and nut trees and building an apiary. The work—as it was for most homesteaders—was ceaseless.

Unlike most homesteaders, however, Curtis recorded his daily routine in small journals that now fill up two boxes in the Special Collections at the Young Research Library, University of California, Los Angeles. Collectively they read as a paean to a life of disciplined toil. "Set stakes for the new trees. Radishes and lettuce begin to show," he wrote in January of 1912. "Finished digging the clearing—400 trees." "Caught a gopher. Shot away many pistol cartridges at the rascal birds. Mended clothes, cut my beard. A little spading." "I worked at a number of things—some chopping, spading and grubbing, some sewing, etc. Shot a thieving bird, and hanged him up for an example." But among all these tasks, none was more important to Curtis than what he described as "bee work."[5]

The pages of the Curtis diaries are replete with descriptions of bees, and they evidently fascinated him, as he would later write *Bees' Ways*, published by Houghton Mifflin in 1948. *Bees' Ways* "is not a useful book for commercial beekeepers," he wrote, but rather a knowledgeable and eloquent treatise on the habits of honeybees. "To reign over eighty thousand faithful and laborious subjects," he wrote of the queen bee, "and to be the mother as well as the queen of every one of them, that indeed is to be royally prolific." "A good queen bee," he marveled, "at the height of her powers, will lay over two thousand eggs in a day, and each of those eggs will in three weeks' time produce a bee." On the question of stings Curtis wrote that his "bees do not show much discrimination; they have stung visitors who were immaculately scrubbed and freshly starched as well as sweaty workmen who were on the wrong side of their Saturday night bath."[6]

East from Curtis's homestead and across the Cuyamaca Mountains was the Imperial Valley. Dewitt Coe and several hundred homesteaders who claimed land in the Imperial Valley just as the Alamo Canal came online reaped the largest rewards. For example, J. M. Cardiff, who settled in the Imperial Valley before the Alamo aqueduct was built, became wildly successful, producing and selling enough alfalfa to leave his family 320 acres and a thriving business when he died in an accident in 1907. A homesteader from Louisiana named Benjamin F. McDonald planted cotton, and by 1903 it grew marvelously, earning accolades from both the Department of Agriculture and from eastern business interests. Hernando J. Messinger came to the Imperial Valley by way of northern Arizona, where he had chiefly traded with American Indians. On leased land he augmented the irrigation system and soon prospered as a grain producer, claimed his homestead, and opened a thriving feed business in 1904. The Arakelian brothers, Armenian siblings who were already successful farmers near Fresno, expanded operations onto an Imperial Valley homestead in 1910.[7]

Yet, from the beginning, the homesteaders of the Imperial Valley chafed at their status as a remote, unaided, and yet fully taxed colony of remote San Diego. Hundreds of homesteaders had claimed land just east of San Diego in the western foothills of the Cuyamacas and in Bear Valley, today known as Pine Valley. There they had relatively easy

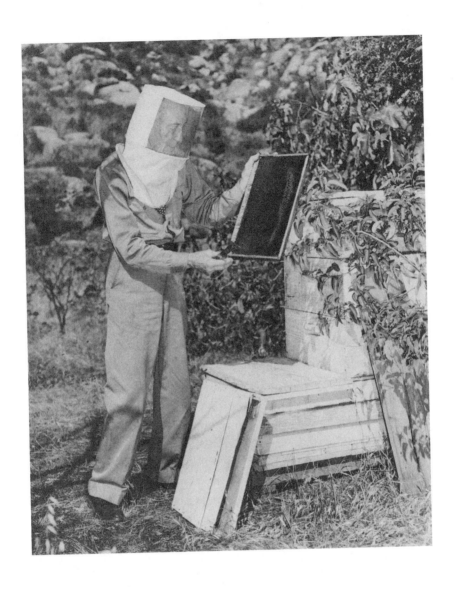

18. Homesteader George DeClyver Curtis in beekeeping attire. S.D. Journal, Photograph by Souligny, George DeClyver Curtis Papers (Collection 1247). Library Special Collections, Charles E. Young Research Library, UCLA.

access to the county services—the courts in particular—in San Diego. But in the far-flung Imperial Valley, any civil or criminal matters had to be dealt with nearly three hundred miles away. Additionally the San Diego sheriff refused to appoint a deputy in the Imperial Valley. It was up to locals to elect a constable of their own: a homesteader named Mobley "Kid" Meadows who had honed his legendary shooting skills as a sidekick to his older brother in a traveling Wild West show. "The residents of the Imperial Valley were so set away from the rest of the world, so cut off from it in every sense of the word, by desert wastes and mountain ranges, that there grew up among them a distinctive comradeship," wrote an enthusiastic chronicler in 1910. "No matter whence they came, a short residence in the Valley, in touch with its ambitions, its ideas and its enthusiasm, fused new comers with pioneers and there developed what may well be called the Imperial spirit." But it also bred in them deep resentment about their forgotten status.[8]

This resentment intensified as a group of wealthy investors from San Diego began speculating on Imperial Valley land in the later part of 1901. A small group of "heavy men," as the newspapers called them, had begun buying up land and water rights with no intention of calling Imperial home or aiding regional development. Particularly troubling to Imperial residents was the fact that outside speculators hired lawyers to try to prove that individual homestead tracts in the valley had not been sufficiently improved and therefore should be returned to the public domain. They failed in these efforts, but not before causing lots of anxiety and forcing homesteaders to defend claims with costly attorneys of their own. Soon after, a group of businessmen in San Diego went as far as to pay "dummy homesteaders" to settle on Imperial Valley land and then quietly deliver the title back to them. After a lengthy court battle, the land office in Los Angeles took the dramatic step of revoking nearly two hundred fifty "dummy" homestead claims. In very few instances were the speculators successful in their chicanery, but the persistence of their efforts—coupled with the homesteaders' long-standing grievance about their taxed isolation—convinced most of the settlers that it was high time to have their own county.[9]

But their plans were temporarily derailed by a man-made, multiyear disaster. George Chaffey had become convinced that the headgate of his irrigation project was too high, thus depriving irrigators of water. He proposed and quickly executed a bypass, one that could be closed during flooding season. But he built the "cut," as it was called, in mudflats because there was no bedrock, and this was a risky move that was then replicated at other points on the waterworks. Frederick Haynes Newell, director of the Reclamation Service, had warned of the consequences of such a practice. "If we go into this depression below sea level and interfere with natural conditions, or—as we say—'develop the country,' we are brought face to face with the great forces of the river and the uncertainty as to whether it will desire to continue in the channel in which we happen to have found it." The Colorado River did not, as it turned out, desire to continue in the channel in which it was found. Instead, on August 9, 1905, the mighty Colorado flooded the Imperial Valley.[10]

Protecting the farmlands of the Imperial Valley was the highest priority for local engineers and specialists brought in from the Southern Pacific Railroad, and after a two-year battle they succeeded in preserving most of the Imperial Valley. Calexico was saved, though the neighboring cross-border town of Mexicali was leveled, the first episode in a long string of glaring inequities between residents on each side of the United States–Mexico border. The most spectacular legacy of the disaster was the creation of the Salton Sea, California's largest lake and its first accidental resort. Half a dozen resort communities would emerge on the beaches of the Salton Sea in the 1950s and 1960s, including now-forgotten places like Salton City and Bombay Beach. But as salinity rose and fishing died off, the towns withered, and today the Salton Sea is a ghost town. Meanwhile the leadership of the Imperial Valley, satisfied that the flood crisis was behind them, finally approached the San Diego County Board of Supervisors in 1907, which was obliged to hold an election, set for August of that year. Support for county division among Imperial Valley residents was overwhelming in 1907, and Imperial County was born, the last county created in California.

But if the settlers of the Imperial Valley were protective of their own rights, they cared little about the humanity of the American Indians they found there. Though their population was in decline by the time homesteaders arrived in the Imperial Valley, about seven hundred Quechan Indians still lived in and around the Fort Yuma Indian Reservation. Their population had once approached seventeen hundred, and they enjoyed a thriving riparian culture and a fierce reputation. In 1781 they revolted against Spanish rule, killing more than one hundred colonists and a priest, and forever ending Spanish endeavors in the region. They even fought back American advances for a time, battling to maintain their historic control of the Yuma crossing of the Colorado, but they were brought under submission of the American military during the Yuma War in 1853. President Chester Arthur issued an executive order establishing a reservation for the Quechan in 1884, by which time they had been thoroughly "pacified," to use the terminology of the era.

The arrival of homesteaders at the turn of the century, and the Yuma Reclamation Project begun in 1903, spelled the last chapter for the Quechan. As efforts to reclaim the Imperial Valley expanded after the construction of the Alamo Canal, the Department of the Interior sought to acquire about sixty-five hundred acres of the original sixteen thousand acres of the reservation for American homesteaders. Likely unaware of the extent of land they were giving away in exchange for irrigation rights, the Quechans agreed to the cession in exchange for water rights and ownership of individual five-acre plots from the original reservation. Meanwhile 173 new farms of much larger acreage were thrown open for homestead entry in 1910, causing a flood of settlers. It was a terrible loss of territory for the Quechan, but one that Anglos easily dismissed. "The Yuma [Quechan] is quiet and docile now," historians Edgar F. Howe and Wilbur Jay Hall wrote in 1910, "but he does not seem to absorb American civilization rapidly, even when young, and there has been found a most discouraging tendency among the tribesmen to return to their heathenish ways when once the heavy hand of the school-mistress is removed."[11]

American Indians on the other side of the Cuyamacas in San Diego County were probably worse off than the Quechan. This was observed most acutely by Reverend Joseph H. Johnson, a Protestant Episcopal bishop of the Diocese of Southern California, who took a ten-day journey into San Diego "Indian country" in 1900 and concluded: "The wretchedness and misery of Indians on most of the reservations in Southern California that I have visited cannot be overstated. If the policy of the government is to exterminate its unfortunate wards, it has made a good start in that direction." Johnson visited ten reservations and was stunned by what he saw. Everywhere, lands were taken up—"little homesteads of the white settlers wherever there was water and good land," the rest left for the American Indian. "Before the homesteaders came and crowded the Indians back, the aborigines had cattle, wheat and other sources of food supply in abundance." To be sure, there is no known evidence that homesteaders ever expressed the slightest remorse for settling on land that had been set aside for American Indians. But as in other parts of California, the homesteaders of the San Diego mountains were really only latecomers to the long process of American Indian dispossession. Sickened or killed at the missions, American Indians in and around San Diego were then driven from their rancherias and into the hills by the hordes of white settlers that arrived after statehood. San Diegans, time and again, left American Indians to the mercy of fate.[12]

Today the Mexican character of the Imperial Valley is striking. Not only does the valley share a border with Mexico, its population is, today, more than 80 percent Latino, and Imperial County has the highest proportion of Latino residents of any of the fifty-eight California counties. This dynamic would have shocked the valley's first homesteaders, who were overwhelmingly white. Even after the irrigation era began, Mexicans only constituted about 10 percent of the population in the 1910 census. But the Mexican Revolution (1910–20) stimulated a mass exodus of Mexicans fleeing violence, poverty, and hunger. Growers and manufacturers in Southern California—and soon the rest of California—became accustomed to the seemingly tireless nature of Mexican labor. After the revolution Imperial Valley growers and their associations encouraged Mexican governors in Mexicali to send more workers, and close to thirteen thousand of them arrived in the Imperial Valley between 1921 and 1924.[13]

As the first generation of homesteaders in the Imperial Valley began to age, they increasingly turned to relatively cheap Mexican labor to perform the tasks that had once been the purview of themselves and their families, and during the 1920s many sold their farms to larger operators with bigger labor forces. Scrappy upstarts were soon replaced by massive family and corporate farms, a prelude to the Imperial Valley of today.

11

Crashing the Orange Gates

Samuel T. Miller was the truest pioneer. Born in North Carolina and raised in Arkansas, he lit out for Texas on his own at the age of seventeen in 1854, searching for work and adventure. He soon joined the legions of other young and daring men driving stagecoaches through the unsettled stretches of the West, often at considerable risk to themselves and their passengers. Having traveled through Mexico many times, Miller settled in San Luis Potosí in north-central Mexico, opened a store, and started his own stage line from Mexico to Monterey in Northern California. But misfortune followed quickly behind. Corrupt Mexican officials, seized with nationalist fervor during the Restoration of 1867, confiscated most of his property. Miller then fled to Texas, where American Indians stole his wagon and killed one of his horses. He decided, wisely, that his stage-driving days were over, and headed for the pastoral life in California in 1873. In the far southern edge of Los Angeles—which would become Orange County in 1889—Miller became an apiarist, got married, and settled on a homestead. In his peak year he produced more than forty tons of honey from 275 stands of bees. After the turmoil of his youth, Miller had found comfort and genuine success in the foothills of the Santa Ana Mountains. "One of the results of these later years of hard, successful work," local historian Samuel Armor wrote in 1921, "is Mr. Miller's ownership today of considerable choice residence property in Santa Ana."[1]

Miller's success was certainly the product of his own acumen, determination, and luck, but it also came from a well-honed instinct for avoiding a fight. He understood that you survived robberies on the Texas range and in the Mexican desert by acquiescing when you were outnumbered; there was no valor in a senseless death. And Miller's decision to claim a homestead in the foothills, rather than in the fertile valley below, was a function of just that kind of calculation. Because in no other region of California were there so few homesteaders, was there so little land to choose from, and were there more egregious schemes designed to defraud aspiring homesteaders, than in Orange County. Miller was exceptional because he quietly accepted what many other homesteaders would not: this was the land of James Irvine.

Irvine's was a quintessential rags-to-riches story, the kind Americans love the most. Born into rural poverty in Belfast in 1827, he fled to the United States during the potato famine of 1845. Though he mined during the gold rush, he found faster success as a merchant selling produce, and he invested those profits into San Francisco real estate. He would be eulogized as the "produce millionaire," but his fortune came decidedly from dealing in land, and his timing was impeccable. During the horrible drought of 1864 he eyed the vast Mexican landholdings in southern Los Angeles. Irvine—in a partnership with the prosperous sheep men Llewellyn Bixby and Benjamin and Thomas Flint—struck one of the best deals in nineteenth-century California when he and his partners bought more than 110,000 acres of former ranchos, including the 47,000-acre Rancho Lomas de Santiago, 13,000 acres of the former Rancho Santiago de Santa Ana, and finally the 50,000-acre Rancho San Joaquin. The total acreage of his holdings amounted to approximately one-third of the entire county. An absentee landowner who lived in San Francisco, Irvine had wheat and barley planted on portions of the ranch and grazed sheep until his death in 1886.

As California's population grew during the 1870s, so did challenges to both the integrity and title of the vast property. First, there was the menace of squatters. "In those days," Irvine Ranch historian Robert Glass Cleland wrote, "hobos, itinerant workers, and 'bindle stiffs,' all called by the generic name of tramps, roamed the southern California countryside in great numbers, especially in winter, and often made themselves a pest to large and small ranchers alike. According to Irvine, the Rancho San Joaquin supported never less than five of these gentry." Irvine and his associates—whom he bought out in 1876—were successful in ejecting squatters through the courts when the ranch managers could not do so with gentle force. Irvine also fought off a challenge by the Southern Pacific Railroad in the 1870s to establish a right-of-way through the property, arguing that there had been a flaw in the original land grant that gave Irvine more than he was supposed to have. He also weathered criticism of his underdevelopment of the land, much of which had been denuded of its fauna in the drought of 1876–77. "This immense estate," the *Santa Ana Herald* chided in 1881, "so dreary and desolate, presents a vivid contrast to the adjoining rancho, which has been made to blossom like a rose in its beauty and luxuriance. The Santa Ana rancho . . . has been cut up and sold out into tracts upon which thousands of happy homes may now be found."[2]

When Irvine died, he left the management of the estate in the hands of trustees until his only son, James Irvine Jr.—eighteen at the time—reached the age of twenty-five. The trustees' decision to sell off portions of the ranch, along with James Jr.'s generous donation of acreage to the public development of Orange County, stimulated wild rumors that much of the land would eventually be thrown into the public domain. One of the first men to believe those rumors, and to believe them most ardently, was a German immigrant and pumpkin farmer named William Schutte. In 1897 Schutte began squatting a one-hundred-acre parcel of land adjacent to Laguna Beach. Ranch managers had tried in vain to eject Schutte, but he resisted, aggressively, and they finally secured a court order for his ejectment. But when the sheriff's deputies delivered him the eviction notice, they "came near being perforated with bullets," according to the *Los Angeles Times*. Schutte listened complacently, and then he "affirmed that the first person who laid hand upon his property would run up against his big Winchester and would be made a target of." They persisted, and he headed for the house to get his gun but was restrained and arrested. In court the next day, he claimed that "a certain wine dealer" had visited on that day "for the sole purpose of making Schutte drunk and unruly" and that he gave him a very liberal supply of "bad wine and thus induced in him a frame of mind that was hostile to the keeping of peace and order." A jury was deadlocked on charges of resisting arrest, but he was eventually ejected from the property.[3]

In Schutte's wine-soaked and "unruly" mind, he was being victimized by Irvine, but in reality he was being victimized by a collective of con men operating under the auspices, alternately, of the Land Settlers' League and the California, Arizona, and New Mexico Settlers' League. Although Irvine's title to the land had been verified by the Land Commission and even confirmed by the United States Supreme Court, this did not stop con men from asserting that the title, which they claimed was flawed and granted more land to Irvine than was originally intended, was under legal review. These swindlers would then solicit aspiring landholders—James Irvine Jr. referred to them sympathetically as "ignorant squatters"—to contribute $50 each toward the retainer of a lawyer, 50 cents a month for the retainer, and another $1.25 per acre once the land was opened. Then the lawyers would collect the fees and go through the motions of challenging the Irvine title, knowing full well that they could not possibly win. The Settlers' League claimed more than thirty-five hundred members, a testament to the desperation of poor Californians to acquire land. Described by the *Los Angeles Times* as "a gigantic fight for 30,000 acres of as fair land as the sun shines on in Southern California, forty-eight square miles of Orange county's wheat and bean land," the scheme ended when the case was dismissed.[4]

A more serious and enduring attempt to break up the Irvine Ranch came again in the 1920s when a federal commission estimated that about eight hundred prospective homesteaders in Orange County spent about $300,000 in a scheme promoted by an itinerant grifter named Dr. William Rosecrans Price. Even by the standards of the twenties, a decade during which the United States witnessed some of its most outlandish frauds and schemes, Price was an exceptional scoundrel. A Tennessean by birth, Price roamed the South in the late nineteenth century, delivering lectures on the "grandest science the world has ever known"—hypnotism. He widely advertised his magazine, *Price's Magazine of Psychology*, and evidently found enough subscribers to pay rent on a building in Atlanta that, he claimed, housed Price's Sanatorium and School of Psychology. He claimed that his brand of hypnotism not only helped patients live longer but also—ironically—helped them "expose fraud."[5]

Price drifted into California shortly after the turn of the century and settled in Long Beach, where he became the pastor of a "psychological temple" called the People's Church. Price's stint as a pastor was likely his most pleasurable, as it involved giving female parishioners what he called a "holy kiss" and then personally bathing them. His wife was displeased by the arrangement and divorced him in 1923, just as Long Beach police began investigating him for embezzling church money. Specifically, Price collected almost one hundred thousand dollars from more than two hundred parishioners to buy a piece of the Irvine Ranch—which, of course, was never for sale—as the site for a religious colony where members might "practice its rites without interruption." As with previous schemes, including soliciting funds for a gold-dredging company, Price remarkably escaped conviction. But the Irvine Ranch scheme evidently whetted his appetite for that particular property because he formulated a new scheme that would be his biggest and his last. This time his prey was the mass of poor men who wanted to homestead on the Irvine Ranch.[6]

In this instance Price cribbed directly from the Schutte incident more than twenty years earlier. Spreading the word among a new and unsuspecting group of aspiring homesteaders who were otherwise unable to claim land in Orange County, Price claimed—as Schutte's promoters had—that the original Mexican grant had been improperly surveyed and therefore the title was in question. For a fee that ranged from $400 to $1500, Price would share "confidential information" about existing homestead plots on the Irvine Ranch and would assist in the preparation of the application. Under the law, the Los Angeles Land Office had to accept the applications before sending them to Washington for approval. This provided enough time to raise the hopes of homesteaders and for them to furnish Price with additional funds to retain Price's attorney,

Ben McClendon. The scheme lasted six months and wrangled more than two hundred aspiring homesteaders in Orange County until the secretary of the interior, Hubert Work, declared all applications null and void. Shamelessly McClendon filed suit against Work, prompting the Senate to order an expensive Committee on Public Lands investigation into the entire affair. The committee, meeting in Los Angeles in 1929, arrived at the same conclusion that the courts had, many times. The title was binding, with no evidence of fraud, and the attacks on the titles were "made by persons seeking to profit financially at the expense of well-intentioned but grossly misled applicants for homestead entry."[7]

But elsewhere in Orange County, the small number of homesteaders—seventy in all—fulfilled both the spirit and the letter of the Homestead Act. It is likely that the small number of homesteaders farming the area gave them each a better opportunity to succeed at the produce markets in the new towns of Tustin, Orange, and Santa Ana. But like Samuel T. Miller, many were just hard pioneers. One of these was Tilford D. Cheney, whose parents traveled with him by mule team to California in 1856, but not before lightning struck him in the Black Hills and knocked him unconscious for three days. His mother miraculously nursed him back to health and he was no worse for the wear. When he later settled as an independent farmer in Tustin, he bought forty acres on loan, raised cattle in the 1870s, and sold the land for $42,000. "In other words," the *Los Angeles Times* moralized, "Mr. Cheney in 11 years made 45,000. He commenced without money and in debt, and accomplished this by work, not speculation. His money was made from alfalfa and stock." He later claimed a homestead ranch in Hidden Hills, Los Angeles, where he retired.[8]

The relative success of Orange County's homesteaders—men like Cheney and a handful of others—who all lived south of the Santa Ana River, depended a great deal on the early efforts of the Santa Ana Valley Irrigation Company. In 1870—long before the Wright Act made every man a potential irrigation district financier—it took men of sufficient capital to support even crude irrigation. In Orange County that man was Alfred Beck Chapman. A Los Angeles city attorney and later district attorney, Chapman began a lucrative real estate law firm with his childhood friend Andrew Glassell in 1866. They acquired significant portions of the former Rancho Santiago de Santa Ana, north of what would become Irvine's holdings. Unlike Irvine, however, Chapman insisted that the land be cultivated, and he had ditches—the biggest known as Chapman Ditch—dug in order to irrigate with water from the Santa Ana River. Chapman and Glassell incorporated the Semi-Tropic Water Company, which was eventually superseded by the Santa Ana Valley Irrigation Company. By charging reasonable rates to surrounding homesteaders for water rights, Chapman and Glassell did well by doing good. Soon the company developed a reputation for efficiency and fair pricing that became the model of civil engineering and infrastructure and regional development. The Chapman Ditch was later remembered as "well watered, sheltered, and above the influence of frosts."[9]

There are no easy lessons to be gleaned from the homesteaders of Orange County, but one of them is surely this: in the late nineteenth century the concentration of capital in the hands of well-heeled whites could work not only against but sometimes for the interests of homesteaders. On one hand, James Irvine's dominance on the landscape severely limited homestead opportunity in the region, and men of low character—like Dr. William Rosecrans Price—easily exploited homesteaders' aspirations. But on the other hand, men like Alfred Beck Chapman brought capital to bear on a dour—and dry—circumstance, to the great benefit of those homesteaders living near the Santa Ana River.

12

Exacting Lives in the Breadbasket

It was often a winding path that brought folks to a California homestead. "The people who have come to the San Joaquin Valley in search of homes," an 1885 promotional pamphlet from the Immigration Association of California explained, "represent every profession, trade and calling, and the causes inducing them to settle here have been as varied." This was true for Samuel D. Hopper, as it was for so many others. Born of Irish stock in Monroe County, Ohio, in 1838, Hopper excelled in school, receiving his teaching certificate at the early age of nineteen. He taught in Ohio for several years until the outbreak of the Civil War, when he enlisted in the Sixty-second Ohio Volunteer Infantry. Fighting in the battles of Fort Wagner and Deep Run—he was shot in the foot at the former conflict—Hopper not only survived but rose quickly to the rank of captain. Captain. It was the title he would insist upon long after the war had ended.[1]

Captain Hopper returned to teaching in Ohio but soon left for Nebraska, met his wife, and started a family there. He continued to teach, supplementing his income by raising cattle. He eventually sold off his stock at a small profit. He had come up, some. But the lure of California burned in him, probably stoked by promotional pamphlets published by the Southern Pacific Railroad in the early 1880s to promote settlement—and passenger travel—to Fresno, the "geographical hub of California." One pamphlet in later years described Fresno as "the paradise of the industrious man of small means." Captain Hopper soon packed up his family and headed to Fresno County, settling on a homestead near the town of Del Rey in 1882.[2]

As was the case in the Kern portion of the San Joaquin Valley, land barons had picked over much of the best land in Fresno. Miller & Lux alone owned close to 700,000 acres there. But for reasons known only to Hopper, he was not discouraged. Instead the captain bought vine cuttings of Muscat and Thompson grapes and planted them in neat rows in order to produce raisins. He joined what was then just a handful of growers in the nascent industry that found Fresno's conditions superb for raisin cultivation. For raisins, Fresno was blessed by nature: grapes thrived in its sandy loam, hot climate, and in the absence of summer rains and cold winter fogs. But it was transformed by irrigation, chiefly through the ditches and canals of the Fresno Canal and Irrigation Company—incorporated in 1871 by land developers William Chapman and Moses J. Church—drawing water from the Kings River. The biggest ditch owned by the company was one hundred feet wide and thirty-five miles long, a massive operation. "In no portion of the raisin-producing portion of the valley," scientist and grape expert Gustav Eisen wrote of the San Joaquin Valley in 1890, "can raisin grapes be grown without irrigation, the natural rainfall being entirely insufficient."[3]

Today about three thousand growers produce 100 percent of American raisins within a sixty-mile radius of Fresno in the San Joaquin Valley. Raisins from Fresno account for about $335 million in California exports (though that pales in comparison to the county's more recent "king" crop, almonds, which account for more than $5 billion in annual exports). Fresno is the undisputed raisin capital of the world, but in the early 1880s, when Captain Hopper arrived, cultivating raisins was still a gamble. Until the late 1870s the raisin was still a Spanish specialty crop—grown chiefly outside of Málaga—sold exclusively to specialty markets in San Francisco. Nonetheless, vine cuttings began making their way to Fresno, and it was in the hot year of 1877 that a farmer named Francis T. Eisen (Gustav's brother) saved his dried-out Muscat grape crop by stemming them, further drying them, and then selling them in San Francisco as raisins, though they marketed them falsely as "Peruvian

Importations." The Fresno raisins were an instant success, and other growers began to experiment with the fruit. Introduced to Fresno in 1878, Thompson grapes—which were plump and had the advantage of being seedless—soon became the industry standard.[4]

As fertile as irrigated Fresno soil was, grape cultivation was still an exacting, often tedious, process, and crop ruination was not uncommon, particularly in the early years of cultivation. Raisin culture "is eminently made up of details," one prominent grower wrote. "None can be carelessly performed or overlooked." First, because hot winds from the northwest could sunscald the grapes, potentially ruining the entire crop, windbreaks had to be planted or built on the northern edge of the field. Then in spring, grape growers needed to cross-plow, level, and weed the land with the goal of planting in June. Furrows had to be plowed and thoroughly irrigated. The cuttings needed to be planted in rows of about eight vines for every ten feet. Though of excellent quality, the soils on Fresno's plains were not seepage soils, meaning they did not retain water on all sides but instead allowed water to sink vertically into the ground, thus requiring careful irrigation.[5]

For Gustav Eisen the importance of neatness in the layout of the vineyard could not be overstated. Sloppy planting would come back to haunt growers when they eventually tried to sell their lands. "In after years, when the proprietor's taste and experience has improved," Eisen wrote, "he finds that his reputation as a careless or ignorant grower cannot be changed; for the vineyard is there to last, and to tell the tale of early ignorance and neglect." Pruning, which was done between December and February, was required to ensure sunlight saturation, but not too much pruning, which would leave the grapes susceptible to burning, and sulphuring the crop several times a season was essential to avoid mildew. Finally, between August and early September, grapes were harvested, stemmed, and placed in "sweatboxes" to dry out. If all went as planned, according to Eisen, growers could expect one hundred to two hundred boxes per acre. And even though the vines would bear fruit in the second and third years, growers could not expect to make a profit until the fifth year.[6]

Even with this laboriousness, "vineyard mania" would soon overtake Fresno. Hopper anticipated it by a few years. In 1882, the year that Hopper started, Fresno only produced about 80,000 pounds of raisins. By 1885 the county produced two million pounds, and by 1889, 9.5 million, with 30,000 acres planted in raisin grapes. But even the spectacular increase masked the challenge of pricing for the grower. In 1891 and 1892, for example, packers and their brokers undercut the prices to growers, and at the end of 1892 the *San Francisco Call* confidently declared that the raisin market was in "bad shape" and "demoralized." Part of the problem was oversupply, though the growers generally rejected that explanation (one did confess that he had so many extra raisins that he used them as horse feed to nurse a tired nag back to robust health). But the bigger problem was that the packers, after collecting commissions, sold the raisins in eastern markets at whatever price they saw fit. In a frenzied competition with other packers, the packers' brokers cut prices to stores, naturally to the detriment of the grower.[7]

Captain Hopper and other raisin growers—homesteaders and not— soon sought a solution to the problem: collective action. Hopper was instrumental in organizing the Raisin Growers Association in the summer of 1892. Under the leadership of Martin Theodore Kearney—known as "The Raisin King" for his 6,720-acre raisin farm, Fruit Vale Estate— the Raisin Growers Association challenged the prevailing system by stabilizing raisin prices, collectively challenging the disproportionate negotiating power of the local packinghouses. "This competition among yourselves in the eastern market at the expense of the grower must now and forever cease," the association declared. "We are strong enough as an association to stop you slaughtering prices. And to those who refuse to come into the association, we are able to render you powerless for evil by refusing to give you any raisins to handle." Soon eighteen of the twenty-two main packers agreed not to cut prices in the "insane and jealous competition among themselves."[8]

No sooner had the growers gained a measure of power than they were hit by the Panic of 1893. Triggered by the overexpansion of industry during the late 1880s and early 1890s, an agricultural depression in the

Midwest, and declining investment in the railroads, the panic lasted well into 1897. Raisin prices tumbled from 5 cents per pound to ¾ cents per pound, leading some frightened and hasty Fresno farmers to pull nearly 20,000 acres of vines in 1894 and 1895. Once they pulled up roots there was "widespread ruin to raisin growers," according to the *Pacific Rural Press*, "and hundreds of mortgages were foreclosed and the farmer and his family turned adrift to compete in an already overcrowded labor market tramping about the State in search of a day's work."[9]

But Captain Hopper was not among those "tramping" through the state. Without a mortgage to pay, the homesteader weathered the storm and joined the returning prosperity in the raisin market in 1889. He and his wife, Rachel, raised their four children on the homestead, and then he raised another child with his second wife after Rachel died. "He never missed a day's work," according to Paul E. Vandor's *History of Fresno County* (1919), "and in this hard work, he may truly claim to have borne the heat and burden of the day." One of his children attended Stanford, another the University of Southern California, and several bought ranches near Fresno. When he entered his eighties, Hopper finally sold off the northern half of his homestead, fetching a tidy profit. By almost any measure, the captain had succeeded.[10]

South of Fresno in Tulare County, homesteaders and other farmers would ultimately propel the county into a leading position in the national cattle, orange, and table grape markets. But in the 1870s many aspiring homesteaders were discouraged when they studied the map of government lands in the land office in Visalia. Much of the valuable farming land in the San Joaquin Valley—with the loamiest soils and the easiest access to irrigation sources—was absorbed in very large land grants to the Southern Pacific Railroad. Standing there in overalls, they strained their eyes to find any open quarter sections and they surely wagged their heads: there were a few quarter sections still left in the San Joaquin Valley, but most were in the Sierra Nevada foothills in the eastern portion of the county. They tapped at the map. That's where they'd go.

But not John J. Doyle. Doyle had a black shock of hair cresting his head, piercing light eyes, and a natural scowl under his pointed beard.

Perhaps he had seen too much to take the long, slow route of a foothill homesteader. Doyle was one of sixteen children raised on an Indiana farm and he moved fast, abandoning Indiana for Ohio at the age of nineteen, and then for California in 1867. He mined and farmed his way through the state, briefly securing a teaching job in Sonoma County, and ultimately buying his own small farm in Tulare by the age of twenty-one. And then in 1870 he read an article in the *Rural Press* by a "lawyer" asserting that because the Southern Pacific Railroad had changed its route between San Jose and Southern California—the original route was coastal—the railroad land grants in Tulare were invalid. The lawyer was wrong. Nonetheless Doyle immediately sold his distant farm and headed to the Mussel Slough area to squat on railroad land in the hopes that it would someday become valuable.[11]

At that time the Mussel Slough area—a branch of the Kings River leading to the now nonexistent Tulare Lake—was largely unsettled frontier. But Doyle changed all that with his settlement, and his pitch. He spread the word that—per his reading of the *Rural Press* article—the odd-numbered railroad quarter sections in the Mussel Slough area were open to settlement, and he sparked a land rush of hundreds of settlers to the region. Meanwhile the young Doyle proved to be an immediate and assertive land speculator: he filed hundreds of homestead, preemption, and cash-purchase claims with the Visalia Land Office. The land office rejected all of them, as did the Department of the Interior, based on the fact that the legality of the railroad's route and land grants had already been clearly established. Doyle continued squatting, nonetheless, encouraging others to join him.[12]

Soon Doyle's followers in the Mussel Slough area built an irrigation works of some significance and began farming. Doyle and other squatters waited for the Southern Pacific Railroad to sell its lands, and in 1878—two years after the completion of the route to Los Angeles—their patience paid off: the company offered them first rights to buy the properties. But the rates—which they expected to be about $2.50 per acre—were, in fact, between $8 to $20 per acre; furthermore they would get no compensation for their improvements to the land, including the waterworks. The Southern Pacific sent several batches of letters to Doyle and the others, repeating the offer to sell the land to them, but the vast majority balked at the cost. Instead, under the leadership of Civil War Confederate major Thomas Jefferson McQuiddy, six hundred settlers organized under the banner of the Settlers Grand League and paraded through Mussel Slough towns with rifles as an active militia.[13]

While most squatters categorically refused to pay the railroad, two settlers—Walter J. Crow and Mills D. Hartt—agreed to the terms of the railroad and bought several quarter sections currently being occupied by squatters, for $25 per acre. Accused by the League of being dummy purchasers for the railroad, Crow and Hartt nonetheless asserted their right to the purchased parcels and called upon law enforcement to eject the settlers from their newly acquired land. Under orders from a federal court in San Francisco, which had upheld the right of the railroad to sell the land at any price the market would bear, United States marshal Alonzo W. Poole and a land appraiser escorted Crow and Hartt to their land on May 11, 1880. They evicted a settler named W. B. Braden, and threw all his furniture out into the road. When news of Braden's fate reached a nearby rally of the Settlers Grand League, a group lit out across the county to defend the next in line, a settler named Henry Brewer, and they waited for Poole, guns ready. When Poole approached, Brewer's would-be defenders started firing, and a shootout ensued. Both Crow and Hartt were killed, though not before Crow—an expert marksman—shot five from the settlers' group. They all died. Poole survived and never even fired his gun.

Public opinion was so lopsided in favor of the squatters that they became instant martyrs; this, despite the fact that they settled on the Southern Pacific's land, refused to buy it, and advocated violent "resistance." But sentiment against the railroad ran so high in the San Joaquin Valley that it blinded people to the untenability of the squatters' grievances. Later Doyle disingenuously claimed that "this trouble was simply a legal fight on our part for our homes," and his obituary perpetuated that myth by declaring him one of the last remaining "survivors of the Mussel Slough tragedy in the fight of the homesteaders to retain their land," despite the fact that it was not "their" land, nor were any of the principal participants homesteaders at the time of the incident. More egregiously the so-called Mussel Slough Five—John J. Doyle, John D. Pursell, James N. Patterson, Wayman L. Pryor, and William Braden— convicted of resisting a federal officer, only served eight-month sentences in San Jose. It was, in historian Richard J. Orsi's words, a "bizarre" eight months, with the Five "coming and going as they pleased from their unlocked cells." One of them even courted the jailer's daughter while imprisoned, eventually marrying her. Today a morally ambiguous California Historical Landmark sits at the spot of the shooting, acknowledging only that it is the site of "a dispute over land titles."[14]

Nor did the Mussel Slough Five suffer long for their transgressions. Instead three of them—Doyle, Pursell, and Braden—became Tulare homesteaders. Pursell claimed a homestead in the southern Sierra Nevada foothills east of Delano in 1890; Braden gave up the valley and moved to homestead in the foothills above Lindsay in 1893. Doyle, the instigator of the entire affair, had come up the most. He eventually agreed to the Southern Pacific's terms, buying the land for $30 per acre, not a bad deal considering that he occupied it for nine years. He sold it for a handsome profit shortly thereafter and bought a parcel of government land east of Springville in 1887 and then homesteaded an adjacent quarter section in 1892. He later divided his holdings into twenty-acre farms, all of which he sold. In Doyle's defense, he also donated one tract for the construction of a schoolhouse.

Meanwhile, about a hundred miles northeast in Madera County (formed from a portion of Fresno County in 1893), poor men worked for the mining companies still blasting into the hard rock of the Sierra Nevada in pursuit of the magic metal a good fifty years after the gold rush. At the turn of the century there was still a rich vein that stretched about twenty miles through Madera. To be sure, the "cleanups" in the southern Sierra Nevada rarely matched those of the gold rush days in the north, when miners brought in more than $2 billion, in 1849 dollars. By contrast, and even after fifty years of inflation, the many mines of Madera County pulled in only about $2.7 million. But there was no going back to 1849. And what the turn-of-the-century Madera region lacked in volume it made up for in access: despite the prevalence of mechanized lode mining in the region, much of the gold lay in placers, deposits of loose gravel in the San Joaquin and Fresno Rivers, accessible by individuals with patience and the right tools. John C. Shay had both.[15]

Shay was the son of Irish immigrants to the gold rush, and the gold bug was in his blood, evidently. He was too prudent to succumb to its influence until middle age, instead building up a thriving blacksmithery in Los Angeles. But then suddenly, at the age of thirty-eight—and presumably in consultation with his wife, Helen—Shay decided to give up the city for the placers of Madera, near a town called Grub Gulch, allegedly because anyone who panned for gold there was guaranteed at least a grubstake. "Like thousands of others," Shay later wrote in his backcountry memoir, "I found myself burning up with the fever for hunting gold." Willing to abandon the urban life with all its comforts, Shay decided to "go out into the mountains and rub up against the rough side of all things" and arrived in the foothills around 1900.[16]

Shay arrived on the downslope of gold mining in Madera. Between the lode and placer mining, the entire cleanup of 1900 only amounted to $104,399. But Shay was able to make a go of it, up to his knees in the riffle, and it brought him great fulfillment. "To have the real legal tender in your hand each night after your day's work," he wrote, "and the comforting thought that you have taken it from old Mother Earth by your very honest labor, brings a satisfaction I have never found in any other line." It also brought him enough money to buy livestock and additional tools and to begin homesteading, and he easily found a site. His property lay adjacent to the main road from the valley to the mines and to Yosemite, and he shrewdly started a roadside blacksmith operation to repair wagons. Between his business, his small orchards, and the increase in his livestock, Shay and his wife soon had plenty. "We had abundance," he later wrote proudly, "at all times."[17]

But if Shay found abundance in mining country, he also observed the perpetual specter of violence. Homesteaders everywhere experienced isolation, and particularly physical distance from formal law enforcement, but in mining country the risk of that isolation was greater because of the proximity of mining camps. There were at least a dozen camps around Grub Gulch, a town with a post office, a hotel, two grocery stores, and five saloons: "These saloons did thriving business; men were coming and going in and out of town daily. One month's work and a good drunk seemed to be all that many of them cared for. Although there were a number of sober, industrious men employed who were settled with their families, the other drifting class was always noticeable."[18]

In addition to the "drifting class" there was also a smattering of Yokut people around Grub Gulch. Their numbers at that time were in steep decline—the 1910 census counted only six hundred in the entire San Joaquin Valley, down from an estimated 18,000 when the Spanish arrived—but they were there. In a tragic story that played out throughout California and much of the Southwest, the Yokuts scraped by on the margins of society, often resented their subordinate status, and were inevitably drawn into conflicts with whites and often among themselves. And though California law forbade the sale of alcohol to American Indians, many nonetheless acquired it, often with baleful results.[19]

In one horrific incident of violence, a Yokut Indian named John Lawrence nearly lost his head. Lawrence enjoyed a positive reputation among both American Indians and whites as generally sober and hardworking and was thus prey for criminals who might relieve him of his hard-earned money. This time it was his American Indian friends who attacked him when he failed to give them money to buy whiskey. As two men held him in a chair, another drew a dull butcher knife and, according to Shay's account, "cut through the flesh to the bone, and severed some of the cords, but fortunately did not sever the jugular vein." Somehow surviving, Lawrence made a harrowing escape: "John in this condition managed to escape from his assailants; but, when he tried to travel through the deep snow, his head would not stay any one place, but kept bobbing around. He found, however, that by holding it in place with his hands, he was able to move along at a fair gait."[20]

In another incident a burly white man who nursed a grudge against a mine foreman "drank heavily all day." "With every round of drinks,"

Shay recorded, "he boasted of how he was going to wipe the road up with the foreman that evening, when the foreman would return from work." When he met the foreman in the road later that evening, the man knocked him to the ground. The foreman tried to stand and the man knocked him down again. Rather than try to stand again, the foreman reached into his pocket, pulled out a pistol, and shot the man through his heart, killing him instantly. In a pithy summary of frontier justice, Shay wrote: "This big bully had consumed lots of booze, and had things his own way for a long time; but that lead pill was too much for him, his career ended here."[21]

The frequency and severity of violence on the mining frontier began to wear on the Shays. John and Helen proved up his claim in 1907, and then they stayed on for the better part of a decade, but the spirit of neighborliness that he had first found in Madera began to erode. "For many years the settlers here seemed to me like one family. There was a real democracy among all. Our sorrows and joys were shared alike by all, but in the last few years evolution has done its work. Personalities have crept in, and men who were seemingly the best of friends are now enemies to each other." It is not clear what precipitated this "evolution," though it is a good bet that the steady decline of gold in the placers made men ornerier and more desperate. But there was also, Shay reported, a greater supply of guns. Settlers had always carried guns, "but in the last few years more attention seems to be given to his habit than at any previous time. Nearly every settler seems to expect to have to use his gun at any time. This spirit," Shay concluded, "is depressing."[22]

13

The Rarified Bay Area

Henry George arrived in San Francisco in 1858, young and penniless. A printer by trade and a Philadelphian by birth, George had left the East in search of employment during the Panic of 1857. He took his chances on the high seas as a merchant seaman and later as a failed miner on British Columbia's Frazer River; now he would try his luck in the most famous city in the West. San Francisco was in an absolute frenzy of growth when George arrived. Between 1849 and 1859 the population grew from under one thousand to more than fifty thousand. Most of them lived in tents or clumsily built wooden houses, while an elite few lived in the substantial brick houses recently dotting the verdant hillsides.

"I have already seen a good deal of the city," George wrote in a letter shortly after his arrival, "and agree 'it is a dashing place,' rather faster than Philadelphia." Indeed the pioneer-era infrastructure could distract a lesser observer from the reality that "dashing" San Francisco was a Gilded Age machine, the churning center of finance in the American West. He already knew that the machine generated inequalities: George could see that just by looking up from the huddled, muddy streets to those brick houses on the hills.[1]

In fact, land speculators had purchased most of the available lots in San Francisco even before the gold rush, as early as 1846, more than a decade before George's arrival. Even after the gold era, land continued to hold its own: "The richest men in San Francisco," an observer wrote in 1854, "have made the best portion of their wealth by possession of real estate." Now, by 1858, land-seekers had pushed well beyond the city limits and into the arable lands of the valleys and plains, the greater region soon known as the Bay Area, and today a nine-county region comprised of Alameda, Contra Costa, Marin, Napa, San Francisco, San Mateo, Santa Clara, Solano, and Sonoma Counties. Because of this early development—relative to Southern California—most of the best land in the Bay Area had been purchased before the Homestead Act was even passed. Indeed if the challenge to homesteading in Southern California was generally water, the challenge to homesteading in Northern California was generally the availability of good farmland. In San Francisco the problem was most acute: there were no parcels of federal land open for homesteading left in the city by the time of the Homestead Act. Ultimately in the entire Bay Area there were only about twenty-six hundred homesteads, most of which were in Sonoma, Santa Clara, and Napa.[2]

Henry George would spend another twenty years in San Francisco, and his observations on land, wealth, and poverty in the region would inform his writings, and particularly his best-selling 1879 book, *Progress and Poverty: An Inquiry into the Cause of Industrial Depressions and the Increase of Want with the Increase of Wealth. The Remedy.* Advocating, among other things, a single tax on land values to prevent speculation and poverty, George was also a fan of the Homestead Act and thought it represented the best use of public lands. But it was being undermined, he consistently argued, by the practice of speculation and preemptory sale. The "growing liberality to the settler," he wrote in 1871, "has been accompanied by a still more rapidly growing liberality to the speculators and corporations, and since the preemption and homestead laws were passed, land monopolization has gone on at a faster rate than ever. . . . Public sales, as a general thing, have been ordered before the line of settlement had fairly reached the land, and thus the speculator has been able to keep in advance, picking out the choice lands in quantities to retail at largely advanced price to hold back from improvements for years."

At that rate, he predicted, by 1890 nobody could possibly "get himself a homestead out of Uncle Sam's Farm, unless he is willing to take a mountain-top or alkali patch, or to emigrate to Alaska."[3]

George's predictions were not quite right, as homesteading in Southern California—most of which occurred well after 1890—proved, but his analysis of the problem was spot on. Sonoma County was a good example of his prediction: even before the passage of the Homestead Act, the county was dominated by an agricultural elite of wine-grape growers, cattlemen, and poultry men who had the best arable and pasture land in the county. By the mid-1850s that elite had consumed an enormous amount of acreage. "A tidal-wave of immigration seemed to sweep over Sonoma County," a historian wrote of the decade, "and it was really a marvel how soon every nook and corner of the county available for farming or grazing was ferreted out and occupied."[4]

As was the case elsewhere, Sonoma's rise as a cornucopia was predicated on the gradual decline of the Californios, in this case the most prominent of whom was General Mariano Vallejo. As the director of Mexican colonization, as well as commandant general of Mexico's northern frontier, Vallejo had enriched himself and his peers mightily during the 1830s and early 1840s. He eventually acquired more than half a dozen ranchos, including the valuable Rancho Petaluma, adjacent to the Petaluma River, which empties into the San Pablo Bay. But the Mexican-American War and the subsequent flood of Yankees ruined him. In 1846, in what became known as the Bear Flag Revolt, American frontiersmen seized him in his home, imprisoned him for two months, and plundered his property. He never recovered from the financial losses and was further beset by adverse legal decisions, in which he lost at least half his landholdings. Perpetually chipping away at remaining holdings were the incursions of Settlers' Leagues, glorified organizations for squatters. He lost the rest when his son-in-law mismanaged his funds, and when Vallejo died in 1890 he owned only the home in which he resided.

As Vallejo lost giant tracts of land after 1846, settlers moved in and generally found the land willing and the climate salubrious to farming. Most significant were the existing vineyards, some of which had been planted by the padres around the mission, but also some by the plantings of an erstwhile Hungarian noble, Colonel Agoston Haraszthy, who imported vines from abroad in the mid-1850s. More significant than his vines was his zealotry: in 1858 he wrote a book about wine production, which the state government of California distributed widely, and for free. Haraszthy's promotions inspired countless genuine farmers, and quite a few speculators, further driving up the price of Sonoma land. By the mid-1870s, the county's wine industry was booming, producing more than 2.5 million gallons of wine annually, just over half of all wine produced in the state.[5]

As George had predicted in his 1871 article "Our Land and Land Policy," there was very little arable land left for homesteaders by the time they came to settle in Sonoma. Those who first did found surveyed home sites east of Glen Ellen and just west of the Napa County line in the heavily wooded canyon surrounding Calabazas Creek, once part of the Vallejo estate. According to historian Arthur Dawson, the first General Land Office survey described the landscape as "very broken" with "but a few places susceptible of settlement or cultivation, the most of it precipitous Chamizo Mountains."[6]

Hugh Nunn was one of the first homesteaders in this "very broken" landscape. Born in Scotland, Nunn immigrated to Texas in the 1830s before joining the rush to California for gold. Working as a merchant rather than a miner, Nunn eventually made enough money to buy a small parcel of land in Sonoma at Calabazas Creek. He claimed a homestead in 1867 and proved it up successfully, receiving his patent in 1872. What Nunn accomplished on his homestead, with the assistance of his wife, children, and brother, was a testament to his sheer force of will. The ranch included a well-built stone house, several other structures, and plantings of eucalyptus to shade the house from the afternoon sun. The Nunns' forty-tree orchard featured apples, pears, peaches, and figs. He also raised and sold livestock in neighboring Glen Ellen, or more distant Petaluma. But after Nunn died in 1875, homesteading in that area died with it: few folks, it seemed, had the grit and temerity to transform the rough landscape into a homestead. Later Nunns' Canyon would become part of the Calabazas Creek Preserve, a state-protected Open Space Preserve.[7]

If homesteading ended at Calabazas Creek, it was about to boom outside of Petaluma. That had everything to do with the arrival of a brilliant young, but ailing, medical student from Canada, Lyman Byce. Byce arrived in Petaluma in 1878 to convalesce in the salty breezes of San Pablo Bay. The son of a chicken farmer, he recognized the potential value of a full-scale poultry industry in the region when he learned that San Francisco needed far more eggs than local farmers were producing. Consequently, San Francisco hoteliers and restaurateurs relied on eggs shipped from the East in un-iced barrels, sometimes with unpleasant results: one bartender confessed to Byce that he had to crack eggs for drinks below the counter because there was a one-in-twelve chance it would contain a chicken instead of an egg.[8]

Lyman quickly recognized that the scarcity of eggs had to do with the poky behavior of the chicken. "She took three or four weeks to accumulate a clutch of eggs," Adair Heig wrote in her *History of Petaluma*, "lolled about on them for three more weeks until they hatched, then frittered away five to ten weeks more raising chicks to the point where they could fend for themselves." For Byce, nature was just too slow.[9]

Ordering five hundred brown Leghorns from the Midwest, Byce and a Petaluma dentist named Isaac Dias began tinkering with an egg incubator. The idea of egg incubation was an old one, but global experiments had failed because of the difficulty of maintaining a consistent temperature. But Byce and Dias hit upon the idea, covering an oil lamp with a diffusing felt covering and an electric regulator to maintain a consistent temperature. Soon they had a working prototype that they presented at the 1879 Sonoma-Marin Agricultural Society Fair. They tinkered with the device for several more years, and at the California State Fair in 1882 they presented a device that held four hundred eggs and hatched 95 percent of them.

The chicken boom was on. Byce and Dias's discovery transformed Sonoma generally, and Petaluma in particular, into California's leading egg-producing region. By the turn of the century egg production dominated small farming. Because it was a low-capital entry business and did not require great arable land, it was appealing to homesteaders, for whom the only remaining land was generally good for small ranching operations but not farming. And whereas traditional agriculture was a young man's game, taking a hard toll on the body, chicken farming was relatively easy. Of course, there was a lot to do: clean the pens, collect the eggs, and feed the chickens, but none of it was backbreaking. William C. Jones appreciated this. Claiming a Sonoma homestead at the age of fifty in 1885, Jones had already seen enough toil in his life. Finding his way to California from Tennessee during the gold rush, he took up work as a gold miner in Placer County in 1853. By that time gold mining was a corporate affair—gone were the days of the independent gold miner. After that he moved to Sonoma County, near the Vallejo adobe, and then near Petaluma. His eighty-acre plot by the turn of the century housed livestock and seven hundred chickens. "Although he is advancing in years," the *History of Sonoma County* recorded in 1911, "he is still caring for his ranch interests with the same interest and enthusiasm as formerly and is as keenly interested in the affairs and happenings in the world at large as he was a quarter of a century ago."[10]

By 1911 there were still more than 88,000 acres of Sonoma land available for the homesteaders, but little of it was arable. Instead many of the Sonoma homesteads were used for ranching. Most were claimed in the 1920s and early 1930s, late in the statewide rush for federal land. Of particular relevance for Sonoma was the Stock Act of 1916, which, as we have seen, had the same residency requirements as the Homestead Act but granted 640 acres for grazing. As the story of Leona Dixon reveals, the Stock Act could sometimes be a buffer against total financial disaster.[11]

Born in Santa Rosa in 1902, Dixon grew up on a family two-thousand-acre ranch west of Healdsburg, raising sheep. Rather than pay the ranch off when he had the money, Dixon's father invested in stock in a coal mine. When the stock market crash of 1929 came, he simply could not afford the mortgage, insurance, and taxes, and sold the large ranch. So in the dark days of 1933 Leona Dixon went to the land office in San Francisco, studied the map, and found a plot that was available for stock entry.

Later Dixon would recall the extraordinary toil involved in simply identifying the boundaries of the surveyed land. "We walked to the survey corner—a pile of rock two feet high and three feet square with a short redwood post set in the center. The post had the section corner numbers chiseled into it." She and her father tied a lariat to it and began to measure out the property step by step, until they found the next surveyor's corner. And then they proceeded to beat back the Depression by felling redwood trees, and cutting and selling redwood railroad ties, posts, grape stakes, split boards, and shakes. She proved it up and received the patent in 1938.[12]

As in Sonoma, finding good land for homesteading in wine-thick Napa was difficult, and the majority of homesteaders lived very modestly if not in actual poverty. This was evident for Charles Glos. Born in Germany in 1858, he left for the United States in 1874, first New York and then San Francisco. He started off as a clerk but then became the manager of a meat market at Montgomery and Market Streets, in the heart of the city. Soon he married Annie M. Ureitch, a fellow German. They decided to try their luck as homesteaders in 1885 and went to Napa, locating a parcel on a mountainside. There was something of a rush during the mid-1880s. The *San Francisco Chronicle* reported that settlement in Napa in 1887 was "exceedingly active."[13]

But the quality of the land was quite poor for farming. The trail to the property was so thick with underbrush "that Mrs. Glos held a flag aloft so that her husband could keep her in sight." They lived in a tent for a year and a half while building a cabin, cutting shakes for the roof and carrying pails of sand for miles to use in lieu of floorboards. According to the *History of Solano and Napa Counties* (1912), "Panthers abounded, also wild cats, foxes and coons. On one occasion Mrs. Glos killed three rattlesnakes. Deer and bear often fell beneath the trusty rifle of Mr. Glos, and in one evening he killed seven skunks, while he also had to his credit the killing of many wild hogs and wild goats." Yet they proved it up and were able to sell it to an eager investor, and made enough money to move to St. Helena and buy thirteen acres in the valley. They improved that property as well, building a substantial house and planting fruit trees and alfalfa.[14]

Part of the population surge in the 1880s could be attributed to the success of Charles Pritchard who planted zinfandel grapes on the boulder-strewn hillside on the east side of Napa in the Vaca Mountains. Proving up in 1883, Pritchard paid $16 for his registration fees, but what he produced was worth much more than that. With his wife and two children, he occupied an eight-room abandoned house, built a thirty-by-fifty-foot barn, a carpenter shop, a blacksmith shop, and most importantly a twenty-acre vineyard. It was one of the first successful hillside operations, and he later sold his homestead to vintners for a tidy sum. Today Pritchard Hill, as it is known, is home of the multiple-award-winning Chappellet Winery.[15]

As was the case in the Santa Clara River Valley in Southern California, some homesteaders found redemption in Napa, perhaps none more acutely than José Jesus (J.J.) Berreyesa. When J.J. was sixteen in 1860, he watched the sheriff auction off the final piece of his family's land. It seemed like the last of many indignities foisted upon the much-beleaguered clan, and it must have made an impression on the young Berreyesa. Like many Californio decedents, he was the heir to bitter family memories.

His great-grandfather, Antonio Berreyesa, had been a legend in his day. A Mexican-born Basque, he had been part of the famous de Anza expedition to California in 1774. He stayed on in California and had nine children, including Nasario Antonio Berreyesa and José de Los Reyes Berreyesa. In 1839 Nasario moved onto the rich land of Las Putas in what would become Napa County. Las Putas—named for the creek running through the fertile valley—was vast, approximately ten miles long and three miles wide. And Nasario made good use of it: according to contemporary accounts he secured the labor of more than one hundred Pomo Indians to tend his herds of cattle and more than twenty thousand horses.

In the fashion of California's Mexican elites of his day, Nasario had simply claimed the land as his own and apparently faced little resistance from the peaceable Pomo people. But his sons—Sexto "Sisto" Antonio Berreyesa and José de Jesus Berreyesa—sought to make the arrangement

19. Rancho de Las Putas on Putas River in Napa County, California. Courtesy the Bancroft Library, University of California, Berkeley.

official and permanent. Maintaining that they owned "a considerable number of cattle and horses" but lacked a "tract of land on which to place them, suitable for their increase," they petitioned the senior military comandante of Sonoma for a land grant in 1842. "The place referred to is vacant, and does not belong to any individual," Sisto and José de Jesus argued. "On the contrary, it lies in the neighborhood of the uncivilized Indians." And in 1843 Manuel Micheltorena, general of the Mexican army, granted the brothers the land, more than 35,000 acres, one of the largest of the Mexican ranchos in California.[16]

Sisto and José de Jesus expanded their father's cattle and horse operations, planted wheat, and had houses built of the adobe-laden soil. The adobe houses they built were "the best they had or desired to have," according to W. F. Wallace's 1901 *History of Napa County*. "Cereals thrive upon" the soil, and the "berry is always plump and full." Locally they became best known for breeding racehorses, a romantic pastime but one that foretold their later demise as heavy gamblers. An article in the *San Francisco Chronicle* referred to them as "two wild and reckless young men." Regardless, it was the arrival of the Americans shortly before the Mexican-American War that truly tore the Berreyesa clan apart and left a fraught legacy for young J. J. Berreyesa.[17]

Shortly after the sacking of Vallejo during the Bear Flag Revolt, John C. Frémont commanded American forces to seize and imprison Californios. Initially the coup was merely degrading, but it soon became a bloody affair. In one of the most egregious episodes of violence, Frémont ordered the execution of two of J.J.'s cousins and his great uncle, José de Los Reyes Berreyesa. Frémont, ever eager to prove his mettle, was patrolling Point San Pedro in San Rafael when the Berreyesa men arrived by boat on their way to Sonoma to check on the condition of imprisoned relatives. Frémont, along with legendary western trapper and guide Kit Carson, approached the unarmed Berreyesas. Carson yelled back to Frémont, asking, "Shall I take these men prisoners?" According to several accounts, Frémont waved his hand and said, "I have got no room for prisoners." Carson understood Frémont's meaning and shot and killed both brothers. José de Los Reyes Berreyesa cried out: "Is it possible that you kill these young men for no reason at all? It is better that you kill me who am old too!" Carson obliged, though he later admitted that he regretted it. The killing of the Berreyesa men inspired "deep meditation" among Californios, according to one of the most prominent, Manuel J. Castro. "Until then, we Californios did not know whether we would have to struggle against savage hordes organized under the Bear Flag . . . or against civilized soldiers." Now they knew.[18]

The arrival of Commodore John Drake Sloat in Monterey the next month brought discipline to the ragtag American forces, and the violence against Californios diminished. But if they no longer paid for American occupation in blood, they did now in land. During the war, and particularly after the gold rush, squatters began to invade Rancho de Las Putas. Although the Supreme Court upheld the patent to Rancho de Las Putas in 1855, Sisto Berreyesa and José de Jesus Berreyesa began selling off parcels to cover gambling debts and to pay attorneys to fight off squatters. In one particularly bad blow the brothers lost 26,000 acres in an auction forced by a judgment against them. José de Jesus's son, J.J., spent his early years watching the family land disappear to Americans until the final sale in 1860. After that the land passed through several hands until a group of American investors bought and then sold off the parcels of the ranch to farmers in 1866 and platted the town of Monticello. Sisto was later found living in a crude cabin in the hills above his former empire.[19]

But J.J. would not go so quietly. What he did during his twenties, no record tells, but he probably worked as a hand on one of the ranches now occupying his family's historic land—then known as Berreyesa Ranch—or in the new town of Monticello as a blacksmith. What is clear is that he intended to get back some of his family's land, for at the age of thirty-three, J.J. claimed a homestead just southwest of the original rancho boundaries. There he built a twelve-by-eighteen-foot house, raised a barn for two horses, sank a well, and planted enough hay to meet the requirements of the Homestead Act. Living with his wife and two children, Berreyesa had only a small family, a far cry from his father's, but it was all his, and maybe there was a virtue in having

20. *Fire Is Part of the Demolition Process, Berryessa Valley,* from the series of photographs in *Death of a Valley.* Photograph by Pirkle Jones, 1956. Copyright Regents of the University of California.

less to lose. He proved up the land, paid the registration fee of $16, and secured his patent in 1882.[20]

J.J. died at the age of seventy in 1914, late enough to hear rumblings about damming the valley, but not long enough to see it happen. At the behest of water-hungry developers in the San Francisco area in 1907, William Mulholland and two other prominent engineers drafted a proposal to flood the valley by building a dam on the southeastern edge at a narrow pass called the Devil's Gate. A drawn-out battle between Napa and Solano Counties over the fate of Berreyesa Valley ensued, and valley farmers resisted the dam vigorously. However, by 1948 the pressures of postwar population growth were such that the Bureau of Reclamation muscled through congressional funding for Monticello Dam. Using the power of eminent domain, the Bureau of Reclamation paid farmers a fair market rate for their properties, but it also killed a once vibrant ranching and agricultural region. The plight of the remaining valley farmers captured the attention of iconic photographers Dorothea Lange and Pirkle Jones who took a series of photographs for a 1956 book called *Death of a Valley*. In one haunting image two silhouettes walk away from a small house they set on fire as part of the mandated demolition process. The photograph is a searing reminder of the impermanence of everything.[21]

The dam was finished in 1958, and the filling of the valley commenced, creating Lake Berryessa (it was a misspelling of the family name, but it stuck) by 1963. Today the Berreyesa estate, the town of Monticello, and J.J.'s homestead are entirely submerged under hundreds of feet of water.

14

Among the Trees of the North Coast

"I stand here today to defend my dignity and my manhood," James N. Barton thundered before the delegates of California's second Constitutional Convention in Sacramento in 1878. "I am a poor man," the Humboldt County homesteader continued. "I have been a citizen of this State long enough to rear a family to manhood and I find myself and my children brought down by force of circumstances." For Barton, the "circumstances" bringing him and his family down were self-evident: competition from Chinese workers in the area's forests and lumberyards, unequal taxation favoring the large land- and mortgage holders, and worst of all "the land-grabbers." "The public lands are the heritage of the people," he concluded, "and ought to be donated to actual settlers in small quantities. Land-grabbing must be stopped."[1]

Of the 152 delegates to the Constitutional Convention, Barton was one of fifty-one from the Workingmen's Party, created only a year earlier in San Francisco. Remembered today chiefly for its activism against Chinese immigrant labor in San Francisco, the Workingmen's Party sprouted chapters in forty of the state's fifty-two counties, each largely responding to the local circumstances in which poor whites found themselves. By the time of the Constitutional Convention in 1878—convened to remedy long-standing complaints about political and corporate corruption in the state—the Workingmen's Party was so influential that political conservatives in both the Republican and Democratic Parties feared that it would control the convention.[2]

The "land-grabbing" to which Barton referred was actually a tangle of problems, one of which was particularly acute in the rich timberlands of Humboldt County. With the possible exception of the San Joaquin Valley, there was no region of California in which corporate interests and individual speculators took so much public land as in Humboldt County. At the core of the land-grabbing tangle was the practice of fraudulent entry, usually perpetrated by large lumber companies. When representatives of California's Public Lands Commission visited Humboldt in 1879, they saw "little huts or kennels built of 'shakes' that were totally unfit for human habitations, and always had been, which were the sole improvements made under the homestead and pre-emption laws, and by means of which large areas of red-wood forests, possessing great value, had been taken under pretenses of settlement and cultivation which were the purest fictions, never having any real existence in fact, but of which 'due proof' had been made under the laws."[3]

California Redwood Company, one of the largest lumber companies in the region, was a most conspicuous offender in this vein. A General Land Office report in 1886 decried its "gigantic scheme." One of the company's agents, operating from a "notorious" saloon, bribed sailors to file homestead claims and then rushed them to the notary public to transfer the claim to a member of California Redwood Company. Worse, "no effort seems to have been made to keep the matter secret." Furthermore homesteaders alleged that the county surveyor took payoffs to delay filing homestead claims to aid the land-grabbing companies. Through these tactics and transfers, the company amassed 64,000 acres of pristine forestland.[4]

By the late nineteenth century, fraudulent entry resulted in extremely inequitable land distribution in the sparsely populated county. As early as 1873 forty individuals or businesses owned more than one thousand acres; five owned more than five thousand acres; and one individual owned more than twenty-three thousand acres. More egregious, homesteading farmers often found themselves working for the big lumber companies in order to provide for their homestead. They labored, many felt, on the very land that had been stolen from under their feet.[5]

Further exacerbating the land problem in Humboldt was tax assessment. One of the chief platforms of the Workingmen's Party was the principle of equal taxation. In particular, it opposed the fact that large lumber companies held mortgages on vast tracts of settled land, drew interest from those mortgages, but paid no taxes on them. Meanwhile, as Barton described it, "when the Assessor comes around, he has no trouble in assessing the man, for his property is all visible, and he assesses it to the full extent."[6]

Taken together, these problems added up to what Barton decried as "landlordism," an arrangement by which even men who owned land paid the way for the large companies. Indeed one of the promises of the West had been the abundance of free or cheap land, and the ability of a man to liberate himself from the strictures of rigid class distinctions in the East. Yet within a decade of the gold rush, historian Daniel Cornford has smartly observed, "disparities of wealth were as marked as in many of the eastern communities from which the pioneers had come."[7]

For Barton and the Workingmen's Party, the Constitutional Convention initially felt like a modest success. Most significantly the new constitution modified California tax structure by requiring mortgage holders to pay taxes on interest and their portion of property, and it created a state board of equalization in the hopes of creating fairer tax assessments on land. The new constitution included a long-sought anti-Chinese article authorizing the legislature to protect California from "aliens, who are, or may become . . . dangerous or detrimental." (Barton described them as "slaves" and "a curse.") Finally, the regulation of the railroad through an elected commission also addressed statewide grievances about "the octopus," as some called the far-reaching railroad. However, as the decades following the Constitutional Convention revealed, corruption continued to reign in Sacramento, and neither equal taxation nor fair assessment occurred in practice. Ultimately the Workingmen's Party only gained one concrete victory in the Constitutional Convention, the banning of the Chinese. Three years after the convention, Congress passed the Chinese Exclusion Act of 1882, prohibiting any new Chinese immigration.[8]

But for the people of Humboldt, many homesteaders among them, a federal immigration ban was not sufficient. Eureka's bustling downtown maintained a significant Chinese community of approximately five hundred through 1885. A few aging Chinese remained from the gold rush days, but most drifted to Humboldt after famously aiding in the construction of the Transcontinental Railroad and the less well-known local short-gauge lumber railroads. Most grew vegetables on small rented plots and worked in the city's fish canneries and were generally not in direct competition with white workers. But enough Chinese remained employed in the timber industry to generate concern. Compounding white animosity toward the Chinese was simple xenophobia: the "un-American" customs of the Chinese were endless fodder for newspaper articles and editorials. Everything from their language to their diets became suspect, and they bore an unreasonable proportion of blame for promoting gambling and prostitution, as if these were practices with which whites had no experience prior to the arrival of the Chinese.

In the winter of 1885 all hell broke loose. In Eureka a stray bullet fired by a Chinese man at his rival struck and killed a city councilman named David C. Kendall. A white mob soon gathered to eject the "almond-eyed intruders," as one more courteous editorial described the Chinese. Despite calls to "hang all the Chinamen," cooler heads prevailed, and within two days the mob herded all the Chinese in Eureka onto a ship awaiting them in Humboldt Bay and shipped them off to San Francisco. Several years later a promotional tract for the county bragged about the victory of Humboldt citizens over the Chinese: "All that portion of Humboldt county which is, so to speak, within the domain of civilization, has been thoroughly, and it is believed permanently, ridded by peaceable means of this objectionable class. . . . Nature's benefactions to Humboldt county have been many, but we pride ourselves on having, by our own efforts, eradicated a festering, putrescent sore from our vitals." Indeed, the Chinese stayed out of Eureka well into the twentieth century.[9]

But surely Humboldt homesteaders quickly recognized that the disappearance of the Chinese scarcely improved their own lives. With the best timberlands owned by the big lumber companies, homesteaders had their pick of redwood stump lands, hillside land, and, about ten miles east of the coast, farmland adjacent to the confluence of the Klamath and Trinity Rivers. "To find Government land," an 1888 promotional pamphlet read, "one must go back beyond the thick settlements, and be content to hew out a home on the outskirts of civilization, and wait patiently till he, by degrees, finds himself in the center of a thriving community." So that is what they did, more than two thousand of them.[10]

Significantly, despite reports of exceptional fruit being produced near the confluence, very little Humboldt land was in cultivation in the late nineteenth century. "We have scarcely begun to use the soil to its full capacity," a California booster and amateur historian named Leigh H. Irvine wrote in 1915. Instead, dairying was second only to lumber in Humboldt's output, followed by stock raising, particularly sheep. And more than a few homesteaders became successful shepherds, producing wool that won awards at local agricultural fairs. Fred S. Bair was a successful shepherding homesteader in Humboldt. Born in Arcata in 1881, the native son labored as a rancher for another family until he made enough money to buy his first plot of land in 1904 in the foothills of Mount Andy about forty miles east of Eureka, deep in Humboldt's backcountry. Within the decade he would augment his small ranch by homesteading another parcel, proving it up in 1917. Irvine visited Bair's ranch and painted an impressive picture of it:

> It is beautifully wooded with pine, redwood, tan and white oak and other varieties of forest trees and abounds in very picturesque scenery. The grass grows luxuriantly and besides ample range and pasture for his flock of eight thousand head of sheep and other stock, Mr. Bair makes an abundance of hay on which to winter his stock. He has large and suitable barns and other buildings and the ranch is well improved for its purpose. His flock is high grade and he secures blue ribbon bucks from the State Fair at Sacramento to head his flocks.[11]

Like many other successful homesteaders in California, Bair availed himself of federal generosity to augment his existing landholdings.

But homesteading in the remote wilderness of the North Coast carried dangers, just as it did in the wide-open, sparsely populated deserts of Southern California. In Mendocino County—just south of Humboldt and sharing a very similar topography, economy, and climate—the isolation of the eastern timberlands region could be inviting for criminals. To perhaps nobody in Mendocino was this clearer than part-time sheriff deputy, shepherd, and homesteader Jeremiah M. Standley. Born in Missouri in 1845, Standley came by ox-train at the age of eight with his family, settling first in Petaluma and then in Ukiah. From a young age he worked on his father's cattle ranch and once nursed a sick cow back to health, earning the lifelong nickname "Doc." Jeremiah "Doc" Standley struck out at the age of sixteen and leased a ranch and began raising sheep. Part of being a good shepherd in Mendocino meant being an excellent shot, and Standley regularly bragged about killing several bears and their cubs in the woods. "It ain't the bear that gives us the most trouble," he later told a writer from *Cosmopolitan*. "It's coyotes. They are a third larger here than in the south, and do more damage to the sheep here than all the other vermints put together." As for trapping them, he said that "he knows more 'bout a trap than the man who sets it. He's the slyest critter on earth." Maybe, but Standley was one of the finest shots in Mendocino County, and it was on this account that the sheriff of Mendocino brought Standley on as a deputy. However, his brief post was not to last: the budget for backwoods law enforcement in the county was so slim that Standley soon found himself laid off. So back to the sheep he went.[12]

Standley settled on a piece of government land in the summer of 1878, and he built a substantial two-story, twenty-eight-by-sixty-foot house and planted an orchard and built a chicken house. He and his wife raised a family of three children, and he even employed several men. But in 1879 Doc Standley's life took a significant turn. Two ex-convicts named Hal Brown and August Wheeler (who also went by "Doc" because he learned dentistry in San Quentin prison when he was serving time for a stage-coach robbery) met in Mendocino in August and immediately put together a team to rob the Mendocino tax collector. Once assembled, the would-be robbers holed up at a camp near Big River, east of Mendocino. They might have remained hidden, even carried out their plot, had it not been for their stomachs: in a nighttime raid they killed a steer belonging to the Mendocino Lumber Company, stringing it up in a tree to cure. Soon a small posse comprised of men from the lumber company and some constables from town tracked the gang through woods, but they were fired upon by Brown and Wheeler, killing two of the posse members and injuring several others.[13]

It was October, and winter would be settling in soon enough, blanketing the backwoods with impenetrable fog and, within a few months, snow. The sheriff needed a capable man who knew the woods and was an expert marksman and tracker. Soon Doc Standley, out east in Sherwood Valley, received a letter re-deputizing him and inviting him to join a posse to catch Brown, Wheeler, and the whole crew. Leaving alone by horse, Standley soon joined the posse near the confluence of Rattlesnake Creek and Eel River. The distance and effort of this journey were staggering, as this account from *The History of Mendocino County* (1880) suggests. Standley's posse traveled from:

> Big river north to Blue Rock; thence east to Bell Springs; crossed Eel river; thence north to Red Mountain; thence north to Mad river; thence west to Kittenchaw valley; thence east, up Mad river to the three forks of the river; thence up the north fork of the main divide between Mad river and the south fork of Trinity river; thence south to the Yolo Bolles; thence across the Yolo Bolles; thence east to the foot-hills on Cold creek; thence south to the Red Banks. . . . This was the end of the first chase, and all parties were now in Ukiah; and it was thought that the gang had eluded the vigilance of the officers. But Standley had his ears always open.

Indeed Standley did. Ultimately spending eight weeks and covering more than a thousand miles in search of the crew, Standley finally found them. Hal Brown, the last to be captured, allegedly said, "God damn it, Doc! Won't you ever quit?"[14]

Standley easily won the next election for sheriff and celebrated by buying a 160-acre plot of government land to augment his homestead.

The writer from *Cosmopolitan* captured the pastoral beauty of sheep ranges in Mendocino:

> The sheep barony, like that of the cattle, belongs to the frontier, and one looks to California's stock-ranges of today. . . . In Northern Mendocino and Humboldt these ranges are of unimaginable wildness and beauty, with forests possessing the canons, streams racing through arcadian valleys, and hills grandly rounded to cloud-troubled summits. These slopes are everywhere set about with picturesque oaks and laurels, and the twisted cinnamon of madroon trunks; while for graceful grouping of the shrubs, there is always the Manzanita, its crimson, satiny arms upholding circular tents of pea-green foliage, each closely cropped next to the ground by sheep.[15]

Doc Standley proved up the land and filed for patent in 1883 with a $16 registration fee, but he had to explain his temporary absences to Ukiah, the county seat where the sheriff's office was located. Even when gone, however, "I have continued the cultivation and improvement of the said land and keep 2 or 3 men employed all the time for that purpose." One of his sons, William Harrison Standley, would go on to military excellence, first proving his mettle as a naval sailor in the Spanish-American War, then as chief of naval operations in the 1930s, and finally as U.S. ambassador to the Soviet Union in the early years of World War II.[16]

Not all North Coast homesteaders had such illustrious careers as the Standleys. Cyrus "Cy" Joseph Cole was a hard worker, but no hero. Cole worked as a timber cruiser—one of the better paid positions in the lumber industry—outside Eureka in Humboldt County. He stayed at the town's hotel, ate at the local tavern, and squirreled away money for when he got his own land. And he was picky: he had filed on a homestead once in 1921 in the forests of Mendocino but could not make a go of it, so he relinquished the land. Tell any Californian today that a man once gave up a 160-acre plot of land in Mendocino and they will call you a liar.

By 1926 Cole was ready to try again and he filed a claim on a remote patch of government land on the north fork of Bear Creek, deep in the backwoods of Humboldt County. It was, he said, "rough and hilly" and barren of timber, not much to look at, except for the forest behind it. But there was enough scrap wood and arable land to succeed, he figured. Today Cole's homestead file sits in a box, as most homestead files do, in the National Archives in Washington DC. When you open the file, you see a record of a man who strove honestly to meet the requirements of the Homestead Act. He built a house, planted an orchard, and made split stuff, posts, and grape stakes out of surrounding Douglas fir and redwoods, like most Humboldt backwoodsmen. He cultivated twelve acres of hay, until it was all "taken by deer and neighbor's stock." Finally, his neighbors vouched for his character. "I have known applicant for over 15 years and know him to be honest and reliable in every way."[17]

But being "honest and reliable" did not preclude also being savvy. What Cole's homestead file does not show is the very thing he was best known for in those parts: making moonshine. During prohibition the Humboldt backwoods proved fertile ground to a number of illegal alcohol operations, Cole's being one of the best known. "He made good 'shine, old Cy Cole," a rancher and rum-runner named Fred Wolf later recalled. "He was something else, goddamn old bugger. I took two guys down there in the evening," Wolf said, "and we didn't get out of there 'til three o'clock. We sure raised hell with a jug of 'shine that he had. But it wasn't too many of 'em went down to see the old boy. Just so goddamn far, had to go up over Wilder and clear into the bottom down there. That was the end of the line. I used to make a trip down there about once every two weeks."[18] And when Wolf was not sampling Cole's wares, he was delivering them. Specifically, he attended the bimonthly dances in nearby Briceland and sold Cole's moonshine by the cup or pint through the late 1920s. "Best thing I know about moonshine was the money," Wolf later recalled. "The money I made from runnin', I was buying this ranch, making the payments. That and helping with the folks, my mother and father."[19]

Long after the end of prohibition, the isolation of Humboldt and Mendocino would continue to prove conducive to illicit activity. In the late 1960s and early 1970s there was a marked migration of young men and women from San Francisco into the Humboldt and Mendocino backwoods, buying inexpensive tracts of land. Many of them identified with the counterculture—the *San Francisco Chronicle* described them as "long haired exiles"—and smoked marijuana. Desirous of self-sufficiency and ever wary of rumors that marijuana from Mexico was treated with pesticides, they began planting their own marijuana, first for personal use, and soon, for sale. They often built their own dwellings and installed irrigation works from local streams and springs. It was all out of code, naturally, and so Humboldt County officials stepped up code enforcement in 1973 to curtail the growing marijuana business. From that time until California legalized the growth of marijuana for medical treatment in 1996, backcountry growers have engaged in a perpetual game of cat and mouse with local and national law enforcement.[20]

15

Under the Shadow of Mount Lassen

E. E. Phelps and F. A. Tipple left Lance Graham for dead, covered in ashes, facedown in the snow. He weighed two hundred pounds, and carrying his body down the hill would slow their own frantic escape from a volcanic crater on Mount Lassen. The three had just crested the rim of the cinder cone and sat down to rest when, without warning, a column of blue-black smoke shot up. A sky full of ash, dust, and rock rained down on them. Phelps ducked under an overhang and Tipple ran for his life, and they both avoided injury. But not Graham: a rock about twice the size of a man's fist struck him in the chest as he turned to run, knocking him unconscious.[1]

Unconscious, but not dead. When Graham awoke, he turned over, painfully, reaching for the wound on his chest, the bones soft underneath. He'd broken an arm, his collarbone, and a few ribs. The volcanic plume above him was massive, visible even in San Francisco, more than two hundred miles away. Graham called out to Phelps and Tipple, but they were long gone, each running, sliding, and tumbling their way to survival.

Born in neighboring Tehama County in 1884, Graham had claimed his homestead in the Shasta County village of Viola in 1911 and worked as a lumberman while proving up his claim. Just as it was in Humboldt and Mendocino Counties, the job was filled with danger and long hours. And the lumber companies were accelerating the pace of work in the lumber camps: just two years before Graham claimed his homestead, a massive strike by seven hundred Italian lumbermen was held in McCloud, a lumber town in neighboring Siskiyou County, about ninety miles north of Viola.[2]

Graham had known the risk of hiking to the rim: the newspapers made a big deal of the eruptions, even publishing retrospectives on the Lost City of Pompeii. Besides, everyone in Viola, Manton, and the more distant Shasta County seat at Redding had worried at least once about Mount Lassen. After close to two hundred years of quiescence, the volcano had rumbled to life two weeks earlier, on May 30, 1914. There were daily rumblings but no new eruptions, so the curious began guardedly hiking up to the rim of Cinder Cone. Graham had not been able to resist the chance to take the trip, but he did not expect the journey to nearly kill him.

Once the rain of rocks subsided, Phelps and Tipple made their way back up the mountain with several other men to recover Graham's body. They were stunned to find him alive, writhing in pain, blood wicking into the snow around him. Using a blanket as a makeshift stretcher, the men successfully transported Graham down the mountain and to a waiting doctor in Viola by about midnight. A surgeon operated on Graham, removing a piece of his shoulder blade and suturing the massive gash on his chest. But the surgeon was not optimistic about Graham's chances of survival, and told the newspapermen as much. "From the best information available at a later hour tonight," according to the *Sacramento Union*, "Lance Graham is still alive, but so seriously injured he is expected to die within a few hours." The *Los Angeles Herald*, more concerned with getting the scoop than waiting for a final prognosis, simply reported that Graham had died.[3]

But Graham pulled through, the surgeon crediting his "extraordinary vitality." When he regained consciousness, Graham told reporters his story: "Just as I turned to leave the crater's rim, there was a puff of blue smoke, followed by a tongue of red flame that resembled the discharge of an old fashioned cannon. . . . I started to pick my way down the mountain, but in a trice I was enveloped in a cloud of smoke, while a perfect hail of small volcanic bombs and cinders beat down upon me."

21. Homesteader Lanson (Lance) Henry Graham, nearly killed by the eruption of Cinder Cone, Mount Lassen, 1915. Tehama County sent Graham to the Panama-Pacific International Exposition in San Francisco that year to show his wounds as the only man ever "hit by an active Made-in-America volcano." California State University, Chico, Meriam Library Special Collections.

Later, he claimed, "I wasn't scared a bit," but admitted, "I'll never climb that peak again."[4]

The next year, in April of 1915, Tehama County civic leaders trotted Graham out to the Panama-Pacific International Exposition in San Francisco. "He will be the only man there that was ever hit by an active Made-in-America volcano, and will be a feature that no state in the union can steal from us."[5] (Tragically the state of Washington did steal that feature in 1980 when the eruption of Mount St. Helens killed more than fifty people.)

About a month after Graham's appearance at the International Exposition, Mount Lassen again erupted. On the nineteenth of May, lava filled the crater, overflowed down the peak, melted the deep snowpack, and started a flood of mud down two creeks. One of them was Hat Creek in Shasta County, and it flowed right past Harvey Wilcox's farm. Wilcox, a forty-five-year-old fireguard for the forest service, bought a quarter section lot on Hat Creek back in 1892 and raised a family there, and would later prove up on a neighboring homestead. At around eleven p.m. he awoke to the sound of horses rushing past his cabin. Realizing what was happening, and shoeless, he gathered his family from the cabin, pushed through the wire fence surrounding the property, and ran, full steam. When he finally stopped running, Wilcox looked back and watched a six-foot wall of mud swallow his cabin.[6]

Settlers on the eastern side of the mountain in Lassen County were certainly used to periodic rumbling. Back in 1889 a reporter from the *Press Democrat* marveled that folks in Susanville had "become so accustomed to the constant trembling of the earth that they pay no attention to it." But the eruptions of 1914 and 1915 changed all that. A local lumberman and stock raiser named Francis M. Garner, who lived on his father's homestead (proved up in 1875) west of Susanville, began frantically writing letters to the land office. "I am a little afraid," Garner wrote, "to stay on the land and improve it while Mt. Lassen and its volcano are so active." And they were not the only victims: stockmen in the Shasta County seat of Redding, complained in April 1915 that cows would not eat vegetation that was covered in ash.[7]

In the foreboding landscape of southeastern Lassen County, close to the Nevada border, Lassen's vibrations punctured the timeless stillness of the high desert. More than a hundred miles east of the volcano, the region was well outside what scientists would later call the pyroclastic-flow hazard zone. Homesteaders must have known that, even without the scientists, because they began settling in the region shortly after the passage of the Homestead Act. The high watermark for settlement was in the years from 1909 to 1919, no doubt stimulated by the arrival of the Western Pacific Railroad to the hamlet of Doyle in 1911, the local stop for the slightly bigger town of Susanville. Doyle, and the Honey Lake Valley more generally, became the site of intense homesteading.

Of course, safety from the volcano did not guarantee success for the homesteader. At a lecture in Mill Valley in 1916, a Berkeley agriculture professor warned against attempting to homestead Lassen. "Generally speaking," the *Mill Valley Record* reported of the lecture, "it should be considered very dangerous from a homesteader's point of view. The great danger is the insufficiency of water." Not for lack of trying, by the way: more than fifty attempts had been made to irrigate the region, none of which succeeded. It would not be until 1921 that irrigation works from Eagle Lake were successfully installed. But that did not stop Ruth Berg from proving up her claim in 1914.[8]

The daughter of German-Jewish immigrants, Berg was born in Nevada and grew up in 1890s Oakland. Why the young University of California, Berkeley graduate and occasional journalist decided to move to the Honey Lake Valley in 1911 we will never know. But it is certain that she made a go of it. "In the fall of 1911 [I] seeded 15 acres to wheat and rye," she wrote on her homestead entry form. "Spring of 1913, reaped about ½ ton to the acre. Plowed 23 acres and seeded part to winter wheat . . . winter wheat good stand. Spring wheat well up. Have about ½ acre in fruit and shade trees and berry bushes. Have 40 trees altogether." Furthermore she built a substantial twelve-by-thirty-six-foot house with "3 rooms & hallway, 5 doors, 5 windows, screened doors & windows. 2 small porches, 2 closets & pantry. Walled cellar, 10 x 10 ft, 2 windows. Corral, Well 282 ft. deep . . . gas engine & pump."[9]

Berg's homestead file is a testament to her honesty, and her loquaciousness. In order to comply with the Homestead Act's requirement of constant residence, the application asked if the applicant had ever been absent from the claim. Most homestead applicants simply wrote the word "no," even when they were absent occasionally for good causes, like searching for outside employment. But not Berg. Instead she carefully detailed her absences: "I was out camping from July 22 to August 29, 1912. Was absent from October 21, 1912 to Mar. 18, 1913. Was absent working to earn a living and to make money to improve my homestead. Was absent from July 5th to August 5th, 1913, camping. Was absent from December 12, 1913 to May 4, 1915, working at my profession again to secure funds to enable me to live upon and improve my homestead." And in 1914 she paid her registration fee of $27.46 and secured the title to her land.[10]

Berg found the remoteness enchanting. In February of 1912 she wrote a letter to her sister in Oakland, frustrated that she had not yet visited her in Lassen. After cooing over the handsome cowpokes—"buckeroos" she called them—who occasionally visited her on her ranch, she pressed her sister. If she did visit, her sister would "soon understand the fascination and revel in the strangeness of this new land. The life here is so contrary to that of our streetbound childhood, our horizon knows only Nature's limits and events are scheduled by days, not minutes. . . . Living near the fog hung bay all our lives, we never knew the real, unadulterated moonlight . . . but I am wiser now that I have lived in the desert." "Come," Berg pleaded, "and come soon, for the old order is changing. Soon the big stretches of country will be cut up, the large claims subdivided; the buckeroo will be gone from the earth, the little homestead shacks will be replaced by houses—real houses—and every lane will have a gate. All here will be patterned as elsewhere. The west will be as the east. Come while we are what we are."[11]

Conclusion

REMEMBERING HOMESTEADING

Today one is hard pressed to find relics of the homesteads in California. New owners and developers tore down the rough-hewn cabins long ago. All of that handiwork, obliterated.

Most of the land was subdivided into countless homes now dotting the California landscape like a stucco constellation. Much of it was absorbed into large corporate operations as indistinct parcels of vast orchards and farms. Some of it ended up back in the hands of the people as gifted acreage to national forests and state parks.

"Most unsettled land goes through the same cycle," California homesteader Elizabeth Campbell observed in the early 1960s. "First, Indians who do not want trappers or cattlemen, then, cattlemen who do not want homesteaders, and finally homesteaders who love quiet, open spaces and do not want subdivisions, billboards or hot dog stands."[1]

Where Bernice Tucker threatened to tar and feather Fred Furniss in Twentynine Palms, there is nothing but an old mailbox and an overnight spot for truckers because it's as good as anywhere else in the Mojave Desert. At Elizabeth Campbell's old ranch there is now a bed-and-breakfast and a spectacular brick house, built after the Campbells sold the property in 1944, by a Hollywood songwriter named Allie Wrubel, who wrote "Zip-A-Dee-Doo-Dah," among other classics. At the intersection of Homestead Drive and Bagley Avenue are the remains of Frank and Helen Bagley's store. The structure still stands, though it has been absorbed into a larger one at the corner of the plaza and is largely indistinguishable. Where Charles Pritchard planted zinfandel grapes on a boulder-strewn hillside in Napa County is today the Chappellet Winery, whose website extols the landscape: "It is their romance with the land that makes the Chappellet story so appealing." The Topanga Canyon land first broken by a Missouri homesteader named Claude Allen in 1901, and occupied by his family through the 1960s, was sold off in 1968, at which point it became the home of Elysium Fields, a nudist camp and massage "sensorium" that contributed to the canyon's reputation as a counterculture haven.

One spectacular exception to general invisibility of homesteads on the landscape is Cabot's Pueblo Museum in Desert Hot Springs, Riverside County. It is the quixotic home of Cabot Yerxa, who claimed his homestead on a remote hillside in 1914. Led there by a series of failed business exploits, Yerxa soon invited his longtime friend, Robert V. "Bob" Carr, to join him in the desert. Carr, a writer who lived in Los Angeles, was inspired by the idea. "We can each take up a homestead of Government land on the desert, no water, no roads, no rain, no neighbors, but we do not have to pay any rent," Carr wrote. "We can eat rabbits, write a few stories, buy a cow, the cow will have a calf, and in time we will be in the cattle business." But if Carr dreamed of pecuniary success on the homestead, Yerxa's goal was to experience a new way of living: "We expanded with delight to be out of cities, and because there was no office to go to, no time card to punch, no city editor to please, and because we were away from people. We rejoiced in being free men (we cared not how poor) in a new clean world, and we were happy." Yerxa vowed to work only enough to earn money so that his homestead would eventually be a studio where he could become a painter and exhibit his work.[2]

Yerxa fulfilled the minimal homestead requirements, building a small cabin and planting barley and corn. Rabbits and heat destroyed most of his crops, but Yerxa's legacy was not destined to be agricultural anyway. Instead Yerxa's legacy was artistic: from 1941 until his death in 1965 he built an extraordinary adobe-style home by hand, integrating materials he had gathered from the desert floor, including fragments of American Indian pottery. The fragments were "the evidence," he later wrote, "that ancient people had preceded me in living on the mesa." Soon he was adding scraps of iron and secondhand windows and western bric-a-brac to the adobe. Known as an "artist hermit" among locals, Yerxa was more exactly a desert bohemian.[3]

Another exception to the invisibility of homesteading in California is a commemorative plaque on Ballard Mountain in the Santa Monica Mountains. For years drivers called the mountain above Malibu "N——head Mountain" after African American homesteader John Ballard, a former slave who moved from Kentucky to Los Angeles as a young man in the 1850s. Ballard started as a farm laborer, raising enough money to buy a parcel of land in El Monte that started him on the "property ladder" to financial comfort. Soon he was a man of influence. He co-founded the First AME Church of Los Angeles in 1869 and rose to prominence within the small black community of the city, even conducting real estate transactions with white buyers and sellers. However, in 1871 his wife died in childbirth, leaving him a widower with seven children, and he suffered significant financial losses in a real estate deal. Emotionally wrought by his wife's death and increasingly vulnerable financially, Ballard decided to pack up his family and move into the Santa Monica Mountains. Ballard bought 160 acres near Triunfo Creek, adjacent to modern-day Agoura Hills and Westlake Village. Later he would expand his holdings by filing homestead entry on land adjacent to this tract.[4]

As his children grew up and moved on, the labor of maintaining the land with his new wife wore on Ballard. Historian Patty R. Colman, who has meticulously reconstructed Ballard's life, explains that the former community leader was reduced to selling charcoal and firewood from his holdings. According to one Ventura County resident who knew Ballard: "He was with his wife and had half a dozen children . . . they would peer out—darky style—and it was equal to a circus. People would cheer and jeer and joke but the old Negro would never crack a smile." Another old-timer recalled how Ballard's cabin had been set on fire "on account of his color," and the promontory nearest his property soon

22. John Ballard in the Santa Monica Mountains. Courtesy the Russell Family.

went by the name "N——head" and "N—— Hill." But Ballard ignored the taunts, proved up his homestead, and was given patent to the land. What he had done to improve it was substantial and included building a house, a barn, chicken coops, corncribs, a well, and a small orchard and vineyard. He died in 1905. Belatedly, in 2010, Los Angeles County supervisor Zev Yaroslavsky pushed to have the name of the mountain near Ballard's homestead changed from its derogatory appellation to Ballard Mountain.[5]

On Palomar Mountain, San Diego State University archaeology students have recently unearthed artifacts from the homestead of Nate Harrison. Under the direction of anthropology professor Seth Mallios, the students have sought clues to the life of the gregarious homesteader. A former slave from Kentucky, Harrison proved up his homestead in 1879 and soon achieved almost mythical status as the first black man on the mountain. Although whites referred to Harrison as "N—— Nate" or "Uncle Nate," he appears to have been beloved, in part because he filed a water rights claim to a freshwater spring on his property. Many a hiker or wanderer drank from "Nate's Well," and stayed to hear him tell a story, of which, apparently, he had many. Harrison was a man of frontier generosity, inviting the weary to stay in his stone cabin for the night. One guest later recalled a pleasant evening with Harrison:

> Arrived in the house, he told me to unroll my blankets and take it easy while he was getting supper. And such a supper! Beef stew, with the beef done just right. Flaky white potatoes with gravy that couldn't be beat. And perfect home-baked bread. The loaves were very thick but thoroughly baked all the way through with a rich, bread. After supper Nate coaxed me into his easy chair beside the fire, and, after putting away the supper dishes, seated himself on a stool nearby and commenced telling stories of his experiences on and around the mountain.

Remembered for his kindness by those who knew him, Harrison also became a minor celebrity in the opening decades of the twentieth

23. Homesteader Nate Harrison outside his cabin in 1917. San Diego History Center.

century: traveling parties would stop to pose for pictures with "N——
Nate." Nate Harrison died in 1919.[6]

The 1934 passage of the Taylor Grazing Act appeared to spell the
end of homesteading. Authorizing the establishment of grazing districts
with up to eighty million acres (later increased to 142 million acres) of
public lands, Congress also empowered the Department of the Interior
to collect fees for permits to graze the range, the proceeds of which
would be used to repair the damaged range. A sensible policy, the Taylor
Grazing Act nonetheless dealt a hefty blow to prospective homesteaders who found much public land now withdrawn from the possibility
of homestead entry. "The bill practically abrogates all of the present
homestead laws," California representative Harry Lane Englebright
complained, "and will take from thousands of our veterans and people
in every State of the Union probably the only chance they will ever have
to acquire a home of their own." Perhaps he was sincere, but it was also
easy to cite the homesteaders in defense of the stockman's position that
the Taylor Grazing Act would produce undesirable "bureaucracy" and
"red tape" for the stockmen. Anyway, the *San Francisco Chronicle* had
already concluded that "there isn't a quarter section of public land in
California on which a homesteader could now make a living farming.

Only a lizard, a grasshopper or a jackrabbit can do it and in some cases even one of these would find it hard picking."[7]

Yet none of these pronouncements mattered, because there were still takers—homestead dreamers—particularly in the Southern California deserts. In 1938 Harry Carr—the *Los Angeles Times* columnist whom we last met flying over Mojave in a chartered airplane in 1931—was so smitten with the desert that he conceived of a "baby homestead" act. "Harry Carr always loved the desert," a friend of his later said, "and saw beneath its frowning exterior a comforting beauty and simplicity. He always felt that the human spirit could be ennobled and uplifted by contact with the desert and the things it represented." And so Carr reached out to his friend Paul Witmer—then mayor of Santa Ana, and later U.S. land commissioner from the Southern California District—to lobby their congressional representatives to pass an act for the purchase of public lands for homes.[8]

Witmer, too, had been inspired by what he saw on a trip toward Palm Springs. "I found the answer in a colony of veterans that had homesteaded the land around the only oasis on the American desert"; "I made the startling discovery that there were several hundred people who were happy and working hard to meet the requirements of homesteading. Yet they were planting a crop which they *knew* was probably doomed to failure. But *I* found a crop—the most valuable in the world. Regained health! Contentment! Leisurely living. That's really what this desert land was really best suited for." Passed by Congress on June 1 of 1938, the so-called Small Tract Act of 1938 gave the secretary of the interior discretion to sell off five-acre plots of surveyed public land for "a home, a cabin, camp, health, convalescent, recreational, or business site." Fairly described by one historian as a "clutter of odds and ends," the parcels available under the Small Tract Act had no known agricultural potential.[9]

Concentrated chiefly in the deserts of eastern San Diego County, as well as San Bernardino, Kern, and Riverside Counties, the parcels also lacked water or other utilities. "The experience of this office for the past 25 years," the new Bureau of Land Management (BLM) explained in a cautious pamphlet accompanying the land application paperwork, "has been the cost of developing water and reclaiming the land is so great that the average person attempting it is doomed to failure and bitter disappointment." Furthermore the BLM put tight restrictions on "uncontrolled, nonconforming uses that conflict with community or area plans of development" and any construction along public highways and scenic areas. Though the small parcels in the deserts got the nickname "jackrabbit homesteads," they were not like the lands granted under the Homestead Act of 1862. In addition to ensuring the tracts' small size, the Small Tract Act made no requirements on their cultivation, and tracts could be leased or purchased outright from the BLM. Subsequent amendments to the 1938 act gave preference to veterans of both World War II and the Korean War. "Although still unheralded in the American Press," one public land expert wrote of the Small Tract Act in 1955, "it is probably the most popular land law passed since the Homestead Act of 1862." That was literally true: almost twenty-eight thousand Small Tract Act parcels were patented, third only to cash sales and homestead entries. If the BLM regarded the lands as worthless, Americans apparently did not.[10]

Initially response to the Small Tract Act was sluggish, mostly because of the rations on building supplies and gasoline during World War II, but the end of the war and the inducements to veterans stimulated a curious boom on this desert land. "Land hunger has reached epidemic proportions in the United States," Small Tract Act homesteader Melissa Branson Stedman wrote in the *Desert Land Magazine* in December of 1945. "It has broken out like a contagious rash in recent months in Southern California, where hordes of people with back-to-the-land yearning, swooped down on the U.S. Land Office in Los Angeles in a mad rush for five-acre desert homelands, anywhere, just so it is earth under foot and space to breath."[11]

Stedman was the first in a wave of Small Tract Act applicants that became part of what the *Los Angeles Times* described as one of "the strangest land rushes in Southern California history," as applicants flooded the land office to file a claim on land released into the public

24. Small Tract Act homesteader Melissa Branson Stedman. The original caption read: "She overcame a childhood-phobia against snakes and skinned this rattler herself." *Desert Land Magazine* (December 1945): 13.

domain in the Mojave Desert after World War II. As the BLM released more "scraps" through the 1950s, the amount of public land available swelled to more than sixteen thousand acres, almost 90 percent of which were in Southern California.[12]

For Stedman and others, claiming land under the Small Tract Act and building a small vacation home was an antidote to urban life, and particularly life in Los Angeles, California's most populous metropolis by far. The men and women who filed on Small Tract Act lands seemed to revel in the foolhardiness of their endeavors, naming their properties Aching Back, Calloused Palms, Canta-Forda Rancho, Dun Movin, Jackass Junction, and Lizard Acres. Indeed Stedman wrote, "A desert homestead is not for the timid or the hothouse grown individual. Resourcefulness, as well as hardihood, and a sincere love of the outdoors and of the wild life are necessary."[13] Steadman already knew this: she had finally confronted her childhood fear of snakes.

> First time I saw a rattler, I put a few slugs of lead into it with my revolver, and let it go at that. But later when a handsome diamondback ambled up the front steps for a drink, I got out the pruning shears and snipped its head off. Then I started skinning the snake. The first touch was a terrible ordeal, but I stoically held on, and found the snake wasn't cold and clammy at all—but warm and almost velvety in my hands. Just when I was becoming adjusted to the feel of it, the reflexes became active, and the body whipped itself around my arm. But I gritted my teeth and took it. Then I started peeling back the skin, and if felt no different from cleaning a rabbit; the meat was clean and white and smelled like the fresh warm body of a newly dressed chicken. The rattlesnake phobia was cured, and I have a beautiful diamondback skin under the glass on my desk as the souvenir of a phobia that is gone forever.[14]

Stedman conquered her fear and conquered the landscape. The "leisure-home boom" as the *Los Angeles Times* called it, lasted well into the early 1960s. By the 1970s the boom was over and many of the simply built homes were abandoned. Despite efforts of local officials to eradicate

25. A Small Tract Act homestead, the Dohmeyer homestead, U.S. Patent No. 1182982. Courtesy Kim Stringfellow.

the shacks, many still stand today. In a curious twist, a community of artists has emerged recently in the Morongo Basin; some artists today inhabit cabins constructed under the Small Tract Act.[15]

But enthusiasm over the Small Tract Act could not stop what was coming for homestead policy. In 1961 President John F. Kennedy appointed three-time Arizona congressman Stewart Udall to the head of the Department of the Interior, where he urged Congress to streamline land laws and to advance the cause of conservation. Udall is properly regarded as a pioneer of environmentalism; he championed the Wilderness Bill, the Wild and Scenic Rivers Act, and the vast expansion of the National Park System, among other environmental achievements. He was a great believer in the value of homesteading, and he gave JFK a miniature plow on the one-hundred-year anniversary of the Homestead Act in May of 1962.

But Udall also recognized that, by the early 1960s, homesteading was an anachronism no longer helpful to man or nature. It was certainly

26. Inspecting a "plow" Stewart Udall (*far left*) gave John F. Kennedy on the one-hundred-year anniversary of the Homestead Act in 1962. Special Collections, University of Arizona Library.

incompatible with long-range preservation planning. "It has been commonplace for many years to say that the 'good' agricultural lands have long since been settled," the subsequent House Committee on Interior and Insular Affairs reported, "that the 'easily' found minerals have been discovered and developed. The inference of these truisms is that the public land laws must be examined to ascertain whether they serve the changed conditions." Congress responded by creating a nineteen-member commission known as the Public Land Law Review Commission in 1964. "We can find no basic reason," its final report, *One Third of the Nation's Land* (1970), concluded, "for maintaining the kind of agricultural settlement policies embodied in the homestead laws." And so in 1976 Congress passed the Federal Land Policy and Management Act, repealing the Homestead Act of 1862, as well as the Desert Land Act of 1877 and the Small Tract Act of 1938. "Suddenly, last year, the American frontier was gone," the *New York Times* editorialized in 1977. "For 114 years, the Homestead Act was both statute and symbol. It meant that there was always a future, as long as there was an American West; there was always fresh land for a fresh start."[16]

As the official homestead era came to an end, fewer and fewer Americans were farming anyway: between 1940 and 1970 the number of Americans living on farms tumbled from thirty million to nine million. As new machines, pesticides, and chemical fertilizers dominated farming, labor demand diminished apace, and small farms had a tough time competing with corporate mergers brokered far away from the soil. The 1954 agricultural report of the census illustrated the extent of agricultural concentration in California: though there were 123,075 farms, a mere 6,248 (about 5 percent) occupied two-thirds of the agricultural land. The days of small farming were long gone and had been for some time. California was again what it once was, "a country of plantations and estates."[17]

But the legacy of homesteading had always been more than agricultural. It was about self-sufficiency and the acquisition of land for poor and lower-middle-class people. Farming was what one did to acquire the land and to survive through the production of food. There was rarely any romance to the dreary task of everyday subsistence, but that has not stopped people from romanticizing. The counterculture of the 1960s inspired various back-to-the-land experiments whose adherents described themselves as "homesteaders." The "new homesteading movement," one scholarly observer wrote in 1972, "is both a way of living and a space in the mind. It may even come to pass that the new homesteading movement will be seen as the beginning of a new or revitalized religious phenomenon which once again makes it possible to experience a sense of cosmic sacrality."[18]

Maybe. But in the meantime folks needed to know how to farm. Like the shady "locators" of yesteryear, there were plenty of writers and publishers eager to capitalize on the back-to-the-land sentiment of the 1960s and 1970s. One of the more popular works was *The Ex-Urbanite's Complete and Illustrated Easy-Does-It First-Time Farmer's Guide: A Useful*

Book (1971) by the eccentric Bill Kaysing, most famous for promoting the theory that the six Apollo moon landings were hoaxes.[19]

For Betty Campbell, whom we met earlier in Twentynine Palms, homesteading was as much a spiritual endeavor as it was a means to prosperity: "To have been friends with homesteaders, to have regained lost health, to have lived close to nature and learned self-reliance, to have found a life interest, to have slept under the stars sharing the silence of the desert nights, means one has known some of the best things life has to offer. There is compensation in the strength that comes from courage acquired down the years. When life hands you some wallop you learn to stand firmly and keep your head up."[20]

The more enduring and problematic legacy of the Homestead Act is the notion that every American can and should own land, regardless of their station in life, their resources, or their abilities. That notion has become so deeply enshrined in the politics, economy, and culture of the United States that it is difficult to imagine Americans ever feeling differently. Of course, we can never know what stirred in the hearts of the dead, whether they pined to own land, hearth, and home. But we do know this much: after the national failure to implement Jefferson's vision of a free fifty-acre plot for every American in the late eighteenth century, about half the population had no reason to believe that land-ownership was a remotely realistic ambition in their lifetime. Perhaps it was the stuff of beautiful and impossible fantasies after a long day's toil, but the reality was always clear: the lenders would never relent! They usually demanded a 50 percent down payment for a short-term loan at an exorbitant rate, particularly in the West, which most eastern financiers viewed as an arid money pit. In the late nineteenth century the home-ownership rate would drop further as new immigrants settled into cities where tenancy prevailed. Thirty years later even President Herbert Hoover—who was bullish on home ownership for Americans—privately acknowledged that there was "utterly no hope" of working-class families buying a house. If the American Dream yet existed in the early twentieth century, it certainly could not include home ownership because such a thing was increasingly unlikely for most Americans.[21]

In 1931 Pulitzer Prize–winning writer and historian James Truslow Adams published *The Epic of America*, an international best seller in which Adams popularized the term "American Dream." For Adams the American Dream was one of "a better and richer life for all the masses of humble and ordinary folk who made up the American nation." "It is not a dream of motor cars and wages merely," he wrote, "but a dream of a social order in which each man and each woman shall be able to attain to the fullest stature of which they are innately capable, and be recognized by others for what they are, regardless of the fortuitous circumstances of birth or position." Significantly, although Adams appreciated the importance of the Homestead Act, he did not view landownership as a significant part of the American Dream. Furthermore Adams warned that Americans had come to see "money-making and material improvement as good in themselves," and that they had taken on the "aspects of moral virtues." "We forgot to *live*," Adams concluded, "in the struggle to 'make a living.'"[22]

But a raft of federal policies designed to stimulate home ownership soon eclipsed Adams's vision and flouted his caution. Just as *The Epic of America* hit newsstands, the Great Depression ravaged the American housing market: countless borrowers lost their jobs and defaulted on their payments, triggering widespread foreclosures across the United States. At the lowest point, the American home-ownership rate dipped just below 40 percent. As a direct response to the crisis, President Franklin Delano Roosevelt signed the National Housing Act of 1934, creating the Federal Housing Administration (FHA), which ensured long-term loans with only a 20 percent down payment and a relatively low interest rate. Coupled with the creation of the Federal National Mortgage Association (Fannie Mae) in 1938 and the rising demand for housing during and after World War II, the FHA stimulated a surge in the home-ownership rate, which reached 55 percent by 1950. Further incentive flowed from the provisions of the G.I. Bill, the chartering of the Federal Home Loan Mortgage Corporation (Freddie Mac), the preservation of the mortgage interest deduction in the United States tax code, and deregulation in the banking sector in the 1980s and

1990s. All the while legions of lobbyists from the National Association of Realtors steered legislators toward agreeable home-ownership polices. A 2001 *Fortune* survey of eighty-seven lobbying groups concluded that the National Association of Realtors was the ninth most influential trade association, just after the National Beer Wholesalers Association and two spots before the National Association of Home Builders. "The dream of homeownership," President George W. Bush declared when signing the American Dream Downpayment Act in 2003, "should be attainable for every hardworking American." Clearly the federal housing policies of the twentieth century had rejiggered the American Dream, first stretching it to include property ownership and then moving that goal to its core.[23]

In the early years of the twenty-first century, the dream became a clinical frenzy. Historically low interest rates, coupled with the rising practice of "flipping"—widely popularized through television shows like *Flip This House* and half a dozen corny imitators—inspired countless investors and aspiring home owners, to say nothing of real estate agents, of whom there were more than 264,000 in California at the peak of the market (more than 20 percent of all realtors in the nation). But it was the proliferation of subprime lending that drove the home-ownership rate to 69.2 percent in 2004, the highest it has ever been in the nation's history. Many hopeful buyers unable to secure conventional loans agreed, en masse, to "adjustable-rate" mortgages with "teaser" introductory rates that soon ballooned, even as home values began to dip. Unable and sometimes unwilling to pay these higher rates, new home owners defaulted, fueling a housing crash in 2007 that ultimately pushed close to eight million homes into foreclosure at a loss of about seven trillion dollars in home equity. It was the largest housing crash in American history, and it sparked the Great Recession. Widely and fairly blamed on banking deregulation, unscrupulous bankers and credit agencies, and subprime mortgages, the crash was also clearly the product of wishful thinking, perhaps naïveté, among American consumers. Conditioned by a century of public policy, excited by the circuslike atmosphere of the real estate market in the early twenty-first century, and eligible for perilous loan products, many aspiring home owners had simply become intoxicated by the American Dream. Awakening was rude: "They have thrown money away," one shrewd journalist observed, "an insult once reserved for renters."[24]

In the end, caveat emptor!

ACKNOWLEDGMENTS

Many good people and institutions helped me produce this book, and it is the least I can do to briefly thank them here, though I'll surely come up short. Steve Hindle, W. M. Keck Foundation Director of Research at the Huntington Library in San Marino, California, was an early and enthusiastic supporter of this project, and I was extremely fortunate to spend a semester at the Huntington as an Andrew Mellon Fellow digging through the case files for land disputes. Anthea M. Hartig, the Elizabeth MacMillan director of the National Museum of American History, encouraged me from the beginning and offered her great insights into the history of California and the United States. Before I even visited an archive, I spent months studying the Bureau of Land Management, Eastern States Office bulk data (available at https:// glorecords.blm.gov/), a collection of five interrelated data sets, the largest of which has close to one million rows of data. I could not have made sense of that data without the assistance and wizardry of Steve Graves, professor of geography, California State University, Northridge (CSUN); and David Deis in the Department of Geography at the university helped me visualize patterns on the California landscape. He also expertly made the maps in this book. The anonymous peer reviewers at the University of Nebraska Press offered exceptional critiques, and others provided insights along the way, including Julia Bricklin, William Deverell, Richard Edwards, Elizabeth Lobb, Michael F. Magliari, Don Pisani, Christopher Thinnes, and Natale Zappia.

Mojave expert Dennis G. Casebier, Robert Marcell and Mark Engler at the Homestead National Monument, and Daniel Fleming at the Bureau of Land Management kindly fielded my questions.

Sarah Brewer, Peter Blodgett, Clay Stalls, as well as archivists at the following institutions were exceptionally helpful: the Bancroft Library; the California Historical Society; the National Archives in Washington DC, San Bruno, and Riverside; Special Collections at the University of California, Los Angeles; San Diego Historical Society; the Kern County Library; the Meriam Library, California State University, Chico; and the Topanga Historical Society. At CSUN, Susan Fitzpatrick-Behrens, Stella Theodoulou, and Jessica Kim were extremely supportive, and I remain grateful for the generous support of the Whitsett Endowment, which defrayed costs associated with photo reproduction, travel, and the great research assistance of Katie Noonan.

APPENDIX

NUMBER OF HOMESTEADS PER COUNTY AND YEAR

Number of Homesteads Per County

County		County		County	
Kern	3,787	Plumas	952	Yolo	376
San Bernardino	2,974	Tuolumne	940	Colusa	362
Los Angeles	2,852	San Benito	909	Glenn	341
San Diego	2,733	Butte	880	Sierra	333
Mendocino	2,391	Sonoma	819	San Joaquin	317
Tulare	2,286	Amador	791	Alameda	277
Fresno	2,235	Lake	780	Del Norte	239
Monterey	2,134	Trinity	748	Contra Costa	233
Humboldt	1,893	Ventura	708	Solano	232
Shasta	1,741	Placer	703	Mono	220
San Luis Obispo	1,642	Nevada	649	Sacramento	220
Riverside	1,586	Inyo	631	Sutter	189
El Dorado	1,536	Imperial	617	Santa Cruz	157
Siskiyou	1,526	Santa Clara	576	Alpine	82
Lassen	1,513	Santa Barbara	537	Orange	71
Tehama	1,420	Yuba	499	San Mateo	34
Calaveras	1,347	Stanislaus	457	Marin	21
Madera	1,291	Kings	432		
Modoc	1,275	Merced	429		
Mariposa	1,124	Napa	402		

Number of Homesteads Granted Per Year

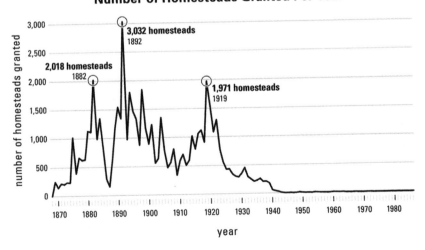

183

NOTES

INTRODUCTION

1. When the Homestead National Monument displayed the original Homestead Act in a 150th anniversary celebration in June 2012, more than 38,000 people visited Beatrice in the first five weeks, and more than 103,000 visited the monument throughout the year. Excluding that anomalous year and 2017—when Americans gathered in the Sandhills of Nebraska to see the total solar eclipse—more than one million people have visited the monument since 2000, an average of about 63,000 annually. The Our Documents initiative is jointly sponsored by National History Day, the National Archives and Records Administration, and the *U.S. News and World Report.* See www.ourdocuments.gov, last modified July 7, 2015; Chris Dunker, "Homestead Act draws 38,000 to Monument," beatricedailysun .com, June 1, 2012, accessed July 29, 2012; and visitation statistics from https:// irma.nps.gov/Stats/Reports/Park/HOME, accessed June 23, 2020.

2. Fraser, *Prairie Fires,* 393; Cannon, "Homesteading Remembered," 9; Owen, *Gen X TV,* 18; Cecil Smith, "Actor-writer-director Michael Landon Is Back on the Prairie," *Los Angeles Times,* March 24, 1974, M2.

3. On the homesteader failure rate, see the estimate of between 37 percent to 45 percent in Edwards, Friefeld, and Wingo, *Homesteading the Plains,* 35. There is a virtual consensus among historians that most homesteaders failed to prove up their claims and that many land claimants were merely "dummy entrymen" for corporate interests that paid them to file claims on the land and then quickly deed the land to the corporation afterward. "After 1862," one historian wrote, "the federal government deeded 285 million acres to homesteaders. Half their claims were fraudulent, backed by false identities, fake improvements, or worse." And in California, where the indisputably corrupt Southern Pacific Railroad hoarded more than eleven million acres of land, historians have been even less charitable: "The Homestead Act of 1862," one widely used California history textbook explains, "encouraged the ownership of land in

small farm units. But in California the operation of that policy was almost entirely thwarted." However, in 2017 economist Richard Edwards and his University of Nebraska–Lincoln research team published their quantitative reassessment of the Homestead Act, *Homesteading the Plains: Toward a New History*, and it was eye opening. They found that the notion that "most homesteaders failed" dated back to a statistical miscalculation in Fred Shannon's widely cited 1945 book, *The Farmer's Last Frontier: Agriculture, 1860–1897*. In fact by correcting this error, Edwards and his team concluded that the majority of homesteaders actually succeeded. Furthermore, on the notion that many homesteaders were just "dummy entrymen" for large-scale corporate interests, Edwards's rigorous case studies from Nebraska demonstrate that such fraud was actually extremely uncommon. With the important exception of the well-publicized homesteading fraud perpetrated by the California Redwood Company in Humboldt and Del Norte Counties in the early 1880s, there is no evidence that fraudulent homestead entries were common in California. For examples of the consensus view, see Warren, *Buffalo Bill's America*, 72; Rawls and Bean, *California: An Interpretive History*, 9th ed., 184; Limerick, *The Legacy of Conquest*, 62. For a more extended discussion of the consensus view, see Edwards et al., *Homesteading the Plains*, 35, 90, 220–21. A notable exception to consensus view can be found in Bogue, "An Agricultural Empire," 289.

4. Researchers and readers seeking the precise number of homesteads in California, or any other state, will be sorely disappointed. My estimate—"more than sixty thousand"—reflects the inconsistency of data sources and definitions. The most authoritative and complete data set on homesteads appears in a work by the United States Bureau of Land Management, *Homesteads*, from 1962. According to *Homesteads* there were 66,738 homestead patents granted in California. Though *Homesteads* is probably the best source, it is not without limitations. Specifically *Homesteads* does not list the initial entry numbers, so there is no way to measure the number of homesteaders who failed to reach the patent stage after the five-year term of settlement. (This has not stopped historians from making sweeping and unfounded claims about the high failure rate of homesteaders.) Paul Gates found a work-around to this limitation by dividing the total number of original entries for the years 1863 to 1880 by the final patents issued and listed in *Homesteads*, thus arriving at the 63 percent figure for California. See Gates, *History of Public Land Law Development*, 413, note 50. Another problem with the *Homesteads* data is that there is no documentation of precisely what constituted a homestead. The figures reported in *Homesteads* clearly include most or all of the patents granted by the Homestead Act of 1862. It is unknown, however, whether the data also includes land granted under subsequent revisions to the Homestead Act, including, among others, the Stock-Raising Homestead Act of 1916 that raised

the allotment to 640 acres for ranching purposes. Despite these problematic limitations, the *Homesteads* data remains the most commonly referenced source, and it informs the tables presented on the website for the National Homestead Monument: https://www.nps.gov/home/learn/historyculture/bynumbers.htm, last modified June 6, 2020. However, to gain a much clearer understanding of the homesteading experience in California, I have relied extensively on state-level "GLO Bulk Data," furnished by the Bureau of Land Management, Eastern States, at https://glorecords.blm.gov/BulkData/default.aspx, accessed November 16, 2018. These data sets are extraordinarily robust and woefully underutilized by scholars. They provide county-level patent dates, land descriptions, individual names of grant recipients, and authority codes—vital for understanding whether the patent was authorized under the original Homestead Act of 1862 or under a subsequent amendment.

1. NOT MUCH ELSE BESIDE

1. Rose Trujillo Wiley, interview with the author, July 31, 2014, Topanga, California.
2. For median income, see "Mapping L.A. Neighborhoods," *Los Angeles Times*, http://maps.latimes.com/neighborhoods/, accessed June 24, 2020.
3. United States Bureau of the Census, 1870 Census: Volume 1, The Statistics of the Population of the United States, 1872, 90; Phillips, "Indians in Los Angeles," 448; Faragher, *Eternity Street*, 17. See also Zetsch, *The Chinatown War*.
4. "Raising the Wind," *Los Angeles Times*, September 30, 1882, 4.
5. Johnson, *The Topanga Story*, 54. Netz, "Great Los Angeles Real Estate Boom," 54–68. My estimate of acreage price comes from figures presented in Dumke, "The Boom of the 1880s," 104.
6. *Illustrated History of Los Angeles County*, 493; *Report of the Commissioner of Agriculture for the Year 1884*, 474.
7. Rose Trujillo Wiley, interview with the author, July 31, 2014, Topanga, California. Route 156 was redesignated as SR 27 in 1964 and runs from the Pacific Ocean to Chatsworth.
8. Morgan, "Slavery and Freedom," 8; Katz, "Thomas Jefferson and Right to Property," 467–88. See also Krall, "Thomas Jefferson's Agrarian Vision," 137–38.
9. Lindert and Williamson, *Unequal Gains*, 38.
10. Frymer, *Building an Empire*, 79–80; Peñalver and Katyal, "Property Outlaws," 1108; Pisani, "The Squatter and Natural Law," 444.
11. Smyth, *Law of Homestead and Exemptions*, 50.
12. Gates, *History of Public Land Law*, 238–39; see also Gates, "The Suscol Principle," 453–71.
13. Deverell, "To Loosen the Safety Valve," 272. Note that I do not include the Desert Land Act of 1877 here because it lacked the residency requirement

of the Homestead Act and its amendments, making it ripe for massive fraud through the use of "dummy entrymen," nowhere more so than in California's Kern County. See also Gates, *Land Policies in Kern County*, 12–13. For a complete list of federal public land laws, see Bureau of Land Management, "Explore the Homesteading Timeline," http://www.blm.gov, accessed November 16, 2018.

14. Bentley, "Condition of the Western Farmer," 27; Welch, "Horace Greeley's Cure for Poverty," 588; Arthur H. Dutton, "The Cost of a Homestead," *San Francisco Chronicle*, March 28, 1909, 4.

15. "Xmas Cheer Tendered Lonely Homesteaders," 3; Lincoln, *Rhymes of a Homesteader*, 27; Bagley, *Sand in My Shoe*, xvii–xviii.

2. A COUNTRY OF PLANTATIONS AND ESTATES

1. Robinson, "A California Copperhead," 215; Hayes-Bautista, *El Cinco de Mayo*, 64.

2. "The Ruing—The Flood," *Los Angeles Star*, January 25, 1862, 2; Pitt, *Decline of the Californios*, 120; Guinn, *Historical and Biographical Record*, 144, 58.

3. Nash, "The California State Land Office," 348; United States Bureau of the Census, *1860 Census*, 34–35; United States Census Office, *Statistics of the United States*, 512; Long, *Wages and Earnings*, 99.

4. "Local Land Office Is Most Important in State," *Los Angeles Herald*, May 17, 1910, 5. See "Letters Sent, 1853–1880," box 1, and "Letters Received, 1853–1921," box 2, RG 49, Los Angeles (California) Land Office, Records of the Bureau of Land Management.

5. Robinson, *Land in California*, 240, 242; Bell, *Reminiscences of a Ranger*, 21–23. Waldron, "Courthouses of Los Angeles County," 352–55. On privatization of public space in Los Angeles, see Davis, *City of Quartz*.

6. "Arousing the People," *San Francisco Chronicle*, March 9, 1879, 8; Pisani, "Land Monopoly," 16; also see Igler, *Miller & Lux*; Rawls and Bean, *California: An Interpretive History*, 9th ed., 186; Vandor, *History of Fresno County California*, 162; McWilliams, *Factories in the Field*, 21, 4. Shelton, *A Squatter's Republic*, 4.

7. Gates, *Land and Law in California*, 5; Bell, as cited in McWilliams, *Southern California*, 61.

8. Gates, *Land and Law in California*, 4; Pitt, *Decline of the Californios*, 253; Robinson, "The Rancho Story," 226; E. Breck Parkman, "Russian Silver in Mexican California," September 23, 2006, https://www.parks.ca.gov/?page_id=24474.

9. Gates, *Land and Law in California*, 15, 5.

10. Pitt, *Decline of the Californios*, 52, 94, 196, 252; Shelton, *A Squatter's Republic*, 16–18; Clay and Troesken, "Ranchos and the Politics," 57–59; McWilliams, *Southern California*, 63.

11. George, *Our Land and Land Policy: Speeches*, 37, 68; California Commission on Immigration and Housing, *Report on Large Landholdings*, 14; Gates, *Land and Law in California*, 252; Fellmeth, *Politics of Land*, 8–9.

12. Grenier, "Officialdom," 145; Nash, "The California State Land Office," 348–49, 353.

13. Peterson, "The Failure to Reclaim," 45, 47; "Swamp Lands," *Sacramento Daily Union*, April 2, 1866, 3; *Reports of the Joint Committees*, 7.

14. *1870 Census*, 125–30; Central Pacific Railroad Company, *List of Government and Railroad Lands*, 3; Olmstead and Rhode, "The Evolution of California Agriculture," 3, 6–7.

15. Land Patent File for Ivar A. Weid, RG 49, National Archives and Records Administration, Washington DC.

16. *Pacific Rural Press*, August 12, 1876, 109; *Pacific Rural Press*, January 24, 1880, 58; *Los Angeles City Directory of 1893*; "How 'Sunset' Blvd. Received Its Name," *Los Angeles Times*, August 12, 1941, A4.

17. *Annual Publication of the Historical Society*, 93–94.

3. INSTANT RELICS

1. "Rancher Is Near Death as Car Hits Wagon," *Santa Monica Bay Outlook*, September 11, 1916, 1; "Strange Ships that Sail in the Skies," *Saint Paul Globe*, May 9, 1897, 18; Bottles, *Los Angeles and the Automobile*, 46.

2. *Fourteenth Census of the United States Taken in the Year 1920*, 14, 43; *Fourteenth Census of the United States: 1920*, 2.

3. The indigenous Tongva people lived in the eastern portion of the Santa Monica mountain range for about seven thousand years, and the Chumash lived for about twenty-five hundred years westward in modern-day Malibu. Costanso, *The Narrative of the Portola Expedition*, 139; King, *Prehistoric Native American Cultural Sites*, x, 44. On homesteading and American Indian dispossession in the Great Plains, see Edwards et al., *Homesteading the Plains*, chapter 5; Hackel, *Children of Coyote*, 262–66, 341; Madley, *An American Genocide*. See also Larson and Knight, "Re-Visiting the Treasure House," 356–72.

4. Land Patent File for Marion Decker, RG 49, National Archives and Records Administration, Washington DC.

5. MacDonald, "Southern California," 1–13.

6. "Santa Monica," *Los Angeles Times*, April 27, 1894, 9; W. S. Lyon, "Orchard, Farm, Rancho and Stockyard," *Los Angeles Times*, July 1899, 13.

7. Arthur H. Dutton, "Uncle Sam," *San Francisco Call*, April 2, 1911, 5.

8. "Proposed Laws for Protection of Game," *Los Angeles Times*, February 4, 1901, 10; "The New Game Laws," *Los Angeles Herald*, April 1, 1901, 4; "Department of

Fish and Game Celebrates 130 Years of Serving California," *Outdoor California,* November–December 1999, https://nrm.dfg.ca.gov/FileHandler.ashx ?DocumentID=23573&inline, accessed June 24, 2020.

9. "Los Angeles County Association," *Forest and Stream,* August 23, 1902, 4; "Campaign for More Members," *Los Angeles Herald,* April 14, 1902, 5.

10. "Venison Out of Season Causes 6 Fines," *Santa Monica Bay Outlook,* July 21, 1916, 1.

11. "Private Snap of Reserve?" *Los Angeles Times,* February 10, 1907, II19.

12. "Private Snap of Reserve?" II19.

13. "Pioneers Testify as to Malibu Road," *Los Angeles Herald,* October 7, 1908, 10.

14. "Court and Jurors Will Inspect All Malibu District," *Santa Monica Evening Outlook,* December 13, 1918, 1; "Progress Threatens to Crumble Ancient Ranch," *Los Angeles Times,* March 25, 1923, II1.

15. "Wilderness Is Invaded: Los Angeles Business Men Become Squatters," *Los Angeles Times,* March 29, 1907, II1.

16. Crutcher, *Tales from Topanga,* 7–8.

4. HARD-BITTEN COUNTRY

1. "Are Indicted for Conspiracy: Government to Prosecute Oil Men in Kern County," *Los Angeles Times,* May 4, 1911, II6.

2. "Are Indicted for Conspiracy," II6.

3. "California Oil Feud," *Petroleum Gazette,* March 1912, 5.

4. See "Edward Doheny, Frank Hogan, Charles Wellborn, et al., ca 1910–1930," in the Edward L. Doheny Family Collection, University of Southern California Libraries, http://digitallibrary.usc.edu/cdm/ref/collection/p15799coll56/id /10, accessed June 24, 2020

5. On the "cult of toughness" in Kern and the broader San Joaquin Valley, see Gregory, *American Exodus;* Gates, *Land Policies in Kern County,* 10–13.

6. *California County Agricultural Commissioners' Report, Crop Year 2016–2017,* 4, 13; for oil numbers, see Shale XP, "Oil & Gas Activity in California," https://www .shalexp.com/california, accessed June 24, 2020.

7. Land Patent File for James M. Elwood, RG 49, National Archives and Records Administration, Washington DC; "Kern River Oil Pioneers," *Petroleum Gazette,* February 1912, 6; see also "The Passing of Tom Means," *Petroleum Gazette,* September 1912, 3; California Department of Conservation, "Oil and Gas Statistics, Annual Report Gas Statistics, 2006," 66, ftp://ftp.consrv.ca.gov/pub/oil/annual _reports/2006/0102stats_06.pdf, accessed June 24, 2020.

8. "Why Kern County Is the Land of Opportunities," *Los Angeles Times,* January 28, 1912, V27.

9. "Oil May Lead to Litigation," *Los Angeles Times,* October 25, 1915, II17.

10. Morgan, *History of Kern County,* 347.

11. Land Patent File for Clarence C. Cummings, RG 49, National Archives and Records Administration, Washington DC.

12. Land Patent File for Clarence C. Cummings, 1531.

5. VIOLENT PARADISE

1. *Jose Cananas vs. Babe Campo*, Case #005145, Superior Court of California, County of Ventura; "Find Poison in Food and Arrest Follows," *Los Angeles Times*, July 5, 1914, 18; "Hand Lacerated; Dies of Tetanus," *Los Angeles Times*, October 4, 1914, III.

2. *California County Agricultural Commissioners' Report, Crop Year 2012–2013*, 4.

3. Menchaca, *Recovering History, Constructing Race*, 268–70.

4. *Santa Paula Water Works vs. Julio Peralta*, Case #001458, Superior Court of the State of California, County of Ventura. For a case summary, see *Pacific Reporter* 45 (St. Paul: West Publishing Co., 1896), 168–70.

5. "Ventura County: The Result of a Cause Celebre," *Los Angeles Times*, December 4, 1897, 3.

6. "Squatter Troubles," *Daily Alta California*, July 12, 1871, 1.

7. Outland, *Sespe Gunsmoke*, 42; see also "The Ventura Murder Case," *Sacramento Daily Union*, August 3, 1878, 8; "More's Murderers," *Morning Press*, August 2, 1878, 1.

8. Blanchard, *Memories of a Child's Early California Days*, 25.

9. Land Patent File for Frank R. Rodriguez, RG 49, National Archives and Records Administration, Washington DC.

10. Land Patent File for Frank R. Rodriguez.

11. "Hands Off the Homesteader," *Los Angeles Times*, June 21, 1891, 4.

12. "200 Dead, 300 Missing, $7,000,000 Loss in St. Francis Dam Disaster," *Los Angeles Times*, March 14, 1928, 2.

13. St. Francis Dam Disaster: Death and Disability Claims and Claimants, 1929, https://scvhistory.com/scvhistory/stfrancis-claims071529.htm, accessed June 24, 2020.

6. SWINDLES AND SALVATION

1. "Antelope Valley: A Section Where Cheap Lands May Yet Be Found," *Los Angeles Times*, September 5, 1891, 4; James, *Antelope Valley*, 3; see also Los Angeles Chamber of Commerce, *Agricultural Survey*.

2. Harry Bowling, "Making our Barren Tracts Productive," *Los Angeles Times*, January 1, 1916, V138; Johnson, *Water Resources of Antelope Valley*, 70–89.

3. Robbins, *Our Landed Heritage*, 329; Adams, *Irrigation Districts in California*, 9.

4. "Boyle Heights: Brief Sketch of a Delightful Suburb," *Los Angeles Times*, August 4, 1889, 10.

5. Johnson, *Water Resources of Antelope Valley*, 12; *Fifth Biennial Report of the Department of Engineering*, 92.

6. Land Patent File for Lewis C. Tilghman, RG 49, National Archives and Records Administration, Washington DC.

7. "More Irrigation Trouble," *Los Angeles Herald*, November 10, 1896, 10; Los Angeles Superior Court, Case #27972, Los Angeles Court Records, Huntington Library.

8. Los Angeles Superior Court, Cases #18226, #21075, #8052, Los Angeles Court Records, Huntington Library; "Wiley Getting Even," *Los Angeles Herald*, May 29, 1897, 6; Los Angeles Superior Court Case #21075, Los Angeles Court Records, Huntington Library; *Reports of Cases Determined in the Supreme Court*, 22.

9. "Land Scheme," *Los Angeles Herald*, August 8, 1897, 7; Smythe, "The Struggle for Water," 648.

10. *United States vs. H. P. Sweet et al.*, folder 1055, box 63, RG 21, National Archives, Riverside CA.

11. Clifton, "History of the Communistic Colony," 80.

12. Land Patent File for Olin L. Livesey, RG 49, National Archives and Records Administration, Washington DC.

13. "The Antelope Valley," *Los Angeles Herald*, April 22, 1896, 16; *Almond Colonies of Southern California*, 30.

14. James, *Antelope Valley*, 5.

15. "The Land," *Los Angeles Times*, October 18, 1901, 10; Greater Antelope Valley Economic Alliance, "Agriculture," socalleadingedge.org/industries/agriculture, accessed June 24, 2020.

7. MEXICAN LANDS IN MEXICAN HANDS

1. "Juan Verdugo: Being Tried for an Assault with a Deadly Weapon," *Los Angeles Times*, September 21, 1887, 1.

2. Pitt, *Decline of the Californios*, 252.

3. Land Patent File for Juan Verdugo, RG 49, National Archives and Records Administration, Washington DC.

4. "Greater Los Angeles Illustrated," as cited in Deverell, *Whitewashed Adobe*, 27.

5. Pubols, *The Father of All*, 14, 209, 292, 301.

6. Land Patent File for Francisco de la Guerra, RG 49, National Archives and Records Administration, Washington DC.

7. Los Angeles Superior Court, Case #01012.5, Los Angeles Court Records, Huntington Library. "Local Brevities," *Los Angeles Herald*, March 31, 1881, 3.

8. Los Angeles Superior Court, Case #05115, Los Angeles Court Records, Huntington Library.

9. Los Angeles Superior Court, Case #331, Los Angeles Court Records, Huntington Library.

10. Land Patent File for Adolfo Albitre, RG 49, National Archives and Records Administration, Washington DC. Note the two different spellings of his name.

11. Los Angeles Superior Court, Case #26766, Los Angeles Court Records, Huntington Library.

12. "Home-Makers Protected: Government Waives Technical Defects in the Final Proof of Homestead Entry," *Imperial Valley Press*, March 20, 1909, 7.

8. FLOODS AND UTOPIAS

1. Vernon, "History of the San Gabriel Mountains, Chapter III," 267.

2. "On Pack Horse to Final Rest," *Los Angeles Times*, August 17, 1914, II6; "Cities and Towns South of the Techachepi's," *Los Angeles Times*, August 24, 1914, II6.

3. "A Mountain Gem," *Trails Magazine* (Winter 1938), 13.

4. Stade, "Loomis Ranch—Last Homestead," 8.

5. Stade, "Loomis Ranch—Last Homestead," 9.

6. Stade, "Loomis Ranch—Last Homestead," 10.

7. Stade, "Loomis Ranch—Last Homestead," 11.

8. "San Bernardino County: Coal Bed Stretching from Colton to Redlands," *Los Angeles Times*, April 28, 1896, 11; James M. Oliver to Mr. A. J. Wheeler, Letter, September 14, 1923, folder HM73802, Wrightwood Papers, Huntington Library.

9. "Wright Ranch, M.S." pg. 6, folder HM73825, Wrightwood Papers, Huntington Library.

10. Smythe, *Conquest of Arid America*, 267.

11. "The Irrigationist," *Pacific Rural Press*, October 21, 1893, 280.

12. Smythe, *City Homes on Country Lanes*, 6, 13.

13. Smythe, *The Little Landers*, 1.

14. Smythe, *The Little Landers*, back cover.

15. Henry Chu, "Instead of Utopia, It Left a Lot of Lots to Be Desired," *Los Angeles Times*, January 8, 1996, B1.

16. "He Shed Tears," *Los Angeles Times*, December 14, 1894, 9; *Journal of the Senate During the Thirty-Ninth Session*, 29.

17. Sides, "The Sunland Grizzly," 36–46.

9. TAMING THE COLORADO DESERT

1. Harry Carr, "The Lancer," *Los Angeles Times*, August 22, 1931, A1.

2. James, *The Wonders of the Colorado Desert*, xix.

3. "The Development of the Great Southwest: In the Fields of Industry, Capital and Production," *Los Angeles Times*, November 5, 1899, 28; J. W. Jeffrey, "The Land: Orchard, Farm, Garden, Rancho and Stockyard," *Los Angeles Times*, August 9, 1901, 12.

4. Smith, *The Mojave Indians*, 97.

5. "Ten Freight Trains to Carry Melons," *Los Angeles Times*, May 28, 1902, 7.

6. "Homestead Rushers Besiege Indio," *Los Angeles Times*, November 24, 1901, B4; George W. Burton, "In Antelope Valley: Where Things Are Not Always What They Seem," *Los Angeles Times*, May 31, 1908, III3.

7. McWilliams, *Southern California*, 98.

8. Lindley and Widney, *California of the South*, 258; "Millionaire Closes Camp: Patients in Desert Resort Must Scatter," *Los Angeles Times*, November 18, 1907, I4; "Rigorous for Consumptives: Would Have the Government Regulate Their Care," *Los Angeles Times*, December 1, 1907, II15.

9. Campbell, *The Desert Was Home*, 18.

10. Campbell, *The Desert Was Home*, 86; James, *Wonders of the Colorado Desert*, xx, xxi.

11. James, *Wonders of the Colorado Desert*, xxi.

12. Campbell, *The Desert Was Home*, 29, 23, 64.

13. Campbell, *The Desert Was Home*, 40.

14. Bagley, *Sand in My Shoe*, 6–7, 3, 21.

15. Bagley, *Sand in My Shoe*, xv–xvi.

16. Bagley, *Sand in My Shoe*, 34, 36; Bagley refers to Tucker pseudonymously as Lillian Potter. "Jury Will Hear of Feud: Armed Desert Homesteaders Pack San Bernardino Courtroom as Tar-and-Feather Party Is Told," *Los Angeles Times*, March 20, 1928, 10; "Tar-Feather Feud Aired: Father and Son Give Version of Asserted Attack by Widow Homesteader of Desert Region," *Los Angeles Times*, April 28, 1928, 5.

17. Bagley, *Sand in My Shoe*, 35.

18. "Tar-Feather Feud Nipped: Woman's Vengeance Fails as Neighbors Balk," *Los Angeles Times*, March 17, 1928, 6; "Woman Gets Freedom in Desert Feud," *Los Angeles Times*, April 30, 1928, 13.

19. Bagley, *Sand in My Shoe*, 218; "Desert Feud Enters Court," *Los Angeles Times*, May 22, 1930, A8; William Endicott, "Rites Set Today for Prospector Desert Bill," *Los Angeles Times*, July 2, 1969, SG1.

20. "Two-Gun Man Again in Court," *Los Angeles Times*, September 10, 1927, 6.

21. Land Patent File for Bob Hollimon, RG 49, National Archives and Records Administration, Washington DC.

22. Land Patent File for Bob Hollimon.

10. IMPERIAL VALLEY DREAMS

1. Howe and Hall, *Story of the First Decade*, 203–4.

2. Wright, *Winning of Barbara Worth*, 12.

3. "Development of the Colorado Delta," *Imperial Valley Press*, June 14, 1902, 1.

4. Wright, *Winning of Barbara Worth*, 12; "Development of the Colorado Delta: Reliable Information and Sound Advice Given by a San Diego Business Man,"

Imperial Press and Farmer, June 14, 1902, 1. On the pace and nature of early twentieth-century railroad construction, Patrick W. O'Bannon has written: "Efficient, oil-burning locomotives, many times more powerful than the old, frail, wood burners, allowed engineers to construct roads over terrain once considered impassable. The disappearance of government subsidies and land grants resulted in the elimination of speed in construction. The roads were laid out with greater emphasis on acquiring the most practical, and profitable, route for the tracks. The de-emphasis on speed also resulted in smaller work crews, with a correspondingly slower pace of construction," O'Bannon, "Railroad Construction," 255–90; Charles Hillinger, "Impossible Railroad Still Operates Daily," *Los Angeles Times,* December 6, 1959, A.

5. "1912 Diary," box 1, George DeClyver Curtis Papers, Special Collections, Young Research Library, University of California, Los Angeles.

6. Curtis, *Bees' Ways,* 3, 65.

7. Farr, *History of Imperial County,* 50, 52, 56.

8. Howe and Hall, *Story of the First Decade,* 163.

9. "Riverside County Wants to Be Independent: Homesteaders Object to Speculators," *Los Angeles Herald,* December 12, 1901, 10; "Land Frauds in Imperial Valley: Prominent Men May Be Implicated in Plan to Swindle Government," *Mariposa Gazette,* August 17, 1907, 2.

10. Howe and Hall, *Story of the First Decade,* 99.

11. Howe and Hall, *Story of the First Decade,* 176.

12. DuBois, *Condition of the Mission Indians,* 9; "The Mission Indians Again," *The Indian's Friend,* February 1901, 7.

13. Andrés, *Power and Control,* 51, 106.

11. CRASHING THE ORANGE GATES

1. Armor, *History of Orange County,* 773, 774.

2. Cleland, *Irvine Ranch of Orange County,* 74, 79.

3. "Orange County: Squatter Schutte Makes Warm Work for the Sheriff," *Los Angeles Times,* August 15, 1897, 29; "Orange County: New Railroad Connection Made at Santa Ana," *Los Angeles Times,* August 20, 1897, 13.

4. "Finish Fight Begun for Land Fortune," *Los Angeles Times,* September 4, 1906, II1.

5. "Get the Best: *Price's Magazine of Psychology*," *Metaphysical Magazine,* December 1901, n.p.

6. "Kisses Only Willing Ones: So Says Psychic Sharp at Long Beach," *Los Angeles Times,* November 9, 1905, I17; "Tells of Bath Given Girl: Wife of Dr. W. R. Price Names Former Guest in Bill of Divorce as Co-respondent," *Los Angeles Times,* July 11, 1923, I8.

7. Robinson, *Land in California,* 131.

8. "Successful Settlers: Men Who Have Done Well in Southern California," *Los Angeles Times*, January 1, 1890, 27.

9. "Founded by Two L.A. Attorneys: Orange Got Its Start as Richland in 1870," *Los Angeles Times*, May 19, 1978, M6.

12. EXACTING LIVES IN THE BREADBASKET

1. Immigration Association of California, *Resources of the Southern San Joaquin Valley*, 59.

2. Vaught, *Cultivating California*, 11.

3. Gates, *Land and Law in California*, 259; McWilliams, *Factories in the Field*, 20; Peffer, *Closing of the Public Domain*, 154; Vaught, *Cultivating California*, 17; Eisen, *The Raisin Industry*, 46; Immigration Association of California, *Resources of the Southern San Joaquin Valley*, 16.

4. California Department of Food & Agriculture, "California Agricultural Statistics Review, 2015–2016," 8, ftp://ftp.consrv.ca.gov/pub/oil/annual_reports/2006/0102stats_06.pdf; Vandor, *History of Fresno County*, 190–91.

5. *Annual Report of the State Board of Horticulture*, 434; Vaught, *Cultivating California*, 21; Eisen, *The Raisin Industry*, 47, 84.

6. Eisen, *The Raisin Industry*, 106.

7. "Market Reports," *San Francisco Call*, December 14, 1892, 6; Vaught, *Cultivating California*, 21; "The Fresno Raisin Producers' Appeal," *Pacific Rural Press*, September 17, 1892, 233.

8. "The Raisin Problem," *Pacific Rural Press*, February 4, 1893, 93; "The Raisin Growers of Fresno," *Pacific Rural Press*, February 11, 1893, 126.

9. Steeples and Whitten, *Democracy in Desperation*, 21, 22; *Seventh Biennial Report*, 39; "The Raisin Victory and Its Lessons," *Pacific Rural Press*, December 23, 1899, 404.

10. Vandor, *History of Fresno County*, 2476.

11. Menefee and Dodge, *History of Tulare and Kings Counties*, 801.

12. Orsi, *Sunset Limited*, 96.

13. Orsi, *Sunset Limited*, 98.

14. "Old Warrior Dies," *Los Angeles Herald*, December 16, 1915, 19; Orsi, *Sunset Limited*, 102.

15. California State Mining Bureau, *Mines and Mineral Resources*, 111.

16. Shay, *Twenty Years in the Backwoods*, 11.

17. Shay, *Twenty Years in the Backwoods*, 28, 47.

18. Shay, *Twenty Years in the Backwoods*, 134.

19. Kroeber, *Handbook of the Indians of California*, 883.

20. Shay, *Twenty Years in the Backwoods*, 109.

21. Shay, *Twenty Years in the Backwoods*, 137.

22. Shay, *Twenty Years in the Backwoods*, 142.

13. THE RARIFIED BAY AREA

1. De Mille, "Henry George," 431. For more on George in California, see Barker, "Henry George and the California Background," 97–115.
2. Lotchin, *San Francisco, 1846–1856*, 63.
3. George, *Our Land and Land Policy, National and State*, 3, 5.
4. *An Illustrated History of Sonoma County, California*, 129.
5. *Fifty-Ninth Annual Report of the California State Board of Agriculture*, 180.
6. Baseline Consulting, *A Homestead Era*, 6, 7.
7. Baseline Consulting, *A Homestead Era*, 12.
8. Heig, *History of Petaluma*, 109.
9. Heig, *History of Petaluma*, 109.
10. Gregory, *History of Sonoma County, California*, 939.
11. "Uncle Sam Still Has California Farms to Give Away for a Song," *San Francisco Call*, April 2, 1911, 5.
12. Cox, *Single Woman Homesteader*, 17–18.
13. "City Real Estate," *San Francisco Chronicle*, September 30, 1887, 5.
14. Gregory, *History of Sonoma County, California*, 341.
15. Land Patent File for Charles Pritchard, RG 49, National Archives and Records Administration, Washington DC.
16. Hillyer, *Reports of Cases Determined*, 514.
17. Wallace, *History of Napa County*, 213; "A Fertile Region: Valleys of Eastern Napa County," *San Francisco Chronicle*, March 17, 1884, 2.
18. Edredge, *The Beginnings of San Francisco*, 406–7; Pitt, *Decline of the Californios*, 30.
19. Gregory, *History of Solano and Napa Counties*, 144, 217.
20. Land Patent File for José Jesus Berreyesa, RG 49, National Archives and Records Administration, Washington DC.
21. *Solano County News*, July 19, 1914, 35; Lange and Jones, *Death of a Valley*.

14. AMONG THE TREES OF THE NORTH COAST

1. Willis and Stockton, *Debates and Proceedings*, 1144.
2. Rawls and Bean, *California: An Interpretive History*, 9th ed., 198.
3. *Report of the Public Lands Commission*, xxxii.
4. Gates, *History of Public Land Law Development*, 418; Farmer, *Trees in Paradise*, 36.
5. Cornford, "To Save the Republic," 137.
6. Willis and Stockton, *Debates and Proceedings*, 1144.
7. Cornford, "To Save the Republic," 131.
8. Rawls and Bean, *California: An Interpretive History*, 9th ed., 198. For a useful synopsis of the failures of the second constitution, see pages 199–200 of their work.

9. *History and Business Directory of Humboldt County*, 91; "The Eureka Outbreak," *Daily Alta California*, January 23, 1886, 1; Carranco, "Chinese Expulsion from Humboldt County," 329–40; Commission to the State and Mechanics' Institute Fairs, *Humboldt County, California*, 9.

10. Commission to the State and Mechanics' Institute Fairs, *Humboldt County, California*, 7.

11. Irvine, *History of Humboldt County*, 1239.

12. Eames, "Upland Pastures," 523–24.

13. Land Patent File for Jeremiah M. Standley, RG 49, National Archives and Records Administration, Washington DC; Boessenecker, *Badge and Buckshot*, 85–86.

14. Palmer, *History of Mendocino County*, 349; Boessenecker, *Badge and Buckshot*, 100.

15. Eames, "Upland Pastures," 519.

16. Land Patent File for Jeremiah M. Standley.

17. Land Patent File for Cyrus J. Cole, RG 49, National Archives and Records Administration, Washington DC.

18. Raphael, *Cash Crop*, 11.

19. Raphael, *Cash Crop*, 12.

20. Richard Goering, "Back to the Land, Phase II," *San Francisco Chronicle*, May 29, 1977, 239; Raphael, *Cash Crop*, 8.

15. UNDER THE SHADOW OF MOUNT LASSEN

1. Holway, "Volcanic Activity of Lassen Peak," 294–95.

2. Hudson, "McCloud River Affair of 1909," 29–35; "American Loggers at McCloud Join Striking Italians," *San Francisco Call*, June 6, 1909.

3. "Outbreaks Sunday More Violent Than Those Preceding," *Sacramento Union*, June 15, 1914, 1; "Snow Saves Party from Fatal Gas," *Los Angeles Herald*, June 15, 1914, 1; "Lassen in Another Eruption," *San Francisco Chronicle*, June 16, 1914, 1.

4. Strong, *"These Happy Grounds,"* 39.

5. "Man Hit by Volcano to Go to Expo," *Red Bluff Daily News*, March 31, 1915, 1; Holway, "Volcanic Activity of Lassen Peak," 86.

6. Strong, *"These Happy Grounds,"* 39; "Lassen Volcano Destroys Home," *Mariposa Gazette*, May 29, 1915, 2.

7. Keeler, *Earthquakes in California in 1889*, 18; "Volcanoes in the Sierra Nevadas," *Press Democrat*, August 27, 1889, 1; "Homesteaders on Mt. Lassen Ask Aid," *Sacramento Union*, November 1, 1914, 1; "Lassen Settlers Fear Active Volcano," *Red Bluff News*, November 6, 1914, 6; "Farmers Fear Ashes from Mt. Lassen Will Block Ditches," *Sacramento Union*, April 10, 1915, 7.

8. "The City Man's Chances in Agriculture," *Mill Valley Record*, March 4, 1916, 8.

9. Land Patent File for Ruth Berg, RG 49, National Archives and Records Administration, Washington DC.

10. Land Patent File for Ruth Berg.
11. "A Girl Homesteader in California," *San Francisco Sunday Call*, February 18, 1912, 28.

CONCLUSION

1. Campbell, *The Desert Was Home*, 67.
2. Gigante and Brown, *Cabot Abram Yerxa*, 28, 36.
3. Gigante and Brown, *Cabot Abram Yerxa*, 93.
4. Colman, "John Ballard and the African American Community," 193–229.
5. Daily, *An Album of Memories*, 162, as cited in Colman, "John Ballard and the African American Community," 221; "Pioneer Gets Proper Tribute: Negrohead Mountain Is Renamed after John Ballard, a Former Slave," *Los Angeles Times*, February 24, 2010, AA3.
6. Asher, "My Palomar," unpublished manuscript, 17; Mallios and Stroud, "Preliminary Excavations," 71.
7. Gates, *History of Public Land Law Development*, 614; *Congressional Record*, 12–13; "Who Wants to Live a Grasshopper's Life," *San Francisco Chronicle*, October 10, 1930, 26.
8. "U.S. Offers 7,000 Acres at Lucerne for Homesites," *San Bernardino Daily Sun*, December 29, 1955, 11, 15.
9. Kursh, *How to Get Land from Uncle Sam*, 37; Peffer, *Closing of the Public Domain*, 291; Library of Congress: Law, "Statutes at Large," Chapter 317, Session 3 (1938), 75th Congress, https://www.loc.gov/law/help/statutes-at-large/75th-congress.php#3, accessed June 24, 2020.
10. "View of Dry Reaches Suddenly in Demand," *Los Angeles Times*, February 25, 1945, A1; United States Department of the Interior, *Small Tracts*, 8; Kursh, *How to Get Land from Uncle Sam*, 38; Peffer, *Closing of the Public Domain*, 291; United States Department of the Interior, *Small Tracts*, 3.
11. "View of Dry Reaches Suddenly in Demand," A1.
12. "View of Dry Reaches Suddenly in Demand," A1; "Public Land Leased," *Los Angeles Times*, March 14, 1948, A5; "U.S. Offers 7,000 Acres at Lucerne for Homesites," *San Bernardino Sun*, December 29, 1955, 10, 15; Ray Herbert, "Land-Hungry Bid for Desert Plots," *Los Angeles Times*, June 16, 1958, 2.
13. Stedman, "Jackrabbit Homesteader," 16.
14. Stedman, "Jackrabbit Homesteader," 16.
15. Doug Mauldin, "Shetlanders Out front in 'Leisure-Home' Boom," *Los Angeles Times*, November 19, 1961, CS7. The last tract of land claimed in California under the Small Tract Act was in 1976. Diana Marcum, "Shack Attack Is Cleaning Up Desert. Communities: Morongo Basin residents have launched a campaign to tear down rickety cabins that litter the area," *Los Angeles Times*, July 11, 1999, 8.

16. *Public Land Laws*, 82; *One Third of the Nation's Land*, 178; "Symbols, Aged and Altered," *New York Times*, May 10, 1977, 26.

17. Cannon, *Reopening the Frontier*, 2; Nash, "Problems and Projects," 327–40.

18. Kaufman, "New Homesteading Movement," 63.

19. Kaysing, *The Ex-Urbanite's Complete and Illustrated Easy-Does-It First-Time Farmer's Guide: A Useful Book*.

20. Campbell, *The Desert Was Home*, 256.

21. The rate of home ownership among whites, for example, dropped from 56.5 percent to 47 percent between 1870 and 1910. See Collins and Margo, "Race and Home Ownership," American Economic Association, 17; see also Collins and Margo, "Race and Home Ownership," *American Economic Review*, 355–59. On typical loan terms, see Vandell, "FHA Restructuring Proposal," 301; Brewer, "Eastern Money and Western Mortgages," 356, 357; Vale, "Ideological Origins of Affordable Homeownership," 34.

22. Adams, *The Epic of America*, 363, 404, 406.

23. Vandell, "FHA Restructuring Proposal," 301–2, 307–8; Ashbee, *U.S. Politics Today*, 259.

24. U.S. Census Bureau, "Quarterly Residential Vacancies and Homeownership, Fourth Quarter 2018," https://www.census.gov/housing/hvs/files/qtr418/Q418press.pdf, published February 28, 2019. David Leonhardt, "A Word of Advice During a Housing Slump: Rent," *New York Times*, April 11, 2007, A1.

BIBLIOGRAPHY

ARCHIVAL SOURCES

Asher, Robert H. "My Palomar." Unpublished manuscript, ca. 1938, 17. Author's collection.

Curtis Collection, George DeClyver. Special Collections. Young Research Library. University of California, Los Angeles.

Death Valley Automobile Trip Collection. Bancroft Library. University of California, Berkeley.

Land Case Files. Bancroft Library. University of California, Berkeley.

Los Angeles Court Records. Huntington Library. San Marino, California.

Los Angeles Land Office Records. Record Group 49. National Archives. Riverside, California.

Records of District Courts of the United States. Record Group 21. National Archives. Riverside, California.

Records of the Bureau of Land Management. Record Group 49. National Archives. San Bruno, California.

Records of the Bureau of Land Management. Record Group 49. National Archives. Washington DC.

Wrightwood Papers. Huntington Library. San Marino, California.

PUBLISHED SOURCES

Adams, Frank. *Irrigation Districts in California, 1887–1915*. Sacramento: California State Printing Office, 1916.

Adams, James Truslow. *The Epic of America*. Boston: Little, Brown, 1931.

Almond Colonies of Southern California: Antelope Valley. Almendro CA: 1893.

Andrés, Benny J., Jr. *Power and Control in the Imperial Valley: Nature, Agribusiness, and Workers on the California Borderland, 1900–1940*. College Station: Texas A&M University Press, 2015.

Annual Publication of the Historical Society of Southern California and of the Pioneers of Los Angeles County, 1903. Los Angeles: Geo. Rice & Sons, 1904.

Annual Report of the State Board of Horticulture of the State of California for 1892. Sacramento: Superintendent of State Printing, 1892.

Annual Report of the State Board of Horticulture of the State of California for 1899. Sacramento: Superintendent of State Printing, 1899.

Arax, Mark. *The Dreamt Land: Chasing Water and Dust Across California.* New York: Vintage, 2020.

Arax, Mark, and Rick Wartzman. *The King of California: J. G. Boswell and the Making of a Secret American Empire.* New York: PublicAffairs, 2003.

Armor, Samuel. *History of Orange County, California: With Biographical Sketches of the Leading Men and Women of the County Who Have Been Identified with Its Earliest Growth.* Los Angeles: Historic Record Company, 1921.

Ashbee, Edward. *U.S. Politics Today.* 2nd ed. Manchester: Manchester University Press, 2004.

Bagley, Helen. *Sand in My Shoe: Homestead Days in Twentynine Palms.* Twentynine Palms: Homestead, 1978.

Barker, Charles A. "Henry George and the California Background of 'Progress and Poverty.'" *California Historical Society Quarterly* (June 1945): 97–115.

Baseline Consulting. *A Homestead Era History of Nunns' Canyon and Calabazas Creek Preserve, c. 1850–1910.* Glen Ellen CA: Baseline Consulting, 2013.

Beasely, Delilah L. *The Negro Trail Blazers of California.* Los Angeles: D. L. Beasley, 1919.

Beers, Terry, ed. *Gunfight at Mussel Slough: Evolution of a Western Myth.* Berkeley: Heyday, 2004.

Bell, Horace. *Reminiscences of a Ranger or, Early Times in Southern California.* Los Angeles: Yarnell, Caystile, and Mathes, 1881.

Bentley, Arthur F. "The Condition of the Western Farmer as Illustrated by the Economic History of a Nebraska Township." *Johns Hopkins University Studies in Historical and Political Science* (July–August 1893): 27.

Blanchard, Sarah Elliott. *Memories of a Child's Early California Days.* Los Angeles: privately printed, 1961.

Boessenecker, John. *Badge and Buckshot: Lawlessness in Old California.* Norman: University of Oklahoma Press, 1993.

Bogue, Allan G. "An Agricultural Empire." In *The Oxford History of the American West,* edited by Clyde A. Milner II, Carol A. O'Connor, and Martha A. Sandweiss, 275–314. New York: Oxford University Press, 1994.

———. "The Iowa Claim Clubs: Symbols and Substance." *The Mississippi Valley Historical Review* 45, no. 2 (September 1958): 231–53.

Bottles, Scott L. *Los Angeles and the Automobile: The Making of the Modern City.* Berkeley: University of California Press, 1987.

Brewer, H. Peers. "Eastern Money and Western Mortgages in the 1870s." *Business History Review* 50 (Autumn 1976): 356, 357.

Burlingame, Michael. *Abraham Lincoln: A Life.* Vol. 2. Baltimore: Johns Hopkins University Press, 2008.

Burmeister, Eugene. *The Golden Empire: Kern County, California.* Norwalk CA: Stockton Trade, 1977.

California Commission on Immigration and Housing. *A Report on Large Landholdings in Southern California with Recommendations.* Sacramento: California State Printing Office, 1919.

California County Agricultural Commissioners' Report, Crop Year 2016–2017. Sacramento: California Department of Food and Agriculture, 2018.

California County Agricultural Commissioners' Report, Crop Year 2012–2013. Sacramento: California Department of Food and Agriculture, 2015.

California State Agricultural Society. *Transactions of the State Agricultural Society During the Year 1882.* Sacramento: California State Printing Office, 1882.

California State Mining Bureau. *Mines and Mineral Resources of the Counties of Fresno, Kern, Kings, Madera, Mariposa, Merced, San Joaquin, Stanislaus.* Sacramento: California State Printing Office, 1915.

Campbell, Elizabeth W. Crozer. *The Desert Was Home.* Los Angeles: Westernlore, 1961.

Cannon, Brian Q. "Homesteading Remembered: A Sesquicentennial Perspective." *Agricultural History* 87 (Winter 2013): 1–29.

———. *Reopening the Frontier: Homesteading in the Modern West.* Lawrence: University Press of Kansas, 2009.

Carranco, Lynwood. "Chinese Expulsion from Humboldt County." *Pacific Historical Review* (November 1961): 329–40.

Central Pacific Railroad Company. *A List of Government and Railroad Lands in California Open to Preemption, or Homestead, or to Purchase, Along the Lines of the Central Pacific, and the California and Oregon Railroads.* San Francisco: Central Pacific Railroad, 1886.

Clay, Karen, and Werner Troesken. "Ranchos and the Politics of Land Claims." In *Land of Sunshine: An Environmental History of Metropolitan Los Angeles,* edited by William F. Deverell and Greg Hise, 52–70. Pittsburgh: University of Pittsburgh Press, 2005.

Cleland, Robert Glass. *The Irvine Ranch of Orange County, 1810–1950.* San Marino: Huntington, 1952.

Clifton, A. R. "History of the Communistic Colony Llano Del Rio." *Annual Publication of the Historical Society of Southern California* 11 (1918), 80.

Collins, William J., and Robert A. Margo. "Race and Home Ownership from the End of the Civil War to the Present." American Economic Association Conference Paper, Denver CO, 2011, 17.

————. "Race and Home Ownership from the End of the Civil War to the Present." *American Economic Review* 101 (May 2011): 355–59.

Colman, Patty R. "John Ballard and the African American Community in Los Angeles, 1850–1905." *Southern California Quarterly* 94 (Summer 2012): 193–229.

————. "Women Settlers in the Santa Monica Mountains." Unpublished manuscript, 2006.

Commission to the State and Mechanics' Institute Fairs. *Humboldt County, California: A Pamphlet Descriptive of Its Climate, Resources and Advantages.* San Francisco: A. J. Leary, 1888.

Congressional Record, 73rd Congress, 2nd Session, March 10, 1934.

Cornford, Daniel. "To Save the Republic: The California Workingmen's Party in Humboldt County." *California History* 66 (June 1987): 130–42.

Costanso, Miguel. *The Narrative of the Portola Expedition of 1769–1770.* Edited by Adolph Van Hemert-Engert and Frederick J. Teggart. Berkeley: University of California Press, 1910.

Cox, Leona Dixon. *Single Woman Homesteader.* Dobbins CA: Inkwell, 1991.

Crutcher, Charles W. *Tales from Topanga.* Self-published, 1927.

Culver, Lawrence. *The Frontier of Leisure: Southern California and the Shaping of Modern America.* New York: Oxford University Press, 2010.

Curtis, George DeClyver. *Bees' Ways.* Boston: Houghton Mifflin Company, 1948.

Daily, Wendell P. *An Album of Memories.* Santa Barbara: Schauer, 1946.

Davis, Mike. *City of Quartz: Excavating the Future in Los Angeles.* New York: Verso, 1990.

Davy, Donald L. *California Homesteads: Accurate Information for the Homesteader, Homeseeker, Tourist.* Fresno CA: D. L. Davy, 1933.

de Mille, Anna George. "Henry George: Early California Period." *American Journal of Economics and Sociology* (July 1942): 431–46.

Deverell, William F. "To Loosen the Safety Valve: Eastern Workers and Western Lands." *Western Historical Quarterly* 19 (August 1988): 269–85.

————. *Whitewashed Adobe: The Rise of Los Angeles and the Remaking of Its Mexican Past.* Berkeley: University of California Press, 2004.

Dick, Everett. *The Lure of the Land: A Social History of the Public Lands from the Articles of Confederation to the New Deal.* Lincoln: University of Nebraska Press, 1970.

DuBois, Constance Goddard. *The Condition of the Mission Indians of Southern California.* Philadelphia: Office of the Indian Rights Association, 1901.

Dumke, Glenn. "The Boom of the 1880s in Southern California." *Southern California Quarterly* 76 (Spring 1994): 104.

Eames, Ninetta. "Upland Pastures." *Cosmopolitan* (March 1896): 519–24.

Edredge, Zoeth Skinner. *The Beginnings of San Francisco from the Expedition of Anza, 1774, to the City Charter of April 15, 1850.* San Francisco: Z. S. Eldredge, 1912.

Edwards, Richard, Jacob K. Friefeld, and Rebecca S. Wingo. *Homesteading the Plains: Toward a New History*. Lincoln: University of Nebraska Press, 2017.

1870 Census: A Compendium of the Ninth Census. Washington DC: Government Printing Office, 1872.

Eisen, Gustav. *The Raisin Industry: A Practical Treatise on the Raisin Grapes, Their History, Culture and Curing*. San Francisco: H. S. Crocker, 1890.

Estrada, William D. *The Los Angeles Plaza: Sacred and Contested Space*. Austin: University of Texas Press, 2008.

Faragher, John Mack. *Eternity Street: Violence and Justice in Frontier Los Angeles*. New York: W. W. Norton, 2016.

Farmer, Jared. *Trees in Paradise: A California History*. New York: W. W. Norton, 2013.

Farr, F. C. *The History of Imperial County, California*. Berkeley: Elms and Franks, 1918.

Fellmeth, Robert C. *Politics of Land: Ralph Nader's Study Group Report on Land Use in California*. New York: Grossman, 1973.

Fifth Biennial Report of the Department of Engineering of the State of California, December 1, 1914 to November 30, 1916. Sacramento: California State Printing Office, 1917.

Fifty-Ninth Annual Report of the California State Board of Agriculture for the Year 1912. Sacramento: California State Printing Office, 1913.

Fogelson, Robert M. *Fragmented Metropolis: Los Angeles, 1850–1930*. Berkeley: University of California Press, 1993 (1968).

Fourteenth Census of the United States: 1920, Bulletin, California. Washington DC: Government Printing Office, 1921.

Fourteenth Census of the United States Taken in the Year 1920, Population. Washington DC: Government Printing Office, 1921.

Fraser, Caroline. *Prairie Fires: The American Dreams of Laura Ingalls Wilder*. New York: Metropolitan Books, 2017.

Frymer, Paul. *Building an Empire: The Era of Territorial and Political Expansion*. Princeton: Princeton University Press, 2017.

Gates, Paul W. "The California Land Act of 1851." *California Historical Quarterly* 50, no. 4 (December 1971): 395–430.

———. *History of Public Land Law Development*. Washington DC: Public Land Law Review Commission, 1968.

———. *Land and Law in California: Essays on Land Policies*. Ames: Iowa State University Press, 1991.

———. *Land Policies in Kern County*. Bakersfield: Kern County Historical Society, 1978.

———. "The Suscol Principle, Preemption, and California Latifundia." *Pacific Historical Review* 39, no. 4 (November 1970): 453–71.

George, Henry. *Our Land and Land Policy, National and State*. San Francisco: Winterburn, 1871.

————. *Our Land and Land Policy: Speeches, Lectures and Miscellaneous Writings*. Garden City NY: Doubleday, Page, 1911.

"Get the Best: *Price's Magazine of Psychology*." *Metaphysical Magazine*, December 1901, n.p.

Gigante, Judy, and Richard E. Brown. *Cabot Abram Yerxa: On the Desert Since 1913*. Desert Hot Springs CA: Cabot's Museum Foundation, 2013.

Gregory, James N. *American Exodus: The Dust Bowl Migration and Okie Culture in California*. New York: Oxford University Press, 1989.

Gregory, Thomas Jefferson. *History of Solano and Napa Counties, California: With Biographical Sketches of the Leading Men and Women of the Counties, Who Have Been Identified with Its Growth and Development from the Early Days to the Present Time*. Los Angeles: Historic Record Company, 1912.

————. *History of Sonoma County, California: With Biographical Sketches of the Leading Men and Women of the County, Who Have Been Identified with Its Growth and Development from the Early Days to the Present Time*. Los Angeles: Historic Record Company, 1911.

Grenier, Judson A. "'Officialdom': California State Government, 1849–1879." *California History* 81, nos. 3/4 (2003): 145.

Guinn, James Miller. *Historical and Biographical Record of Southern California: Containing a History of Southern California from its Earliest Settlement to the Opening Year of the Twentieth Century*. Chicago: Chapman, 1902.

Haas, Lisbeth. *Conquests and Historical Identities in California, 1769–1936*. Berkeley: University of California Press, 1995.

Hackel, Steven. *Children of Coyote, Missionaries of Saint Francis: Indian-Spanish Relations in Colonial California, 1769–1850*. Chapel Hill: University of North Carolina Press, 2005.

Hamm, Lillie E. *History and Business Directory of Humboldt County, Descriptive of the Natural Resources, Climate, Scenery*. Eureka CA: Daily Humboldt Standard, 1890.

Hayes-Bautista, David E. *El Cinco de Mayo: An American Tradition*. Berkeley: University of California Press, 2012.

Heig, Adair. *History of Petaluma: A California River Town*. Petaluma: Scottwall, 1982.

Hillyer, Curtis J. *Reports of Cases Determined in the California Supreme Court*. Vol. 21. San Francisco: Bancroft-Whitney, 1906.

History and Business Directory of Humboldt County: Descriptive of the Natural Resources, Delightful Climate, Picturesque Scenery, Beautiful Homes. Eureka CA: Daily Humboldt Standard, 1890.

Holway, Ruliff S. "Preliminary Report on the Recent Volcanic Activity of Lassen Peak." *Bulletin of the American Geographical Society* 46 (1914): 740–55.

————. "The Volcanic Activity of Lassen Peak, California." *Popular Science Monthly* 86 (March 1915): 274–89.

Howe, Edgar F., and Wilbur Jay Hall. *The Story of the First Decade in Imperial Valley, California*. Imperial CA: Edgar F. Howes, 1910.

Hudson, James J. "The McCloud River Affair of 1909: A Study in the Use of State Troops." *California Historical Society Quarterly* 35 (March 1956): 29–35.

Huffman, Margaret. *Wild Heart of Los Angeles: The Santa Monica Mountains.* Niwot CO: Roberts Rinehart, 1998.

Humboldt County, California. Eureka: Eureka Printing, 1915.

Igler, David. *Miller & Lux and the Transformation of the Far West, 1850–1920*. Berkeley: University of California Press, 2005.

Illustrated History of Sonoma County, California. Containing a History of the County of Sonoma from the Earliest Period of Its Occupancy to the Present. Chicago: Lewis, 1889.

Illustrated History of Los Angeles County. Chicago: Lewis, 1889.

Immigration Association of California. *California*. San Francisco: Chicago and North-western Railway, 1882.

———. *Resources of the Southern San Joaquin Valley, California: Fresno, Tulare, and Kern Counties.* San Francisco: Immigration Association of California, 1885.

Irvine, Leigh H. *History of Humboldt County, California, with Biographical Sketches of the Leading Men and Women of the County Who Have Been Identified with Its Growth and Development from the Early Days to the Present.* Los Angeles: Historic Record Company, 1915.

James, George Wharton. *Antelope Valley: Los Angeles County, California.* San Francisco: Southern Pacific Railroad, 1917.

———. *The Wonders of the Colorado Desert.* Vol. 1. Boston: Little, Brown, 1906.

Johnson, Harry R. *Water Resources of Antelope Valley.* Washington DC: Government Printing Office, 1911.

Johnson, Michelle (ed.). *The Topanga Story.* Topanga CA: Topanga Historical Society, 2011.

Journal of the Senate During the Thirty-Ninth Session of the Legislature of the State of California, 1911. Sacramento: Superintendent of State Printing, 1911.

Katz, Stanley N. "Thomas Jefferson and Right to Property in Revolutionary America." *Journal of Law & Economics* 19 (October 1976): 467–88.

Kaufman, Maynard. "The New Homesteading Movement: From Utopia to Eutopia." *Soundings: An Interdisciplinary Journal* 55 (Spring 1972): 63–82.

Kaysing, Bill. *The Ex-Urbanite's Complete and Illustrated Easy-Does-It First-Time Farmer's Guide: A Useful Book.* New York: Straight Arrow, 1971.

Keeler, James Edward. *Earthquakes in California in 1889: Department of the Interior Bulletin of the United States Geological Survey.* Washington DC: Government Printing Office, 1890.

Kindall, Cleve E. "Southern Vineyards: The Economic Significance of the Wine Industry in the Development of Los Angeles, 1831–1870." *Historical Society of Southern California Quarterly* 41 (March 1959): 26–37.

King, Chester. *Prehistoric Native American Cultural Sites in the Santa Monica Mountains.* Topanga CA: Topanga Anthropological Consultants, 1994.

Kneipp, Leon F. *Land Planning and Acquisition, U.S. Forest Service: Oral History Transcript / and Related Material, 1964–1976.* Berkeley: Bancroft Library Regional Oral History Office, 1972.

Krall, Lisi. "Thomas Jefferson's Agrarian Vision and the Changing Nature of Property." *Journal of Economic Issues* 36 (March 2002): 137–38.

Kroeber, A. L. *Handbook of the Indians of California.* Washington DC: Government Printing Office, 1925.

Kursh, Harry. *How to Get Land from Uncle Sam.* New York: W. W. Norton, 1955.

Lange, Dorothea, and Pirkle Jones. *Death of a Valley.* Rochester NY: Aperture, 1960.

Larson, Eva, and Albert Knight. "Re-Visiting the Treasure House, CA-VEN-195." *Proceedings of the Society for California Archaeology* 28 (March 2014): 356–72.

Lebergott, Stanley. "Wage Trends, 1800–1900." In Conference on Research in Income and Wealth, *Trends in the American Economy in the Nineteenth Century,* 449–500. Princeton NJ: Conference on Research in Income and Wealth, 1960.

Limerick, Patricia. *The Legacy of Conquest: The Unbroken Past of the American West.* New York and London: W. W. Norton, 1987.

Lincoln, Elliot Curtis. *Rhymes of a Homesteader.* Boston and New York: Houghton Mifflin, 1920.

Lindert, Peter H., and Jeffrey G. Williamson. *Unequal Gains: American Growth and Inequality since 1700.* Princeton: Princeton University Press, 2016.

Lindley, Walter, and J. P. Widney. *California of the South: Its Physical Geography, Climate, Mineral Springs, Resources, Routes of Travel, and Health-Resorts, Being a Complete Guide-Book to Southern California.* New York: D. Appleton, 1896.

Long, Clarence Dickenson. *Wages and Earnings in the United States, 1860–1890.* Princeton: Princeton University Press, 1960.

Los Angeles Chamber of Commerce, Agriculture Department. *Agricultural Survey of the Antelope Valley.* Los Angeles: Chamber of Commerce, 1924.

Los Angeles City Directory, 1893. Los Angeles: W. H. L. Corran, 1893.

Lotchin, Roger W. *San Francisco, 1846–1856: From Hamlet to City.* New York: Oxford University Press, 1974.

MacDonald, Glen M. "Southern California and the Perfect Drought: Simultaneous Prolonged Drought in Southern California and the Sacramento and Colorado River Systems." *Quaternary International* (2007): 1–13.

Madley, Benjamin. *An American Genocide: The United States and the California Indian Catastrophe, 1846–1873.* New Haven: Yale University Press, 2017.

Mallios, Seth, and Sarah Stroud. "Preliminary Excavations at the Nate Harrison Site." *Proceedings of the Society for California Archaeology* 19 (2006): 71–74.

Marks, Bernard. *Small-Scale Farming in Central California.* San Francisco: Crocker, 1882.

McWilliams, Carey. *Factories in the Field: The Story of Migratory Farm Labor in California.* Berkeley: University of California Press, 1999 (1935).

———. *Southern California: An Island on the Land.* Layton UT: Peregrine Smith, 1980 (1946).

Menchaca, Martha. *Recovering History, Constructing Race: The Indian, Black, and White Roots of Mexican Americans.* Austin: University of Texas Press, 2001.

Menefee, Eugene L., and Fred A. Dodge. *History of Tulare and Kings Counties: Biographical Sketches of the Leading Men and Women of the Counties Who Have Been Identified with Their Growth and Development from the Early Days to the Present.* Los Angeles: Historical Record Company, 1912.

Miller, Bruce W. *The Gabrielino.* Los Osos CA: San River Press, 1991.

Morgan, Edmund S. "Slavery and Freedom: The American Paradox." *Journal of American History* 59 (June 1972): 8.

Morgan, Wallace Melvin. *History of Kern County, California with Biographical Sketches of the Leading Men and Women of the County Who Have Been Identified with Its Growth and Development from the Early Days to the Present.* Los Angeles: Historic Record Company, 1914.

"A Mountain Gem." *Trails Magazine,* Winter 1938, 13.

Nash, Gerald D. "The California State Land Office." *Huntington Library Quarterly* 27 (August 1964): 348–49, 353.

———. "Problems and Projects in the History of Nineteenth-Century California Land Policy." *Arizona and the West* 2, no. 4 (Winter 1960): 327–40.

Netz, Joseph. "The Great Los Angeles Real Estate Boom of 1887." *Annual Publication of the Historical Society of Southern California* (1915–16): 54–68.

O'Bannon, Patrick W. "Railroad Construction in the Early Twentieth Century: The San Diego and Arizona Railway." *Southern California Quarterly* 61 (Fall 1979): 255–90.

Olmstead, Alan L., and Paul W. Rhode. "The Evolution of California Agriculture, 1850–2000." In *California Agriculture: Dimensions and Issues,* edited by Jerome B. Siebert, 1–28. Berkeley: University of California Press, 2004.

One Third of the Nation's Land: A Report to the President and to the Congress. Washington DC: Government Printing Office, 1970.

Orsi, Richard J. *Sunset Limited: The Southern Pacific Railroad and the Development of the American West, 1850–1930.* Berkeley: University of California Press, 2005.

Outland, Charles E. *Sespe Gunsmoke: An Epic Case of Rancher Versus Squatters.* Norman OK: Arthur H. Clark, 1991.

Owen, Rob. *Gen X TV: The Brady Bunch to Melrose Place.* Syracuse: Syracuse University Press, 1997.

Pacific Reporter 45. St. Paul: West, 1896.

Palmer, Lyman L. *History of Mendocino County, California: Comprising its Geography, Geology, Topography, Climatology, Springs and Timber.* San Francisco: Alley, Bowman, 1880.

Peffer, E. Louise. *The Closing of the Public Domain: Disposal and Reservation Policies 1900–1950.* Stanford: Stanford University Press, 1951.

Peñalver, Eduardo Moisés, and Sonia K. Katyal. "Property Outlaws." *University of Pennsylvania Law Review* (May 2007): 1108.

Peterson, Richard H. "The Failure to Reclaim: California State Swamp Land Policy and the Sacramento Valley, 1850–1866." *Southern California Quarterly* 56, no. 1 (Spring 1974): 45, 47.

Phillips, George Harwood. "Indians in Los Angeles, 1781–1875: Economic Integration, Social Disintegration." *Pacific Historical Review* 49 (August 1980): 448.

Pisani, Donald J. *From the Family Farm to Agribusiness: The Irrigation Crusade in California and the West, 1850–1931.* Berkeley: University of California Press, 1984.

———. "Land Monopoly in Nineteenth-Century California." *Agricultural History* 65, no. 4 (Autumn 1991): 16.

———. "The Squatter and Natural Law in Nineteenth-Century America." *Agricultural History* 81 (Fall 2007): 444.

Pitt, Leonard. *The Decline of the Californios: A Social History of the Spanish-Speaking Californians, 1846–1890.* Berkeley: University of California Press, 1998 (1966).

Prior, Jan M. "Kinship, Environment and the Forest Service: Homesteading in Oregon's Coast Range." Master's thesis, Oregon State University, 1998.

Public Land Laws: Hearings, Eighty-Eighth Congress, Second Session, on H.R. 5159 and 8087, June 29, and 30, 1964. Washington DC: Government Printing Office, 1964.

Pubols, Louise. *The Father of All: The de la Guerra Family, Power, and Patriarchy in Mexican California.* San Marino: Huntington Library and University of California Press, 2010.

Raphael, Ray. *Cash Crop: An American Dream.* Mendocino CA: Ridge Times, 1985.

Rawls, James J., and Walton Bean. *California: An Interpretive History.* 8th ed. Columbus OH: McGraw-Hill, 2001.

———. *California: An Interpretive History,* 9th ed. New York: McGraw Hill, 2008.

Report of the Commissioner of Agriculture for the Year 1879. Washington: Government Printing Office, 1880.

Report of the Commissioner of Agriculture for the Year 1884. Washington: Government Printing Office, 1884.

Report of the Public Lands Commission: Public Lands in the Western Portion of the United States and to the Operation of Existing Land Laws. Washington: GPO, 1880.

Reports of Cases Determined in the Supreme Court of the State of California. Vol. 117. San Francisco: Bancroft-Whitney, 1906.

Reports of the Joint Committees on Swamp and Overflowed Lands and Land Monopoly. Sacramento: G. H. Springer, 1874.

Rindge, Frederick Hastings. *Happy Days in Southern California.* Cambridge and Los Angeles: Self-published, 1898.

Robbins, Roy M. *Our Landed Heritage: The Public Domain, 1776–1936.* Lincoln: University of Nebraska Press, 1962 (1942).

Robinson, J. W. "A California Copperhead: Henry Hamilton and the Los Angeles Star," *Arizona and the West* 23, no. 3 (Autumn 1981).

Robinson, W. W. *Land in California: The Story of Mission Lands, Ranchos, Squatters, Mining Claims, Railroad Grants, Land Scrip, Homesteads.* Berkeley and Los Angeles: University of California Press, 1948.

———. "The Rancho Story of San Fernando Valley." *Historical Society of Southern California Quarterly* 38 (September 1956): 226.

Seventh Biennial Report of the State Board of Horticulture of the State of California, 1899–1900. Sacramento: State Printing Office, 1901.

Sharp, Maud Morrow, and Margaret Sharp Moore. *Maruba: Homesteading the Landfair Valley.* Goffs CA: Mojave Desert Heritage & Cultural Association, 2004.

Shay, John C. *Twenty Years in the Backwoods of California.* Boston: Roxburgh, 1923.

Shelton, Tamara Venit. *A Squatter's Republic: Land and the Politics of Monopoly in California, 1850–1900.* Berkeley: University of California Press/Huntington-USC Institute on California and the West, 2013.

Sides, Josh. "The Sunland Grizzly." *Natural History* (June 2014): 36–46.

Skillen, James R. *The Nation's Largest Landlord: The Bureau of Land Management in the American West.* Lawrence: University of Kansas Press, 2009.

Smith, Gerald A. *The Mojave Indians.* Bloomington CA: San Bernardino Museum, 1977.

———. *The Mojaves: Historic Indians of San Bernardino County.* San Bernardino County Museum Association, 1977.

Smyth, John H. *The Law of Homestead and Exemptions.* San Francisco: Sumner Whitney, 1875.

Smythe, William E. *The Little Landers of . . . Los Angeles.* Los Angeles: House of the Little Landers, 1913.

———. "The Struggle for Water in the West." *Atlantic Monthly* 86 (1900): 646–54.

Smythe, William Ellsworth. *City Homes on Country Lanes: Philosophy and Practice of the Home-in-a-Garden.* New York: MacMillan, 1921.

———. *The Conquest of Arid America.* New York: Harper & Brothers, 1900.

Stade, Odo B. "Loomis Ranch—Last Homestead." *Trails Magazine,* Spring 1938, 8–11.

Stedman, Melissa Branson. "Jackrabbit Homesteader." *Desert Magazine,* December 1945.

Starr, Kevin. *Inventing the Dream: California Through the Progressive Era.* New York: Oxford University Press, 1985.

Steeples, Douglas, and David O. Whitten. *Democracy in Desperation: The Depression of 1893*. Westport CT: Greenwood, 1998.

Stephenson, George M. *The Political History of the Public Lands from 1840 to 1862*. New York: Russell & Russell, 1967 (1917).

Street, C. H. *Colony Lands and Abridged Catalogue of Country and City Real Estate, for Sale*. San Francisco: C. H. Street, 1889.

Strong, Douglas Hillman. *"These Happy Grounds": A History of the Lassen Region*. Red Bluff CA: Loomis Museum Association, 1977.

United States Bureau of the Census. *1860 Census: Population of the United States*. Washington DC: Government Printing Office, 1864.

United States Bureau of the Census. *1870 Census: Volume 1, The Statistics of the Population of the United States*. Washington DC: Government Printing Office, 1872.

United States Bureau of Land Management. *Homesteads*. Washington DC: Government Printing Office, 1962.

United States Census Office, *Statistics of the United States in 1860*. Washington DC: Government Printing Office, 1866.

United States Department of the Interior, Bureau of Land Management. *A History of the Rectangular Survey System*. Washington DC: Government Printing Office, 1983.

———. *Small Tracts*. Washington DC: Government Printing Office, 1958.

United States Public Lands Commission. *Report of the Public Lands Commission*. Washington DC: Government Printing Office, 1905.

Vale, Lawrence J. "The Ideological Origins of Affordable Homeownership Efforts." In *Chasing the American Dream: New Perspectives of Affordable Homeownership*, edited by William M. Rohe and Harry L. Watson, 15–40. Ithaca NY: Cornell University Press, 2007.

Vandell, Kerry D. "FHA Restructuring Proposal: Alternatives and Implications." *Housing Policy Debate* 6 (1995): 301.

Vandor, Paul E. *History of Fresno County California with Biographical Sketches of the Leading Men and Women of the County Who Have Been Identified with Its Growth and Development from the Early Days to the Present*. Los Angeles: Historic Record Company, 1919.

Vaught, David. *Cultivating California: Growers, Specialty Crops, and Labor, 1875–1920*. Baltimore: Johns Hopkins University Press, 1999.

Vernon, Charles Clark. "A History of the San Gabriel Mountains, Chapter III." *Historical Society of Southern California Quarterly* 38 (September 1956): 263–88.

Vollman, William T. *Imperial*. New York: Penguin, 2010.

Waldron, Granville Arthur. "Courthouses of Los Angeles County." *Historical Society of Southern California Quarterly* 41 (December 1959): 352–55.

Wallace, W. F. *History of Napa County*. Oakland CA: Enquirer, 1901.

Warren, Louis. *Buffalo Bill's America: William Cody and the Wild West Show.* New York: Vintage, 2016.

Welch, Rodney. "Horace Greeley's Cure for Poverty." *The Forum* (January 1890): 588.

White, Richard. *"It's Your Misfortune and None of My Own": A New History of the American West.* Norman: University of Oklahoma Press, 1993.

Willis, E. B., and P. K. Stockton. *Debates and Proceedings of the Constitutional Convention of the State of California, Convened at the City of Sacramento, Saturday, September 28, 1878.* Vol. 2. Sacramento: State Printing Office, 1878.

Wright, Harold Bell. *The Winning of Barbara Worth.* Chicago: Book Supply Company, 1911.

Wynalda, Stephen A. *366 Days in Abraham Lincoln's Presidency: The Private, Political, and Military Decisions of America's Greatest President.* New York: Skyhorse, 2010.

Zetsch, Scott. *The Chinatown War: Chinese Los Angeles and the Massacre of 1871.* New York: Oxford University Press, 2012.

INDEX

Page numbers in italics indicate illustrations.

Adams, James Truslow, 177

Agoura Hills CA, 165

Agricultural Entry Act (1914), 47

agriculture: in Antelope Valley, 62, 65, 67; in Berreyesa Valley, 145; in Coachella Valley, 92; failed attempts at, 35, 87–88; in Fresno, 123–24; as homestead requirement, 10–11, 56, 164, 174; in Humboldt County, 150; in Imperial Valley, 106, 108, 111, 113–14; in Kern County, 43, 44, 47; knowledge about, 175–76; land for, in California, 27, 30, 37, 45, 50–51, 135–38, 168, 169; in Napa County, 139, 142; in Northern California, 134; in Orange County, 120; and Panic of 1893, 125–26; production between 1940 and 1970, 175; promotion of, 7, 85, 86, 87; in San Diego County, 107; in San Gabriel Mountains, 76; in San Joaquin Valley, 126; in Santa Monica Mountains, 6, 36. *See also* alfalfa; almonds; eggs; grapes; melons; oranges; wheat

Alameda County, 134

Alamo Canal, 106, 108, 112

Alder Creek, 82

alfalfa, 48, 62, 67, 92, 108, 120, 139

Allen, Claude, 164

almonds, 45, 67, 123

Alta California, 23, 70

Alvitre, Adolfo, 71, 73

Alvitre, Tomas de Los Innocentes, 71, 72, 73

American Dream, xiv, 12, 176, 177, 178, 179

American Dream Downpayment Act (2003), 178

American Indians: attack on stagecoach, 115; burial sites of, 41; in California, 35, 93, 131; dispossession of land, 112–13; guides for, 101; as laborers, 24, 93; in Napa County, 142; natural springs used by, 91; trade with, in Arizona, 108; water ditch built by, 72. *See also* Chumash Indians; Pomo Indians; Quechan Indians; Tataviam tribe; Tongva Indians; Yokut tribe

Antelope Valley: Christian colonies in, 66–67; cooperation in, 60; first land sale in, 21; population of, 58–59; postmaster in, 62; successful homesteaders in, 65; water supply in, 59, 61, 64, 91, 92

Antelope Valley Poppy Reserve, 65
Arakelian brothers, 108
Arcata CA, 150
Argay, Joe, 80
Arizona, 107, 108, 173
Arkansas, 115
Armor, Samuel, 115
Arthur, Chester, 112
Articles of Confederation, xii
Atlanta GA, 119
Atlantic Monthly, 63
Austria, 85

Bagley, Frank, 98–99, *99*, 163
Bagley, Helen, 98–99, 163, 194n16
Bair, Fred S., 150
Bakersfield CA, 44, 47
"Bakersfield sound," 45
Baldwin, Elias "Lucky," 72
Ballard, John, 165–67, *166*
Ballard Mountain, 165, 167
Banning CA, 101
Bard, Thomas R., 54
Barton, James N., 146, 148
Battle of Puebla, 19
Bay Area, 134. *See also* Oakland CA; San Francisco CA
Beale, Edward Fitzgerald, 21
Bear Creek, 153
Bear Flag Revolt, 135, 142, 143
bears, 88–89, 151. *See also* wildlife
Bear Valley, 108
Beatrice NE, xi, 185n1
beekeeping, 67, 107–8, *109*, 115. *See also* honey
Bees' Ways (Curtis), 107
Belfast, Ireland, 116
Bella Union hotel, 21
Benioff (homesteader), 100, 101

Bentley, Arthur Fisher, 11
Benton, Thomas Hart, 10
Berg, Ruth, 160–61
Berreyesa, Antonio, 140
Berreyesa, José de Jesus, 140–43
Berreyesa, José de Los Reyes, 140, 142–43
Berreyesa, José Jesus (J.J.), 140, 142, 143
Berreyesa, Nasario Antonio, 140
Berreyesa, Sexto "Sisto" Antonio, 140–42, 143
Berreyesa Ranch, 143
Berreyesa Valley, 144
Bigler, John, 20, 28
Big River, 151
Big Rock Creek Irrigation District, 60–65
Big Tujunga Creek, 88
Bixby, Llewellyn, 116
Blacks, 165–67
Blanchard, Nathan Weston, 54
Blanchard, Sarah Eliot, 54
Boehmer, Fritz, 63
Bombay Beach CA, 111
Bowling, Harry, 59
Boyle Heights, 61, 81
Braden, W. B. (William), 128, 129
Bratt, Benjamin, 2
Brewer, Henry, 128
Briceland CA, 154
British Columbia, 133
Brown, Hal, 151, 152
Bureau of Land Management, 169–70, 172, 186n4
Bureau of Reclamation, 111, 144–45
Bureau of Water Works, 57
Bush, George W., 178
Butch Cassidy's Wild Bunch, 102
Byce, Lyman, 137

Kenliworth Ostrich Farm, *3*
Kennedy, John F., 173, *174*
Kentucky, 35, 165, 167
Kern City CA, 46
Kern County, 12, 43–48, 56, 67, 123, 169
Kern River, 45
Kern River Oilfield, 46, 47
Keys, William "Desert Bill" F., 101–2
Kings Canyon, 67
Kings River, 22, 123, 127
Klamath River, 150
Korean War, 170

labor strikes, 94
La Cañada, 68
Laguna Beach, 117
Lake Berryessa, 145
Lake Katrina, 67
Lancaster CA, 58, 59
land: classification of, 103–4; James
    Irvine's dealings in, 116–18; losses
    of, 72, 113, 135, 143; quality in
    Napa County, 139; sale in Sweet
    irrigation district, 61, 64; sale of
    Little Landers colonies, 86; use
    at Manzana Colony, 65; value of,
    xiii–xiv, 94, 133, 136; near Wright
    coal strike, 84. *See also* public land
Land Commission, 26, 118
"land monopoly," 22–23, 29, 134
land offices, 55. *See also* General Land
    Office; Los Angeles Land Office;
    San Francisco Land Office; U.S.
    Land Office; Visalia Land Office
Landon, Michael, xii
Land Ordinance of 1785, 9, *13*
landownership: in agricultural areas,
    51; Californios' effect on, 27;
    complexity in California, 23; in
    1880s California, 3, 4, 78; of John

Ballard, 165; in Kern County, 48; by
    lumber companies, 146–48; after
    Mexican-American War, 24–25;
    obstacles to, 9, 56, 185n3; under
    Preemption Act, 10; promotion of,
    86, 87; significance to Americans, 7,
    176, 177; and social class divisions,
    27, 45. *See also* home ownership;
    split estates
"land pirates," 22, 23
land sales, 20–22
Land Settlers' League, 118
Lanfair Valley, 103
Lange, Dorothea, 145
Las Putas, 140
Lassen County, 159–61
Latinos, 113. *See also* Mexicans
Lawrence, John, 131
Lincoln, Abraham, xi, 10, 11, 19, 29
Lincoln, Elliot C., 16–17
Lindley, Walter, 95
Lindsay CA, 129
Little House on the Prairie series, xii
Little Landers colonies, 86–88
Livesey, Olin L., 65
Llano CA, 61, 63, 64
Llano Del Rio, 64–65
Long Beach CA, 119
Loomis, Grace, 81, 82
Loomis, Lester, 81–82
Loomis Ranch, 82
Los Angeles Aqueduct, 57
Los Angeles Board of Public Utilities, 33
Los Angeles CA: agricultural labor
    from, 93; Bernice Tucker's trip
    to, 100; blacksmithery in, 130;
    cattle companies in, 102, 103;
    Christian colonies contrasted with,
    66; Clarence Cummings in, 49;
    employment in, 94; enforcement

Sespe Settlers League, 53
Settlers Grand League, 128, 135
Shannon, Fred, 185n3
Shasta CA, 20
Shasta County, 156, 157, 159
Shaw, Lucien, 63
Shay, Helen, 130
Shay, John C., 130–33
sheep, 150, 151. *See also* ranching
Sheep Hole Mountains, 99
Shenandoah Valley, 19
Sherman, William T., 23, 26
Sherwood Valley, 152
Shippey, Lee, 82
Sierra Madres, 84
Sierra Nevada Mountains, 22, 126, 129
Silva, Santos, 2
Sinaloa, 20
Siskiyou County, 157
Sloat, John Drake, 143
smallpox, 93
Small Tract Act (1938), 169–74, *173*,
    199n15
Smith (homesteader), 100, 101
Smythe, William Ellsworth, 63, 85–88
Snepp, Bernard L., 44, 47, 48
Solano County, 134, 144
Soledad Township, 69
Somis CA, 50
Sonoma CA, 23, 127, 134, 135, 136, 138,
    139, 142
Sonoma-Marin Agricultural Society
    Fair, 137
Sonora, 20
Sonoratown, 2
South El Monte, 72
Southern California: agriculture in,
    30, 35, 36, 87, 113; airplane tour of,
    90; American Indian population in,
    35; coal mining in, 83; connection
to Central California, 45; grizzly
bears in, 89; homestead land in,
135; Indian reservations in, 113;
land surveying in, 27, 30; Mexican
homesteaders in, 71; number of
homesteads in, 12, 59, 91; poem
from homesteader in, 16; quality
of land in, 94, 134; railroad route
in, 127; rainfall in, 61; real estate
market in, 78
*Southern California: An Island on the
    Land* (McWilliams), 95
Southern Pacific Railroad: accidents
of, 73; challenge of James Irvine,
117; effect on Los Angeles
population, 29; homesteaders'
transportation by, 107, 122; in
Imperial Valley, 111; land boom
inspired by, 3; landownership by, 59,
185n3; land sales of, 66–67, 127–29;
in San Joaquin Valley, 126
Soviet Union, 153
Spain, 23, 25, 68, 73, 112, 123
Spanish-American War, 44, 153
Spanish missions, 35, 93
split estates, 56
Sprague, Frank, 53–54
Springville CA, 129
squatters: appeals to Los Angeles
    Land Office, 21; harassment of
    homesteaders, 74; land rights of,
    9–10, 26, 51, 103; occupation of
    Mexican ranchos, 24, 135, 143;
    on railroad land, 127; near Sespe
    ranch, 53; in Southern California,
    116–17
Stade, Ordo B., 81, 82
Standley, Jeremiah M. "Doc," 151–53
Standley, William Harrison, 153
Stanford University, 48, 126